An Introduction to Women's Studies

This book is dedicated to the memory of our mothers
'Gwyn', born Gwyneth Ada Jeremy (1903–1985)
'Meg', born Elizabeth May Taylor (1905–1993)

An Introduction to Women's Studies

Edited by

Beryl Madoc-Jones and Jennifer Coates

B

BLACKWELL

Oxford UK & Cambridge USA

Copyright © Blackwell Publishers Ltd, 1996

First published 1996

2 4 6 8 10 9 7 5 3 1

Blackwell Publishers Ltd
108 Cowley Road
Oxford OX4 1JF
UK

Blackwell Publishers Inc.
238 Main Street
Cambridge, Massachusetts 02142
USA

British Library Cataloguing in Publication Data

A CIP catalogue record for this book is available from the British Library.

Library of Congress Cataloging-in-Publication Data

An introduction to women's studies / edited by Beryl Madoc-Jones and
Jennifer Coates.
   p. cm.
   Includes bibliographical references and index.
   ISBN 0–631–19254–9 (hbk. : acid-free paper). -- ISBN 0–631–19255–7
(pbk. : acid-free paper)
   1. Women's studies. I. Madoc-Jones, Beryl. II. Coates, Jennifer.
HQ1180.I576 1996
305.4--dc20   95–11994
                                                      CIP

Typeset in Garamond $10\frac{1}{2}$ on $12\frac{1}{2}$pt by Photoprint, Torquay, S. Devon
Printed in Great Britain by T. J. Press Ltd, Padstow, Cornwall

This book is printed on acid-free paper

Contents

Contents

List of Plates

List of Boxes

Contributors

Margaret L. Arnot gained her first two degrees from the University of Melbourne and her Ph.D. from the University of Essex. She is based in the History Department at Roehampton Institute, London, where among other things, she teaches women's and gender history. She researches women's and gender history in nineteenth-century England. At the moment her particular interest is gender and crime, and she also works on the history of medicine. She is currently writing a book on infanticide in nineteenth-century England.

Lyndie Brimstone is a lecturer in Women's Studies at Roehampton Institute. She has special interests in the areas of representation and sexuality and has published a number of articles in these fields.

Beverly Clack lectures in the Philosophy of Religion and Modern Theology at Roehampton Institute. Her main interest is feminist philosophy of religion and she is currently working on two books in this field.

Jennifer Coates is Professor of English Language and Linguistics at Roehampton Institute. She chaired the Working Party which planned and then set Women's Studies at Roehampton. She continues to contribute to the course offering two options in the Women's Studies undergraduate programme. She is internationally known for her work in the field of language and gender, notably for her books *Women, Men and Language* (2nd edn 1993) and *Women in their Speech Communities* (edited with Deborah Cameron, 1989). She is currently writing up her long-term research project on the talk of women friends, to be published early 1996 under the title *Women Friends Talking*.

Susanne Greenhalgh is Senior Lecturer in Drama and Theatre Studies at Roehampton Institute and has also been a lecturer on Women's Studies Programme at the Institute, which she helped to establish. She has written on teaching as a feminist, on seventeenth-century witch trials and women terrorists.

Valerie Hey is a feminist researcher based at the Social Science Research Unit, Institute of Education, University of London. She is currently working on a project exploring the gendered construction of special educational needs. She is also writing a book about girls' friendships due to be published in 1995/6 by the Open University Press. It is provisionally titled *The Company She Keeps: An Ethnography of Girls' Friendships*. She has contributed to Roehampton Women's Studies as a visiting lecturer.

Louise Jackson is an Academic Assistant in the History Department at Roehampton Institute, and has a background training in both History and Women's Studies. She is currently researching a Ph.D. project on child sexual abuse in Victorian London.

Beryl Madoc-Jones has been involved with the establishment of the Women's Studies undergraduate degree at Roehampton Institute since its inception. She is currently Head of Department. Her original discipline was sociology. Among her research interests are a study of the progress of Access students in higher education, and issues in feminist pedagogy and the development of the Women's Studies curriculum.

Melanie Mauthner works as a Research Officer at the Social Science Research Unit, Institute of Education, University of London. She is currently researching the way that families talk about health issues for a study funded by the Health Education Authority. Her main research interests are in feminist methodology and the sociology of female friendships which she is pursuing in an exploratory study of sisters' relationships for her Ph.D.

Lorraine Radford is Senior Lecturer in Social Policy and Women's Studies at Roehampton Institute. She is an experienced researcher of the law, social policy and violence against women and has published a number of articles in this area. At present she is directing three major projects on women and violence: a study of mediation and domestic violence, and research into inter-agency initiatives and crime prevention in Surrey.

Kimberley Reynolds is Senior Lecturer in English and Director of The Children's Literature Research Centre, Roehampton Institute. Her interests include women's autobiographical writing, nineteenth-century women novelists and gender in children's fiction. Her book *Girls Only? Gender and Popular Juvenile Fiction in Britain 1880–1910* (Harvester, 1990) explores many of these issues.

Joanna Thornborrow is a lecturer in the English Department, Roehampton Institute. As a linguist she became interested in issues relating to Women's Studies through her work in critical discourse analysis and stylistics, particularly in the field of representation of women in media texts. She published in the field of discourse and gender. A recent publication is a chapter in Sara Mills (ed.), 1994, *Gendering the Reader*.

Jo-Anne Whitcomb has worked as a visiting lecturer in the Department of Theology and Religious Studies at Roehampton Institute, where she taught World Religions. Her main research interests relate to the study of Moslem women. She is studying for a Ph.D. in Moslem women in contemporary literature and media.

Christine Zmroczek is lecturer in the Department of Women's Studies at Roehampton Institute and Managing Editor of *Women's Studies International Forum*. Her current research interests include women and technology and social history of working-class women in the twentieth century. A recent publication is 'The weekly wash', in Oldfield, Sybil (ed.) 1994, *This Working-day World: Women's Lives and Culture(s) in Britain 1914 to 1945*, Taylor and Francis.

Acknowledgements

This book has arisen from the experiences of staff and students involved in the setting up and development of the Women's Studies Programme at Roehampton Institute, London. Beryl and Jennifer would like to thank everyone who has contributed to what we and our team have learned about Women's Studies and Feminist Pedagogy. We thank Nannette Herbert and Helen Jacobs for helping us with the manuscript and special thanks go to Angela Ross, administrative secretary in Women's Studies for her skill, patience and good humour as she worked with us to prepare the final draft.

The authors and publishers wish to thank the following for permission to use copyright material:

Blackwell Publishers for material from Dorothy Jerrome, 'Good company: the sociological implications of friendship', *Sociological Review*, 32, 4 (1984), 696–715.

Giles Coren for an extract from *The Times*, 14.11.94.

Guardian News Services Ltd for material from various editions of *the Guardian*.

The Islamic Foundation for an extract from Yusuf Ali's translation of *The Holy Qur'an* (1975), 25–6.

Penguin Books Ltd and Tessa Sayle Agency on behalf of the author for material from Ann Oakley, *Housewife*, Allen Lane (1974), 129, 131–2; Copyright ©1974 Ann Oakley.

Bloomsbury Publishing plc and Peters Fraser and Dunlop on behalf of the author for material from Joanna Trollope, *The Rector's Wife* (1991), 56–8.

Princeton University Press for material from Robinette Kennedy, 'Women's friendship on Crete: a psychological perspective', in Jill Dubisch (ed.), *Gender and Power in Rural Greece* (1986); Copyright ©1986 by Princeton University Press.

Acknowledgements

Random House UK Ltd and Watson, Little Ltd on behalf of the author for material from Lynne Reid Banks, *The L-Shaped Room* (1961), Chatto & Windus, 35, 163–4.

The Society for Promoting Christian Knowledge for 'God our Mother: A Prayer from the St Hilda's Community', from *Women Included* (1991), originally in Janet Morley, *All Desires Known*.

The Women's Press Ltd for material from Jill Miller, *Happy as a Dead Cat* (1983), 26–8; and Gilda O'Neill, *A Night Out With The Girls: Women Having A Good Time* (1993), 43–5, 63.

Yale University Press for Olga Broumas, 'Little Red Riding Hood' from *Beginning with O* (1977).

Zed Books for material from Nawal el Sa'adawi, *Women in the Arab World* (1980), 44–6.

Every effort has been made to trace all the copyright holders, but if any have been inadvertently overlooked the publishers will be pleased to make the necessary arrangement at the first opportunity.

CHAPTER
1 Introductory

Beryl Madoc-Jones and Jennifer Coates

To Our Readers

This book has been written for and addresses you as students starting on your explorations of Women's Studies – as newcomers to higher education, as participants in adult education classes (including Access courses), or as independent students wanting to find out what Women's Studies is about.

In this opening chapter, we are trying to do several things. We want to frame the central chapters by giving you a brief overview of our subject (this is the section called 'What is Women's Studies'). In the section called 'Background to Writing the Book' we clarify what kind of textbook this is, and tell you something about how we, the women writing the book, came together to do it. In the last part of the chapter we look at the main themes and topics dealt with in the book, and discuss the role of theory. The chapter ends with some brief hints on how to get the most out of the book.

What Is Women's Studies?

Women's Studies is *about women*. A major impetus which has led to the emergence of Women's Studies in the academy has been the recognition by women as feminist scholars working in a wide range of disciplines, that academic knowledge about women has been marginalized. Thus, a first aim of Women's Studies has been to focus on women. This process is described in a variety of ways, for example allowing women 'to find a voice', 'to claim space for themselves', or 'to render women visible'. Many women scholars have pointed out that men have failed to acknowledge that women have their own history, have distinctive ways of 'knowing' (see Belenky et al. 1986). Women's exclusion in this sense stems from **male domination** [for an explanation of bold text see page 10 of the construction of Western knowledge. Male domination refers to the nature of power relations between women and men which have advantaged men. Feminist scholarship has made us aware of the scale and extent of men's ability to control women and to place us in a subordinate relationship to them. Men's power in relation to women is referred to as **patriarchal** control, which has resulted in the widespread oppression of women. One aspect of this oppression has been the failure to recognize women's knowledge in standard forms of received knowledge. This situation is being redressed by the acceptance of Women's Studies in the academy. These issues have been expressed by Mary Bateson (1990: 71) in the following way: 'The values and potentials of excluded groups need to be made visible and accessible to

3

stimulate the imaginations of those who have always assumed that their way . . . is the best.'

Women's studies is not only *about* women but it is *for* women. Participating in Women's Studies is a political engagement. The recovery of knowledge that belongs to women has political implications. This recovery promotes change by challenging traditional views about received knowledge; it fosters the agency of women to be in control of their own lives; it implicates the institutions in which we study and work since Women's Studies challenges not only received notions of what should be taught but *how* it should be taught (Humm, 1991); it empowers women collectively, leading to changing them as people (Griffin, 1994).

Women's Studies is about *experience*. Women's experience, both individual and collective, is at the heart of women's knowledge (Griffin, 1994). It is a rich resource for a Women's Studies curriculum. We have chosen to make considerable use of this resource in the design of the book. You will find that much of the material presented to you in the following pages is based on personal accounts and fictional representations of women's experiences. This material is drawn from a wide range of sources, including biographical writing, sociological studies in which women have been given a space through interviews to record their experiences, historical records, and creative writing (stories and poems). We also give you an opportunity through exercises (described in detail below) to record and reflect on your own experience. 'Reflect' is a key word here since the attention that we have given to experience as a valid form of knowledge needs careful justification for a place in Women's Studies as an academic endeavour. Individual experience has its own authority (for a discussion of this issue see Kitzinger, 1994). However, we need to look further than experiential authority for an adequate explanation of women's experiences. We take the view with others (Humm, 1991; Kitzinger, 1994) that women's lives are to an important extent 'socially constructed', meaning by this that our ideas, identities and actions are shaped and modified by the social contexts in which we have been positioned. The implication of this is that we need to go outside ourselves and locate our experience in complex social orders. By doing this we can begin to interpret our own apparently unique experience through understanding the connections and relationships between individual experience, shared experience and different experience. In other words we proceed to understanding by theorizing. The importance of theory will be discussed later in this chapter.

The focus on experience opens up another aspect of Women's Studies. It is about *difference*. In the earlier years of the development of Women's Studies, the influence of the unifying notion of 'sisterhood' was strong. While commonalities between women remain important and a source of power for women, more recently developments in Women's Studies have revealed the extent and significance of *diversity*. Increasing attention has been given to the diversity of women's experience, particularly in relation to class, race and ethnicity, and sexuality. The tensions and connections between these aspects of women's lived realities have raised major theoretical issues and they open up new possibilities for a meaningful global feminism.

Women's Studies is about *celebration*. While much of the intellectual energy stimulating the growth of Women's Studies has been used to unpack the basis of women's oppression (from a variety of different theoretical perspectives), an equally important outcome of rendering women's knowledge visible has been to facilitate recognition of women's achievement. Achievement can be understood in many different ways. Aspects of women's achievement which we think are particularly important are our ability to gain control over our lives (personal autonomy); our ability to sustain positive feelings of self-worth; the influence that women have had through the exercise of creative human potential on the course of human history; our contribution to the growth of human knowledge.

What Kind of 'Textbook' is This?

A range of Women's Studies textbooks has emerged over the last few years. The earlier ones (for example, Tong, 1989; Gunew, 1990, 1991) have attempted to acquaint the student with the complex range of feminist theoretical perspectives which underpin Women's Studies. Most recently has come Diane Richardson and Victoria Robinson's *Introducing Women's Studies* (1993) which sets out to provide a comprehensive and accessible source book, offering 'an overview of past, present and future developments in feminist knowledge and theory' (p. xvii). Such a source book is invaluable for negotiating your way through increasingly sophisticated levels of study. Our aim is different. We do not set out to provide a comprehensive source book or a survey of theoretical perspectives, but a *taster*. We hope that what you will gain from using this book as a learning resource is a basic understanding of what Women's Studies is about and a sense of excitement about its possibilities to take with you into more advanced studies.

Background to Writing the Book

From the mid 1970s Women's Studies has flourished world-wide in a variety of contexts. Since the early 1980s it has become part of the academy in Britain, finding a place for itself in the structure of university-based intellectual inquiry. In their 1991 survey of Women's Studies in British Higher Education, Christine Zmroczek and Claire Duchen drew attention to the small group of institutions offering undergraduate opportunities, led by the then Polytechnics of East and North London, and Lancaster University. But since 1990 the proliferation of undergraduate degree course opportunities has been remarkable. A major development here has been the provision of Access courses for adults in preparation for entry to higher and professional education. The predominance of women among returners to adult learning has meant a push toward women-centred learning in relation to both the epistemology (what counts as knowledge) and the teaching methodolgy of Access courses. In order for you to understand our approach, we would like to share a number of issues with you that arise from our experience and that have provided the major impetus for the project to write a text to meet the needs of students starting their Women's Studies. First of all, women who teach on Women's Studies undergraduate courses rarely have a full-time appointment in this field but are based in other departments in their institutions and teach in associated specialist areas. This was a situation we experienced at the beginning of our undergraduate teaching. We have since then been able to gain some full-time appointments but recognize that this is unusual. We still depend on the expertise and goodwill of our colleagues in other departments. The pressure on academic staff working in more than one area is very great and especially so when they are involved in a relatively underdeveloped field – a curriculum for undergraduate Women's Studies. This book is based on our experience which we want to share.

Secondly, the composition of the student body enrolling in undergraduate courses in Women's Studies differs in significant ways from both other undergraduate groups of students and postgraduate Women's Studies students. Gabrielle Griffin (1994) has reminded us that postgraduate courses in Women's Studies 'introduced a new type of student into the academy' (p. 28), i.e. the female mature student who does not typically enter her postgraduate degree course in Women's Studies fresh from completion of a first degree. In the same way, undergraduate courses in Women's Studies have attracted large numbers of 'mature' students ('mature' for institutional purposes meaning 21 years old and over), most of whom do not come with prior learning experiences rooted in standard forms of knowledge. Undergraduate courses in Women's Studies also share with postgraduate courses significant numbers of 'non-traditional' students – students who come not with an A level package but with other forms of knowledge gained from life experience. In this way, as a result of its appeal to mature and non-traditional students, a typical undergraduate class in Women's Studies has a profile different from many other undergraduate classes. At the same time, expansion of undergraduate studies throughout the UK has meant that Women's Studies is now widely available to the student coming from school. This pattern of recruitment is encountered in particular at higher education institutions which have a tradition of national recruitment. It means that the age range of students in undergraduate Women's Studies is very wide indeed. For example, a recent cohort of Women's Studies students at Roehampton Institute, London, ranged in age from 18 to 65 years.

A third and related issue that has concerned us in the preparation of an appropriate undergraduate curriculum is the level of understanding and expectations which you, as new students, may have with regard to feminist perspectives in Women's Studies. Many women attracted to Women's Studies come to such courses because of previous engagement with feminism. The past histories of older students may include memories of the excitement of the Women's Liberation Movement of the 1960s and 1970s, participation in feminist consciousness-raising groups and active involvement in women's organizations at the present time. On the other hand, many women (of all ages) enter our courses with a very hazy notion of the relevance of feminism to Women's Studies. In our experience, attitudes towards feminism run the gamut of possibilities from a radical commitment to feminism, curiosity, lack of awareness, indifference, anxiety to outright hostility. (For a further discussion of this see Griffin, 1994.) Many younger students do not connect with feminist politics and question the relevance of feminist theory for understanding their positioning of themselves and others in womanhood and society.

A fourth issue which we have taken into account in our planning and design of this book is the recognition that the conditions within higher education under which undergraduate courses must work are changing. Classes are getting larger while at the same time tutors are under increasing pressure both from administrative demands and from the desire to be active in research. This means that student-centred learning (which has always been important in Women's Studies) is fundamental to our approach.

Structure and Organization of the Book

The book consists of eleven substantive chapters, each highlighting a particular area of women's lives, framed by this Introduction and by a Conclusion. We have selected for our central chapters eleven topics which we hope will give you an insight into the scope of contemporary Women's Studies. These topics relate to particular aspects of women's lives such as work or health or leisure. We have also decided to give sex and sexuality a chapter in its own right since it is at the heart of women's gendered reality. Inevitably, we've had to be selective – there's a limit to how much can be included in any book – and we recognize that certain important topics have been omitted. The topics we have chosen are those we have worked on with our own students; they reflect our own interests and expertise which we hope to share with you, the reader.

These eleven chapters share a common structure in that each one addresses a set of underlying parameters and themes. We conceptualize a **parameter** as a marker defining the scope and reality of women's lives. The ones which we have selected are the following: The Body, Lifecycle, Class, Race. Each of these parameters could have been treated as a topic for a chapter. (Equally, some of the topics – sex and sexuality, for instance – could have been included as one of the parameters.) We have chosen to think of them as parameters shaping experience in every aspect of our lives and we have therefore included them in every chapter.

In addition to working with the selected parameters, we have identified a set of themes which we believe to be central to the understanding of the ways in which we construct our identities and the variety of our life experience. They are: space, history (time), power, and cross-cultural perspectives. These themes thread their way through our texts. They are important for introducing concepts which will facilitate explanation (theoretical analysis). Space may be conceptualized in a number of ways, ranging from physical to ideological (room for new ideas). Locating women in history is crucial for the task of interpreting past experience and relating it to the present and the future (change). Power is a key concept which we have already talked about in this chapter. Our emphasis will be on power relations between women and men (patriarchal power). Cross-cultural perspectives focus our attention on both the commonalities between women arising from a shared gender category and on the significance of difference.

These eleven chapters also reflect the fact that Women's Studies is multi-disciplinary. This means that feminist scholars from a wide range of academic areas of knowledge (disciplines) participate in the study of women and are concerned with all aspects of women's lives. Each of us writing for this book approaches her topic from her own perspective, for example, sociological enquiry or literary criticism. However, all of us have attempted to incorporate into our own chapters as wide a range of material as possible, so that you will gain a sense of the variety of ways in which women's experiences can be studied. The chapter on Schooling (chapter 4), for example, has drawn upon school reports, autobiography, sociological studies, historical accounts and novels. All play their part in the construction of women's knowledge. In this way we try to demonstrate the richness and diversity to be found in multi-disciplinary studies. At the same time, the disciplinary background of each individual writer is often visible. Some chapters draw heavily on sociological and historical studies (crime, chapter 11) while others are grounded in literary studies (growing up, chapter 2, and mothers, chapter 3).

We have attempted to introduce you to the main ideas/debates and more important substantive knowledge relating to our topics by writing in the following format. Every chapter includes a selection of extracts, from a variety of written sources. Most of these provide you with a snapshot of a moment in a woman's (or women's) experience. We have endeavoured to write a text around these extracts. These linking passages comment on and interpret and develop the ideas found there. In this way you are introduced to some of the very significant issues and debates in the topic being studied. This style of writing, making use of fairly extensive extracts is costly in terms of space: we have deliberately chosen to foreground certain aspects of each topic and to deal with others briefly or not at all. This is an important way in which our textbook differs from the more conventional text which would set out to provide the student with a comprehensive overview. One of our aims is to facilitate the development of skills in reading extracts and to use them to build up an understanding of the topic. We know that students in the early stages of their academic careers have considerable demands made on them. This is particularly acute when entering a new field of study. You may have only limited time for reading complete works; this means that the ability to read and analyse extracts becomes an important intellectual tool.

After these eleven chapters comes a Conclusion (chapter 13). This final chapter pulls together the main theoretical ideas that have been introduced to you in the course of the book. It aims to provide in a more concentrated way a map of the theoretical developments that have been important in the intellectual history of Women's Studies.

The Place of Theory

Now that we've established what we mean by Women's Studies, and have discussed the structure and organization of the book, we need to return to the question of the theoretical framework our material will be presented in. More generally, we want to discuss the role that theory will play in this book.

To begin with, we need to ask what we mean by 'theory'. Is it a word that fills you with dread? Did you feel like putting the book to one side when you saw the heading 'theory'? All of us have at one time or another reacted negatively to the word. We associate the term 'theory' with words like 'difficult', 'dry', 'distant', 'impersonal', not with words like 'accessible', 'friendly', 'personal'. It is our aim in this book to help you to feel more comfortable with theory and with theoretical issues. Theory does not have to be difficult or impersonal.

In answer to our question, 'What do we mean by theory?', we can say that a theory is just a framework or set of ideas for making sense of the world. A theory allows us to *explain* in a systematic way the things we observe and experience in our everyday lives. One of the reasons that we, as women, have reacted negatively to the term may be because most theories have been developed by men. Some theories, like Marxism, are explicitly associated with an individual man; others, like Liberal Humanism, are more vaguely associated with great white male thinkers of the past.

Feminist theory has arisen in the twentieth century as we, as women, try to make sense of our lives. One aspect of feminist theory which is unique is its emphasis on the link between theory and practice, embodied in the slogan 'The personal is political'. Maggie Humm (1989) describes feminist theory like this:

A fundamental goal of feminist theory is to understand women's oppression in terms of race, gender, class and sexual preference and how to change it. Feminist theory

9

reveals the importance of women's individual and shared experiences and our struggles. It analyses how sexual difference is constructed within any intellectual and social world and builds accounts of experiences from these differences. (Humm, 1989: x)

The phrase 'feminist theory' suggests that we're talking about one unified theory. In fact there is a range of perspectives included under this umbrella term, so we should more accurately talk about **feminist theories**. 'Feminist theory is not one, but many, theories or perspectives and . . . each feminist theory or perspective attempts to describe women's oppression, to explain its causes and consequences, and to prescribe strategies for women's liberation' (Tong, 1989: 1).

In this book we have deliberately drawn on a range of feminist perspectives, feminist theories. These are all linked, in that they are all feminist in orientation. We want you, the reader, to get some experience of these different ways of making sense of our lives. But because we want women's lived experience to be at the heart of our book, theory will be used to help to explain particular topics and particular themes; it will not be the main focus. (The exception will be the concluding chapter in which, as we have already indicated, we will try to pull together the theoretical strands that have emerged in the book, and will attempt to show how feminist theory relates to Women's Studies.)

What we have tried to do in this book is to introduce you to a range of perspectives by making you familiar with particular *theoretical concepts*. As the concepts arise in the various chapters of the book, they will be printed in **bold**, and their meaning will be explained in the surrounding text.

EXERCISE

As you read this book, build up a glossary of new terms by writing words which are new to you (or words which are used in a new way), together with their definitions, in a notebook. You will find this a useful resource as you move from chapter to chapter, and when you read more widely.

Besides introducing theoretical concepts in the text, chapters will highlight one or more *theoretical debates* related to the topic dealt with in the chapter. These theoretical debates will appear in boxes, that is, in framed sections of text set off from the main body of the chapter. For example, in the next chapter, 'Growing Up', the box is on 'Theories of identity formation' (see box 2.1, pages 18–20) – it introduces theories which try to explain the ways in which we develop an identity. This type of theoretical material is set apart from the main text for the following reasons:

- to allow you a first reading of the text without getting bogged down in theoretical material
- to make theoretical discussion distinct from the main text
- to allow you as a reader to return to these debates on your own, without necessarily always tying them in with the surrounding text
- to allow those of you who want to follow them up, to take them further at your own pace.

Language

The discussion of theory brings us neatly to the question of language. One of the reasons that we so often shy away from theory is because of the language used. Much academic discourse (that is, the language typically used in academic books and articles, and also used in spoken discussion by some members of the academic world) involves a style which favours complex sentence structure and polysyllabic words. By complex sentence structure we mean sentences (the chunks of print between one full stop and the next) which are long and which involve many clauses (the sub-sections of sentences). Such sentences are more difficult to understand, because they take longer to process in your mind. (But don't forget that one of the advantages of writing over speech is that we can go back and reread written sentences – they don't disappear after they are produced.)

Examples of polysyllabic words are: theoretical, feminist, polysyllabic – such words are more typically found in written language, in particular in academic prose, than in everyday speech. They differ from everyday words not only in being longer or polysyllabic, but also in their origins: they have been borrowed from classical languages (Latin and Greek) and are not part of the original Anglo-Saxon wordstock. Everyday words such as, 'woman', 'man', 'book', 'write', 'read' are Anglo-Saxon in origin, and have a very different feel about them.

There is no reason why academic books should be written in complex sentences using classical vocabulary – it's just a convention. But to say 'it's just a convention' is to ignore the fact that this convention is very convenient for those people who want to exclude others from academic discourse. By writing in a style that is complex and which draws on Latin and Greek-derived words, writers (sometimes thoughtlessly, sometimes deliberately) address a particular audience, an intellectual elite. We can describe such a style as mystifying rather than clarifying and enlarging understanding. It is one of our aims in this book – and is an aim of many feminist writers – to challenge mystification when we find it, and to write in a style that is accessible. This means that we have avoided long complex sentences wherever possible, preferring shorter, simpler ones. We have also favoured everyday vocabulary over arcane or obscure words. But as you may have noticed, the polysyllabic words we used as examples in the previous paragraph – theoretical, feminist, polysyllabic – have all been used in this chapter, as well as the more everyday words. What this demonstrates is that it is not possible to write about complex issues using only everyday words.

So although we have chosen everyday words where such words express what we mean, we have also had to use more learned terminology in places. However, as already explained, it is one of our aims to familiarize you with new theoretical perspectives and this means introducing you to a whole range of theoretical terms. We have tried to define these terms clearly as we go along, and to strike a balance between simple and complex expressions, avoiding, we hope, both the excesses of formal academic prose and over-simplification.

We have also made a positive effort to speak to you, the reader, directly. In other words, we have tried to open up a dialogue with you, to encourage you to engage with the book in an active rather than a passive way. We want you to respond to what we say with your own ideas and your own examples.

How to Use this Book

We have tried not to make too many assumptions about you, the reader of this book. The one thing we can be sure of is that you, an individual, have chosen to engage – if only briefly – with this book. We can also be reasonably sure that you have some interest in, or curiosity about, Women's Studies. Beyond that we are assuming very little. Since we cannot assume that you belong to a group or class who will share your interest in Women's Studies, we have designed the book to be read by someone on their own, in isolation. In other words, it is not necessary for you to discuss the ideas you meet as you read the book in a group or class (though of course it would be a bonus if you were able to do so). Similarly, the exercises you will meet in the text are designed to be done by you alone. As you will see, some of the exercises ask you to reflect on aspects of your personal life which you might be reluctant to reveal to others. We do not expect you to expose yourself to others. Your notes and answers are for your eyes alone. If, however, you do read the book as part of a class, then we expect that you and other members of the class (and your teacher, if there is one) will come to an agreement about what is to be shared and what is to be kept private.

We have already said that we have attempted to write in an interactive way to enable you to feel involved in what you read. Ideally, you should experience reading this book as participating in a dialogue with us, the authors. This means that we have used the pronoun 'you' to address you, the reader directly through-out the book. We have also used the pronouns 'I' (where there is one writer) or 'we' (where there is more than one writer) to refer to ourselves.

The various exercises are a vital part of this interaction – have pencil and paper to hand and take time out from your reading to carry them out. It is a good idea to get into the habit of putting the book down from time to time to think about issues that have arisen in the text, whether or not there is an exercise to do. The exercises will often ask you to draw on your own experience and to relate this experience to discussion in the text: in our experience, students find it helpful to make these links. The writer or writers of each chapter will discuss briefly possible answers to exercises when appropriate, but don't be tempted to look ahead at this de-briefing before you have carried out the exercise yourself. And don't forget: there are no right answers. Your responses to particular tasks and to particular questions may be just as valid as the ones given by the authors; our comments are just there to help you to evaluate your own response.

Although we expect you to read this introductory chapter first, and to read the concluding chapter last, there is no necessary reason why you should read the other eleven chapters in any particular order. We have had to put them in a particular order, and we think there are some logical connections between partic-ular topics – for example, between the chapter on work and the chapter on leisure – and this has affected our decisions about what to put where. But we can think of many other ways the chapters could be ordered. This means that you could start with any chapter you like: none of the chapters assumes that you have read any of the others. However, remember that a concept is highlighted with a brief explana-tion where it is introduced. This means that you may need to refer to the index to find that first reference.

As you read the various chapters, we hope that you will be stimulated to follow up works referred to in the text that particularly interest you. These may be works of fiction or autobiography – we have used extracts from such works in all our chapters, because we feel that story-telling, in all its guises, is an important strategy that human beings use to make sense of the world (Le Guin, 1989; Johnstone, 1993) – or they may be academic books and articles. Every chapter has a complete list of works referred to at the end, with all the information you need to track them down in your local library. It's important that you move on from this introductory text in Women's Studies to wider reading: this process will help to establish you as a Women's Studies student.

We hope you will enjoy reading this book as well as learning from it. Our main goal in writing it has been to provide those with an interest in Women's Studies a point of entry to the subject area. But another important goal is to stimulate you to continued study in the area. If we have done that, then we shall be more than satisfied – and we wish you good luck in your continuing journey of discovery in Women's Studies.

Beryl Madoc-Jones and Jennifer Coates

REFERENCES

Bateson, Mary Catherine 1990: *Composing A Life*. New York: Plume.

Belenky, Mary, Clinchy, Blyth, Goldberg, Nancy and Taruh, Jill 1986: *Women's Ways of Knowing*. New York: Basic Books.

Griffin, Gabrielle 1994: *Changing Our Lives*. London: Pluto Press.

Gunew, Sneja (ed.) 1990: *Feminist Knowledge*. London: Routledge.

Gunew, Sneja (ed.) 1991: *A Reader in Feminist Thought*. London: Routledge.

Humm, Maggie 1989: *A Dictionary of Feminist Thought*. London: The Women's Press.

Humm, Maggie 1991: Thinking of things themselves: theory, experience, Women's Studies. In Jane Aaron and Sylvia Walby (eds), *Out of the Margins*, London: Falmer Press.

Johnstone, Barbara 1993: Community and contest: midwestern men and women creating their worlds in conversational storytelling. In Deborah Tannen (ed.), *Gender and Conversational Interaction*, Oxford: Oxford University Press.

Kitzinger, Celia 1994: Experiential authority and heterosexuality. In Gabrielle Griffin (ed.), *Changing Our Lives*, London: Pluto Press.

Le Guin, Ursula 1989: Some thoughts on narrative. In Ursula le Guin, *Dancing at the Edge of the World*, London: Victor Gollancz.

Richardson, Diane and Robinson, Victoria (eds) 1993: *Introducing Women's Studies*. Basingstoke: Macmillan Press.

Tong, Rosemary 1989: *Feminist Thought A Comprehensive Introduction*. London: Routledge.

Zmroczek, Christine and Duchen, Claire 1991: What are those women up to? Women's Studies and feminist research in the European Community. In Jane Aaron and Sylvia Walby (eds), *Out of the Margins*, London: Falmer Press.

CHAPTER
2 Growing up

Susanne Greenhalgh

Plate 1 Suzanne Valadon, *The Abandoned Doll*, 1921, oil on canvas, 51 × 32 in, The National Museum of Women in the Arts; Gift of Wallace and Wilhelmina Holiday. DACS 1995.

In this chapter we will look at growing up and the difference that gender makes to the way that girls relate to adulthood. Although this is the first substantial chapter of the book it could just as easily have been the last. Much of what you will touch upon in this chapter will be developed further and differently in the other chapters. Experience of mothers, schools, work, the media, sex and so on are all part of what constructs 'growing up' – a complex and cumulative process involving many different stages, ingredients, and influences, which has happened in various ways, in particular societies and times. We will look in particular at the way in which women have recalled youthful experiences in autobiographical and fictional writing, and suggest that such memories often remain a touchstone throughout women's lives. By the end of this chapter the concept 'growing up' will no longer be one you take for granted. You will have thought about what 'growing up female' means, and will have gained experience in the close analysis of texts as a means of illuminating a specific subject of investigation. You will also have approached growing up from a number of different disciplinary perspectives – literary, historical and sociological.

Becoming a Woman/Staying a Child

Before we go any further, it is worth thinking a little more about the ideas raised by the very words *growing up*.

EXERCISE

Write down any words that you connect with growing up. You might want to group some of these under opposite headings, such as 'Grown up'/'Not grown up'. If you do this you will start to think about the possible *results* of growing up and its role as a process of change from one state to another.

EXERCISE RESPONSE

You may have ended up with some quite long lists. Perhaps you focused on the type of experience growing up can be – 'hard', 'essential', 'rewarding', 'endless', and so on. You may have come up with linked words or ideas, such as 'adult', 'child', 'adolescence', 'maturity', 'development', 'experience', 'responsibility', 'power', 'freedom'. You may have picked specific representative events, such as a first period, eighteenth birthday, passing a driving test, starting a job, getting married, having a child. Or, like me, you might have been interested by the different *images* conjured up by the phrase. Why 'up'? Do we think of it as a natural process, like a plant growing towards the light? Or as a hierarchical progression, moving upwards from a lower stage to a higher one? And from this wide range of ideas we can start to see that our understanding of growing up is often the result of a **comparative** process – we think about childhood in relation to, and as different from, adulthood. This also allows us to imagine a state which is neither still being a child nor yet being an adult – what anthropologists call a **liminal** stage (from the Latin word for 'threshold') – betwixt and between two worlds. We even have words for these years in people's lives – 'teenage', 'adolescence'.

In historical terms, however, both childhood and adolescence are relatively new concepts, emerging in Western Europe only within the last five hundred years or so. Before then – as in many Third World countries today – children were apprentice adults, carrying out grown up tasks as soon as they were physically able, and learning social roles by imitating the activities taking place in the extended 'family' (which might include non-related members such as servants or workmates) around them. Changes in political and psychological ideas about the individual (see box 2.1 on 'Theories of identity formation') together with the increased role of schooling in the **socialization** (a process by which human beings acquire a self-identity on the basis of which social relations are established) of children led to the development of childhood and youth as a distinct and lengthy period. This stage combined freedom from social responsibilities with continuing subordination to adults (Stone, 1979). According to Shulamith Firestone (1971: 90–1), however, this was a class and gendered 'myth of childhood', which applied only to boys. Commenting on the emergence of a three-stage clothing code for male children – from baby swaddling clothes, to feminine skirts, to a miniature version of male adult dress (often uniform) – Firestone argues that girls and working-class boys had no such costume changes because, even when grown, they remained in a lower, non-adult class in relation to men.

BOX 2.1	THEORIES OF IDENTITY FORMATION

Ever since Simone de Beauvoir (1949) famously asserted that one is not born but becomes a woman, it has been possible not only to view gender identity as constructed rather than innate but also to recognize the extent to which models of human development and identity formation – growing up – have mainly been explored in terms of masculinity. The 'modern' European view of the individual developed out of the changes in ideas about religion and the nature of the state that began in the sixteenth century. A picture of human life as given and shaped by God, in a society powerfully influenced by the Church, gradually gave way to an emphasis on an autonomous being, capable of choosing his own moral path, of shaping his own identity, to whom belonged certain kinds of natural rights in his relations with the state, expressed in laws and political processes (such as Parliament). My use of the masculine pronoun here is deliberate for in both theory and practice women were only problematically part of this category of active subject. The name given to this still powerfully influential model of personal and political identity is **humanism**. During the twentieth century, however, a complex of ideas have arisen to challenge this idea of a fixed unified human subject at the centre of things. Sigmund Freud theorized an unconscious which came into being through the emotionally and sexually charged family relationships of infancy, expressing itself in drives which were continually repressed by the requirements of social living. And research into the nature of language led to emphasis on identity as the product of language rather than language as the expression of a pre-existing 'essential' self. The changed viewpoint brought about by these and other ideas is often termed **post-modernist**.

Psychological Theories of Identity Formation

As regards development and identity-formation, Freud hypothesized a 'normal' pattern in which a child's initial closeness to the mother must give way to identification with the father, as representative of the world outside the home and family. For boys this involved a stage of desire for the mother and consequent rivalry with the father (the famous 'Oedipal complex', taking its name from the Greek tragedy King Oedipus, which tells the story of a man doomed unknowingly to murder his father and marry his mother). Eventually 'normal' boys found an acceptable mother-substitute in heterosexual relationships. Girls' development was far less easy to account for, however, since not only must they detach themselves from their first (female) love-object but must also transfer attachment from their fathers to another male figure. Freud came to see the persistence of girls' first emotional attachment to a member of the same sex as the cause for what he considered to be their failure to develop fully, as expressed in a reliance on emotion and feeling rather than impersonal objective judgement.

Feminist psychologists such as Nancy Chodorow (1978) have reassessed the role of women in childcare and its impact on the emotional development of girls and boys. According to Chodorow this means that girls' sense of self is based on connection and empathy (in the first place with the mother) while a boy's ego and sense of masculinity comes into being through separation and strongly defined individuation. (For further discussion of Chodorow's ideas see chapter 3, pages 46–7; also box 9.1 on 'Connection and separateness' page

199–200.) Carol Gilligan has used Chodorow's ideas to argue against models of human growth and development based on a (masculine) ideal of the autonomous individual. Instead she argues for a 'self in relationship', an 'interdependence of attachment' that could empower both the self and others, responding to others' needs without sacrificing their own (Gilligan, 1986: 249–50).

Post-modernist Theories of Identity

Theorists influenced by post-modernist ideas have fundamentally questioned the ideal of a unified continuous self – whether male or female – and have emphasized multiple identities, multiple subject positions taken or enforced through discourses, as the means by which individuals exist in and experience the world. Judith Butler (1990) has argued that 'being female' is a cultural performance that creates the illusion of naturalness and coherence.

> Gender ought not to be construed as a stable identity of locus of agency from which various acts follow; rather gender is an identity tenuously constituted in time, instituted as an exterior space through a stylized repetition of acts. The effect of gender is produced through the stylization of the body and, hence, must be understood as the mundane way in which bodily gestures, movements, and styles of various kinds constitute the illusion of constantly gendered self. . . . That gendered reality is created through sustained social performances means that the very notions of an essential sex and a true or abiding masculinity or femininity are also . . . part of the strategy that conceals gender's performative character. (Butler, 1990: 140–5)

For Butler, linear models of growth or development are inevitably built in terms of 'masculine domination and compulsory heterosexuality' and these restricting frames must be disrupted by the 'performative possibilities for proliferating gender configurations' (Butler, 1990: 27).

During the eighteenth and nineteenth centuries a gendered way of viewing youth was reflected and developed in novels and other writing. Youth came to be seen as a period of restless experimentation, a journey of rebellion and self-discovery which ended in acceptance of the demands of society, usually in the form of marriage (Moretti, 1987). Such stories of adventures in search of a 'sentimental education' away from home were essentially boys' stories, however. A girl's growing up, based in the home of her family or employers until marriage, largely excluded from education, and often rigorously protected from sexual encounters, did not take the same form, either in fiction or in fact. To a large extent girls were not seen as part of this new category of 'youth'.

This historical association of girls with the home also made them less prominent in public, on the streets, where they were out of place and even at risk. As a result girls were thought of as less of a public problem than boys. Indeed the term 'youth' came to have predominantly masculine and delinquent connotations and adolescence, viewed as a phase of achieving a separate, individual identity, often through rebellion against family or social conventions, came to be typified by the sort of teenage boy played by James Dean in 1950s films such as *Rebel Without a Cause*. For girls, however, such adolescent attempts to take charge of their sexuality and other aspects of their lives conflicted with the socially preferred feminine goals of being carers, dependants and sex objects (Lees, 1993: 15, 17, 21)

I have already mentioned the view that boundaries between girlhood and womanhood are far less clear-cut and pronounced than those between boyhood and manhood. Firestone (1971: 8) points out that women and children are always mentioned in the same breath and that the link between them is one of shared oppression.

The black American writer Alice Walker rejects this notion of womanhood as prolonged childhood with her coinage of the word 'womanist':

> WOMANIST: from *womanish*. (opp. of 'girlish' i.e. frivolous, irresponsible, not serious).
> A black feminist or woman of color. From the colloquial expression of mothers to daughters, 'You're acting womanish', i.e. like a woman. Usually referring to outrageous, audacious, courageous or *wilful* behavior. Wanting to know more and in greater depth than is considered 'good' for one. Interested in grown-up doings. Acting grown-up, being grown-up. Interchangeable with other colloquial expressions: 'You're trying to be grown'. Responsible. In charge. *Serious* . . . (Walker, 1983: xi)

Notice how the qualities that Walker celebrates in 'womanist' women combine in an interesting way ones that we might connect on the one hand with adolescence and youth – 'outrageous', 'audacious', 'courageous', 'wilful', 'wanting to know more' – with words that are more usually associated with adult behaviour – 'responsible', 'in charge', 'serious'.

Does this suggest that girlhood is a stage that truly grown-up women should overcome and put behind them? Or that being grown up as a woman can retain some of the experimental, questioning attitudes associated with youth? I'll come back to these questions later on, when we consider some women's autobiographical and fictional writing about growing up.

Sugar and Spice: Growing up Different

The idea that boys and girls are different categories of human beings is so familiar to us that we may take it for granted. Pink and blue baby clothes are still manufactured and purchased, even if they don't always end up on the 'right' sex. If you look at toy catalogues or the commercials during children's television you

21

will still find playthings labelled in much the same way as in this nineteenth-century verse, part of a collection 'for school boys, during their leisure hours at boarding school'.

Mamma and Miss Ann

Mamma. Go and buy a Toy, Ann.
Ann. I can buy a gun.
Mamma. A gun is not fit for you, Ann.
Ann. Why is a gun not fit for me?
Mamma. A gun is only fit for a boy.
Ann. May I buy a top?
Mamma. No, but you may buy a mop.
(Arnold, 1969: 19)

The fact that this dialogue is targeted in the first instance at *boys* also underlines how vital it is for males as well as females to recognize inappropriate conduct since this will ensure that they keep to their own gender roles, by avoiding behaviour that could be labelled 'feminine'. In other words we need to think about the relationships *between* boys and girls and *between* masculinity and femininity if we are to understand how and why this sense of difference operates.

In Margaret Atwood's (1989) novel *Cat's Eye* the heroine, Elaine, confronts a doorway to the different worlds of boys and girls:

At the back are two grandiose entranceways with carvings around them and ornate insets above the doors, inscribed in curvy, solemn lettering: GIRLS and BOYS. When the teacher in the yard rings her brass handbell we have to line up in twos by classroom, girls in one line, boys in another, and file into our separate doors. The girls hold hands; the boys don't. If you go in the wrong door you get the strap, or so everyone says.

I am very curious about the BOYS door. How is going through a door different if you're a boy? What's in there that merits the strap, just for seeing it? My brother says there's nothing special about the stairs inside, they're plain ordinary stairs. The boys don't have a separate classroom, they're in with us. They go in the BOYS door and end up in the same place that we do. I can see the point of the boys' washroom, because they pee differently, and also the boys' yard, because of all the punching and kicking that goes on among them. But the door baffles me. I would like a look inside. (Atwood,1989: 45–6)

What intrigues Elaine is that although this division is only temporary – the children end up in the same classroom – it is maintained by the threat of punishment and the door separates and distinguishes between the sexes in a way that has no obvious connection with any differences of male and female anatomy or behaviour. Her brother tells her that there's 'nothing special' behind the door, but Elaine senses that it is the labelling process itself that is important. The lettering is 'solemn' because it ensures that the categories of 'boy' and 'girl' are kept separate and significant even within a situation – schooling – which claims to treat all children equally.

Elaine is well placed to notice the existence of these categories. She and her brother have had an identical upbringing, on the move in wartime Canada, rarely attending school for more than a few months. The schoolbooks they study, with their pictures of comfortable homes, a father who goes out to work, a mother who wears a dress and apron, and a little girl who wears 'pretty dresses and patent-leather shoes with straps' (p. 29) are far removed from Elaine's childhood experiences. When the family settle in Toronto Elaine both longs for and fears the prospect of having girlfriends at last:

> So I am left to the girls, real girls at last, in the flesh. But I'm not used to girls, or familiar with their customs. I feel awkward around them, I don't know what to say. I know the unspoken rules of boys, but with girls I sense that I am always on the verge of some unforeseen, calamitous blunder. . . . I begin to want things I've never wanted before: braids, a dressing-gown, a purse of my own.
>
> Something is unfolding, being revealed to me. I see there's a whole world of girls and their doings that has been unknown to me and that I can be part of it without making any effort at all. I don't have to keep up with anyone, run as fast, aim as well, make loud explosive noises, decode messages, die on cue. I don't have to think about whether I've done these things well, as well as a boy. All I have to do is sit on the floor and cut frying pans out of the Eaton's catalogue with embroidery scissors, and say I've done it badly. Partly this is a relief. (Atwood, 1989: 47, 54)

EXERCISE

What would you say are the differences that Elaine finds between boys' and girls' play?

EXERCISE RESPONSE

The differences are mainly expressed through a contrast in activities. Boys are described as being constantly in action, playing wargames, competing with each other. Girls, on the other hand are linked with appearance and possessions – hairstyles, clothes, accessories like handbags associated with grown-up status. Instead of physical activity they are pictured sitting quietly carrying out finicky tasks such as cutting out kitchenware from shop catalogues. Rather than learning assertiveness and self-reliance they are self-deprecating even about their 'feminine' skills. We can begin to see that whereas masculinity is constructed as *active* femininity tends to be connected with *passivity*.

Susanne Greenhalgh

Sweet Dreams: The Culture of Femininity

Atwood's character describes the discovery of femininity as an unfolding revelation of an unknown world that had lain hidden around her, something that she can be part of 'without making any effort at all'. This process of being won over to a particular belief system, by a variety of means – from family example to fairy tales, from advertisements to comic books, from soap operas to films – is often referred to as **ideology**. A set of power relations which privileges some people at the expense of others is made to seem inevitable and even desirable by the languages or **discourses** of images, words, gestures, clothing, or the values and attitudes expressed in such institutions as the media, schools and workplaces. Femininity can be regarded as one such, very powerful, ideology: a code of dos and don't-dos often masquerading as free choices.

Jamaica Kincaid's 'Girl' (1986) encapsulates from a West Indian perspective the variety of languages and codes of behaviour that construct femininity. Read the passage and then try to answer the questions below.

> Wash the white clothes on Monday and put them on the stone heap; wash the colour clothes on Tuesday and put them on the clothes-line to dry; . . . on Sundays try to walk like a lady and not like the slut you are bent on becoming; don't sing benna in Sunday school; you musn't talk to wharf-rat boys, not even to give directions; don't eat fruit on the streets – flies will follow you; *but I don't sing benna on Sundays at all and never at Sunday School*; this is how to sew on a button; this is how to make a buttonhole for the button you have just sewed on; this is how to hem a dress when you see the hem coming down and so prevent yourself from looking like the slut I know you are so bent on becoming . . . this is how to behave in the presence of men who don't know you very well, and this way they won't recognize immediately the slut I have warned you against becoming; be sure to wash every day, even if it is with your own spit; don't squat down to play marbles – you are not a boy, you know . . . this is how to make a bread pudding this is how to make duokona; this is how to make pepper pot; this is how to make a good medicine for a cold; this is how to make a good medicine to throw away a child before it even becomes a child . . . this is how to bully a man; this is how a man bullies you; this is how to love a man, and if this doesn't work there are other ways, and if they don't work don't feel bad about giving up . . . this is how to make ends meet; always squeeze bread to make sure it's fresh; *but what if the baker won't let me feel the bread?*; you mean to say that after all you are really going to be the kind of woman who the baker won't let near the bread? (Kincaid, 1986: 326–7)

EXERCISE

Now answer these questions on Kincaid's 'Girl'.

1. Who do you think is the advice-giver?
2. What areas of life does the advice cover?

3. What will happen if the girl fails to learn her lessons successfully?

EXERCISE RESPONSE

One likely answer to question 1 is that the advice comes from the girl's mother, or another close female relative: a grandmother, an older sister, or an aunt. Whoever she is, she is certainly female – her inside knowledge tells us that – and involved in making sure that the girl 'grows up right'. In chapter 3 on 'Mothers' you will find further discussion of the 'reproduction of mothering'; here I want to stress the way in which codes of feminine conduct form part of a process by which true self-worth as a woman comes to be regarded as only possible through acceptance of a caring, nurturing role. Another possibility is that this is the voice of the girl herself, mimicking the wise sayings she has heard so often, perhaps in order to criticize or distance herself from these 'rules'. Or is it the inner voice that results from having unconsciously **internalized** ('reproduced') the advice that she has continually heard from so many different sources in her culture?

When answering question 2 I hope you noticed how much of the instruction is to do with caring for others – cooking, cleaning, sewing, how to run a household efficiently. But there is also a lot of advice about sexual conduct. Although the speaker gives some useful advice about contraception and getting your way with a man, sexuality mainly appears as something that must be kept under control.

In response to question 3, she will lose her reputation as a 'good' woman and be regarded as a slut. This is an interesting word, originally applied to women who were lazy and careless about housework or their appearance – 'slatterns' – which came to refer to sexual carelessness as well. Throughout the extract the speaker makes a similar connection between physical and moral cleanliness. She also seems to assume that the girl has a wilful tendency to become exactly the wrong kind of woman, 'the kind of woman who the baker won't let near the bread'. There is a contradiction here. As a woman she is expected to keep dirt at bay on behalf of her family, but breaking the rules outlined to her will make her 'dirty'. In many cultures women are regarded as being at the boundaries of what is regarded as clean, 'pure', and thus safe, and that which is unclean, and potentially dangerous – and therefore in need of control (Douglas, 1978). Certain female physiological processes – childbirth, menstruation – are often regarded as times when women are especially contaminated and contaminating. What is important just now is to notice the connection with women's sexuality.

As suggested by the Kincaid extract, girls' freedom is powerfully controlled by the vocabulary of sexual abuse. Sue Lees (1993) has termed this the language of 'slags and drags'. She found that the behaviour and attitudes of young girls are continually influenced by the danger to their reputation implied by being named as a 'slag'. She also found that this term was very ambiguous, being used in a variety of situations where sexual behaviour was only marginally at issue. In other words it acted as a control of all kinds of 'deviant' behaviour, by signalling complete failure of the ideal of femininity (Lees, 1993: 266–93).

But if the language of slags and drags is a stick for the growing girl there are carrots as well. Romance plays a special role within the ideology of femininity.

> Being constituted as feminine involves girls in discourses of feeling and emotion, and more specifically the culture of romance. . . . Children learn the standard pattern of romance from such sources as fairy tales. Through such sources, as well as conversations [with other girls etc.] they are learning nuances of meaning through which they make sense of emotions and relationships. (Jackson, 1993: 46)

Other teenage 'reading', such as comics, magazines, romantic novels, and even films and soap operas, also 'proffer a "happy ever after" situation in which the finding of the prince . . . comes to seem like a solution to a set of overwhelming desires and problems' (Walkerdine, 1984: 163).

Here is an example of a girl 'decoding' the message of *Beauty and the Beast*, from Jeanette Winterson's (1985) novel, *Oranges are not the Only Fruit*.

> Slowly I closed the book. It was clear that I had stumbled on a terrible conspiracy.
> There are women in the world.
> There are men in the world.
> And there are beasts.
> What do you do if you marry a beast?
> Kissing them didn't always help.
> And beasts are crafty. They disguise themselves like you and I. Like the wolf in 'Little Red Riding Hood'.
> Why had no one told me? Did that mean that no one else knew?
> Did that mean that all over the globe, in all innocence, women were marrying beasts? I reassured myself as best I could. The minister was a man, but he wore a skirt, so that made him special. There must be others, but were there enough? That was the worry. There were a lot of women, and most of them married. If they couldn't marry each other, and I didn't think they could, because of having babies, some of them would inevitably marry beasts. (Winterson, 1985, 1990: 72–3)

This girl interprets the fairy story as a warning about sexual choices. However, she is more struck by the beast than the handsome prince, the usual focus of romantic narratives and the dreams they produce. In some ways she is a 'resisting reader': she senses there's a message, but finds a different one from the obvious moral that 'love will be rewarded', so that she ends up suspicious of marriage. In fact, as you can read in the chapter on sexuality (chapter 7), she will end up selecting women as partners, but this is a possibility that none of her childhood reading – from fairy tales to *Jane Eyre* – points to. Romance and the happy ending lie with heterosexuality.

The languages that create the ideal/fantasy of perfect womanhood in our culture may be inescapable but we must be careful about assuming that femininity is monolithic and unchanging. In her study of young black women and achievement Heidi Mirza (1992: 15) argues that this 'culture' does not apply in the same way to all cultural groups. White observers often perceive black girls as displaying significantly different behaviour from white girls, labelling them 'unfeminine' and 'sexually overt'. In fact, Mirza claims, there is a specific form of black femininity among young black women characterized by relative autonomy among the sexes 'which produces significant differences in attitudes to school, work and marriage' (p. 164). Black girls have a stronger sense of self-worth and a greater appreciation of female role-models than their white counterparts. When asked whom they most admired 48 per cent of black girls named themselves and 20 per cent their mother or other female relative or friend: the figures for white girls were 25 per cent and 8 per cent respectively (pp. 54, 187, 199). Children and career are not seen in conflict, and 'few distinctions were made between male and female abilities and attributes with regard to possible jobs' (p. 147). If different versions of femininity exist in our own culture – and if a strong sense of a specific kind of femininity can in certain circumstances help to overcome racial and economic oppression – we need to be aware that femininity is a complex and often contradictory concept.

'Powerlessly in Harness': Spaces of Knowing for Young Girls

As Jacqueline Rose (1983: 9) has argued, 'most women do not slip painlessly into their roles as women, if, indeed, they do at all'. Youthful reading – whether of books or television – shapes desires and fantasies in certain directions, but there are other ways in which girls learn to become women, perhaps most importantly through their developing sense of their own bodies.

EXERCISE

Think for a moment or two about the way you felt about your body as a young girl, and jot down any words that help sum up those feelings.

I expect you had some uncomfortable recollections there. Girls' relationship with their own bodies is made far from easy. According to Shirley Ardener, physical space and its social perception are 'mutually affecting spheres of reality' for women, who often feel they do not deserve to take up space or time (Ardener, 1981: 32; Rich, 1977: 242–3). Iris Young (1989) argues that as girls learn they are girls, they also learn specific style of moving and presenting their bodies. Because they become aware that they continually face the prospect of being seen and used by others primarily as *body* rather than an intentional, active self, they come to look at and treat their own bodies as mere things. Doubts about the power of their bodies to have an effect in and on the world lead, Young (1989: 65–7) suggests, to doubt in their powers of understanding and leadership, which may influence the decisions they make about education and employment.

Cindi Katz (1993) has termed these connections between the space and freedom given to girls 'spaces of knowing'. Comparing the daily movements of girls in US cities and rural Sudan, not only did she find significant restrictions on girls' mobility in both environments, but also that girls had considerably less freedom of movement than boys. Like Young she argues that restrictions on girls' access to and control over space are implicitly linked to the social codes that control sexual access to female bodies. This leads not only to an internalization of fear, and thus eventual self-restriction, but has implications throughout the entire life-course. For instance, different rates in the development of spatial, mathematical, cognitive and mapping skills in boys and girls may be linked with the greater spatial restrictions girls experience in and outside the home. (See Katz, 1993: 103–5.)

The New Zealand writer Janet Frame (1971) gives a powerful self-portrait of being restricted and controlled, combined with being looked at, surveyed, like a prisoner:

> My memory of myself contains now myself looking outward and myself looking within from without, developing the 'view' that others might have, and because I was my body and its functions and that body was clothed during most waking hours in a dark grey serge tunic that I hated increasingly because it was far too tight now in the yoke, it was rough, scratchy material; and in long black stockings with their sealing effect; and in blouses, pure white in summer, grey flannel in winter, all with cuffs buttoned tightly over my wrists and pointed collars closing with pearl buttons high upon my neck, completing the seal; and in the black shoes laced in complete capture of my feet; in the regulation gloves, hat, or beret; and, as a final imprisonment, in the red and black tie knotted round my neck and the green Gibson House Girdle also specially knotted around my waist, because of these clothes I saw myself as powerlessly in harness. Added to that view was my sisters' opinion of my 'figure' seen free and naked before the bedroom mirror, compared and contrasted with theirs and with the film stars and with the ideal . . . (Frame, 1983: 143–4)

Notice how Frame's choice of words – 'far too tight', the 'sealing effect' of 'long black stockings', 'cuffs buttoned tightly', 'collars closing . . . high upon my neck,

completing the seal', 'shoes laced in complete capture' and the 'final imprisonment' of the school tie and House girdle – help us to recognize that the function
of the school uniform is to suppress both spirit and sexuality. But her 'free and
naked' body seen in the mirror of the ideals of female attractiveness that circulate
in her society is equally imprisoned. John Berger (1972) has shown how 'ways of
seeing' in Western culture are different for men and women.

> A woman must continually watch herself. She is almost continually accompanied by
> her own image of herself . . . Men look at women. Women watch themselves being
> looked at. This determines not only most relations between men and women but also
> the relation of women to themselves. (Berger, 1972: 46–7)

Frame's phrase 'powerlessly in harness' sums up for me the impact that the combination of spatial and bodily restriction with the sense of being an object to be
viewed can have on a young girl's sense of independence and identity.

Frame's investigation of her image in the mirror, like that of the girl in the
painting by Suzanne Valadon reproduced at the beginning of this chapter, is a
private way of marking the change from girl to woman but this transformation
can take more public forms – what anthropologists call 'rites of passage'. These are
forms of ritual behaviour which mark the transition of people from one life-stage
to another. They display the separation that most societies make between such
categories as young and old, male and female. Women's rites of passage often
centre on the life-cycle in terms of sexuality and fertility, and such key events as
menstruation and childbirth.

Here are two accounts of such rites of passage. One is a description of the
footbinding undergone by upper-class Chinese women until this century. The
other is the true story of an African girl being circumcized – suffering the removal
of parts of her genitals. Such material not only makes painful reading but also
poses special problems of interpretation. Because we may not be familiar with the
culture that produced such customs we may see the values they encode as utterly
different from our own – 'other', 'barbaric' where we are 'civilized' – and dismiss
their relevance to our own situation. Or, on the other hand, we may regard such
ceremonies as exactly equivalent to rituals of our own; for instance to the manipulation of the body that is encouraged by the beauty industry in Western societies. While taking note of connections and similarities with our own lives we must
give full value to our sense of *difference*; not in order to reject or belittle, but rather
to acknowledge that becoming a woman takes varied forms in different cultures.
In this way we can try to avoid empty generalizations about 'Woman' and her
universal experiences.

The first extract is from Jung Chang's (1991) bestseller *Wild Swans: Three
Daughters of China*, an account of three generations of women's lives by a woman

who has herself traversed two cultures, from Maoist China to the capitalist West.

> My grandmother was a beauty . . . But her greatest assets were her bound feet, called in Chinese 'three-inch golden lilies' (*san-tsun-gin-lian*). This meant that she walked like 'a tender young willow shoot in a spring breeze,' as Chinese connoisseurs of women traditionally put it. The sight of a woman teetering on bound feet was supposed to have an erotic effect on men, partly because her vulnerability induced a feeling of protectiveness in the onlooker. My grandmother's feet had been bound when she was two years old. Her mother, who herself had bound feet, first wound a piece of cloth about twenty feet long round her feet, bending all the toes except the big toe inward and under the sole. Then she placed a large stone on top to crush the arch. My grandmother screamed in agony and begged her to stop. Her mother had to stick a cloth into her mouth to gag her. My grandmother passed out repeatedly from the pain. The process lasted several years. Even after the bones had been broken, the feet had to be bound day and night in thick cloth because the moment they were released they would try to recover. For years my grandmother lived in relentless, excruciating pain. When she pleaded with her mother to untie the bindings, her mother would weep and tell her that unbound feet would ruin her entire life, and that she was doing it for her own future happiness. (Chang, 1991: 30–1)

The second passage is the testimony of a girl known only as 'P.K.'.

> Very early the next morning, as my mother was too easily upset to have anything to do with the proceedings, my two favorite aunts took me to the hut where the excisor was waiting with some younger women . . . Once I was inside the hut, the women began to sing my praises, to which I turned a deaf ear, as I was so overcome with terror . . . 'Lie down there,' the excisor suddenly said to me, pointing to a mat stretched on the ground . . . I felt my thin frail legs tightly grasped by heavy hands and pulled wide apart . . . Two women on each side of me pinned me to the ground . . . Suddenly . . . I was already being excised: first of all I underwent the ablation of the labia minora and then of the clitoris. The operation seemed to go on forever, as it had to be performed 'to perfection'. I was in the throes of endless agony, torn apart both physically and psychologically. It was the rule that girls of my age did not weep in this situation. I broke the rule. I reacted immediately with tears and screams of pain. I felt wet. I was bleeding. The blood flowed in torrents. Then they applied a mixture of butter and medicinal herbs which stopped the bleeding. Never had I felt such excruciating pain. After this, the women let go their grasp, freeing my mutilated body. In the state I was in, I had no inclination to get up. But the voice of the excisor forced me to do so. 'It's all over! You can stand up. You see, it wasn't so painful after all!' (Thiam, 1986; cited in Walker and Parmar, 1993: 105–7)

EXERCISE

What similarities can you find between these rituals in two different periods and cultures?

EXERCISE RESPONSE

The first point you may have made is that both rituals are intensely painful, and involve permanent mutilation of the body. Both also restrict the girl's future freedom – simply to move around easily in the case of footbinding, or to enjoy sexual intercourse or give birth without problems in the case of circumcision (in some cases this practice includes the sewing up, as well as removal, of parts of the female genitalia). Both are intended to make the girl more marriageable – small feet were regarded as sexually attractive in China, and circumcision seeks to ensure the chastity of a girl for her future husband. Both rituals are performed by women – often relatives – who have themselves gone through the process. Even knowing the pain involved they still consider it beneficial for younger women. (But notice that P.K.'s mother cannot bear to attend and that Yu-Fang's mother weeps, even though she is convinced that she has acted in her daughter's best interests.)

As women of colour Alice Walker and Prabitha Parmar squarely confront the issue of respect for cultural tradition which is often made in defence of such customs, by women themselves.

> Women literally abolish themselves as women and take on a male persona in order to participate in the ritual . . . deeply rooted patriarchy perpetuates this violence by turning women into heroes for withstanding the terrible pain of mutilation . . . The complexity of this web of denial and distancing demonstrates women's ability to embody, embrace, and reinforce patriarchal power. Unfortunately the phenomenon of 'colonizing' and oppressing one's own kind is not new or unique, nor is it rare. (Walker and Parmar, 1993: 179)

According to this analysis these 'feminine' cultural traditions, though controlled and celebrated by women, are actually a manifestation of patriarchal power, literally inscribing itself on female bodies, so as to bring about an inner colonization which can only be challenged and overcome by mental **decolonization**, a process requiring the rejection or remaking of the cultural symbols, values and practices which maintain the status quo (Lesage, 1988).

In the last section I shall look at the ways in which women writers have begun to remake the cultural symbols of femininity, through their exploration of girl-hood wounds.

'Something Else to Be': The Fiction of Growing up

In their study of fictional treatments of female development, Elizabeth Abel, Marianne Hirsch and Elizabeth Langland (1983) argue that women's writing on growing up differs significantly from men's. Whereas boys' experience of school and travel orients them to achievement and autonomy the goals that girls strive to reach in order to become women centre on community and empathy with others. (See the discussion of Carol Gilligan's work in box 2.1 on 'Theories of identity formation', pages 18–20.) And, as we found when considering adolescence and femininity, these two sets of goals are frequently in conflict, so that the heroine's refusal to accept adulthood on masculine terms is often expressed through her death. In George Eliot's novel *The Mill on the Floss* (written in 1859), for instance, the drowning of Maggie Tulliver ultimately comes about through the irreconcilable opposition between loyalties to family and friends and the desire for self-realization through study and sexuality.

In contemporary women's writing, however, other outcomes have become possible. Alice Walker's (1983) novel *The Color Purple* begins with the words of a father who has raped his daughter and taken away the babies that resulted: 'You better not never tell nobody but God' (Walker, 1983: 3). The rest of the novel is in the form of letters, to God, to and from her absent sister, by the abused girl, Celie. By telling her life-story in secret, Celie defies the physical, sexual and economic power embodied in the unnamed father, and the silence he tried to impose upon her, and wins her way to a happy ending in middle age, when she learns that her assailant was not her real father, and is reunited with her lost children. Celie's first words are 'I am fourteen years old. I am I have always been a good girl. Maybe you can give me a sign letting me know what is happening to me' (p. 3). The whole novel is a quest to understand 'what is happening' to her, once she is thrust brutally out of the identity of 'good girl', signified by the crossed out words. After long years of loveless drudgery in a marriage of convenience she finds physical and emotional satisfaction with her husband's lover, the blues singer Shug, who teaches her to celebrate the pleasures and beauties of the world symbolized by 'the color purple'. At the end of her story Celie reflects:

> I feel a little peculiar round the children. For one thing, they grown. And I see they think me and Nettie and Shug and Albert and Samuel and Harpo and Sofia and Jack and Odessa real old and don't know much what going on. But I don't think us feel

old at all. And us so happy. Matter of fact, I think this is the youngest us ever feel.
Amen.
(Walker, 1983: 244)

Celie has acquired her knowledge of 'what going on' through pain and hardship but paradoxically she doesn't feel aged by these experiences but rather as though her life has run backwards, arriving at last at the youth and happiness stolen from her in girlhood. Nor does her quest for self-knowledge result in achievement and autonomy at the expense of community and empathy. At the end of the novel she is a successful businesswoman, but she is also surrounded by a community of loved ones, in which even her husband can be included.

Maxine Hong Kingston's (1977) *The Woman Warrior*, subtitled 'Memoirs of a girlhood among ghosts', also starts with an order not to tell: ' "You must not tell anyone," my mother said, "what I am about to tell you" ' (p. 3). Through a complex sequence of fictional, factual and legendary stories Kingston seeks out the secrets of her family history through the experience of a girl growing up between different cultures and languages in a Chinese immigrant community on the West Coast of America.

> My American life has been such a disappointment.
> 'I got straight A's, Mama.'
> 'Let me tell you a true story about a girl who saved her village.'
> I could not figure out what was my village. And it was important that I do something big and fine, or else my parents would sell me when we made our way back to China. In China there were solutions for what to do with little girls who ate up food and threw tantrums. You can't eat straight A's. When one of my parents or the emigrant villagers said, 'Feeding girls is feeding cowbirds,' I would thrash on the floor and scream so hard I couldn't talk. I couldn't stop.
> 'What's the matter with her?'
> 'I don't know. Bad, I guess. You know how girls are. "There's no profit in raising girls. Better to raise geese than girls." '
> 'I would hit her if she were mine. But then there's no use wasting all that discipline on a girl. "When you raise girls, you're raising children for strangers." '
> 'Stop that crying!' my mother would yell. 'I'm going to hit you if you don't stop. Bad girl! Stop!' . . . 'I'm not a bad girl,' I would scream. 'I'm not a bad girl. I'm not a bad girl.' I might as well have said, 'I'm not a girl'. (Kingston, 1977: 46)

Kingston's search for identity is built around a series of identifications with and exploration of real and legendary women: the nameless aunt who committed suicide with her illegitimate child before the family left China; the woman-warrior of the title, who saves her village but returns from her heroic adventures to resume her daughterly duties; her mother, who trained as a doctor in China and achieved fame as a 'tamer of ghosts'; another aunt, who is destroyed by the conflict of customs between east and west and becomes one of a series of 'crazy ladies' who drift, ghostlike, through the book's pages; and finally a warrior and poetess who was captured by barbarians and translated their music into Chinese poetry. Kingston tries to make sense of an upbringing that taught her on one hand that 'we failed if we grew up to but wives or slaves. We could be heroines, swordswomen' (p. 19), on the other that 'there is a Chinese word for the female *I* – which is "slave"' (p. 47). Like Walker's (1983) novel, her narrative is fragmented, divided into different stories and voices, linking past and present to suggest the complexity of identity formation: 'I continue to sort out what's just my childhood, just my imagination, just my family, just the village, just movies, just living' (Kingston, 1977: 205).

Maggie Humm (1989) has compared the ways in which male and female adult returners to higher education composed the autobiographies required as part of their course. She concluded that men never seemed to admit to childhood in what they wrote, typically starting their 'real' stories in adolescence. Women on the other hand 'use the tension of childhood experiences as the basis of adult analysis' (Humm, 1989: 43–4). In the examples of women's writing discussed above we can also find evidence not only that girlhood experiences are central to women's adult lives but that they remain a vital source of ideas for the future. Instead of passively accepting the patriarchal concept of women as perpetual children these writers have redefined womanhood to combine youthful vision with the accumulated experience of different generations and, often, cultures. In the process the clear boundaries between youth and adulthood are abandoned and a new definition of 'grown up' begins to emerge:

> My mother is not like the other mothers, she doesn't fit in with the idea of them. She does not inhabit the house, the way the other mothers do; she's airy and hard to pin down. The others don't go skating on the neighbourhood rink, or walk in the ravine by themselves. They seem to me grown up in a way that my mother is not. (Atwood, 1989: 156)

As Humm found with her students, these writers 'exploit a rhetoric of uncertainty about themselves and about the role of women, and record feelings not accomplishments' (Humm, 1989: 45). 'Becoming a woman' is envisioned as a constantly transformative, provisional process rather than a fixed goal: 'like someone making herself up as she goes along . . . improvising' (Atwood, 1989: 301). (See the discussion of Judith Butler in box 2.1 on 'Theories of identity formation' on pages 18–20.)

EXERCISE

I have one final exercise for you, to be completed after you have read all the chapters of this book.

Draft your own life story, your own memories of growing up. Whether you simply make notes or end up with a full history I believe that you will find the process an invaluable aid to thinking critically about the experience of becoming a woman.

Conclusion

In this chapter I have tried to emphasize both the restrictions and freedom of growing up female and to suggest that we need to redefine the very concept of being 'grown up' if we are to understand what it means for women today. As Sue Lees has concluded at the end of her study:

> For many years girls were brought up to develop 'only' a woman/female identity directed to the reproductive function and caring for a husband, with a subjectivity that was constructed as muted or suppressed . . . Today such clear delineation has gone and what comprises womanhood is misty, confused and contradictory. (Lees, 1993: 263)

We can see both challenge and opportunities in this dissolution of the sharp contours of what it is to be a woman, in becoming 'hard to pin down' rather than pinned to our sex.

It is also important to remember that we are not defined solely by our gender. We are spoken to (and about) not just as 'girls' or 'women'. Other identities – such as 'citizen', 'consumer' or 'worker' – are offered to us through the educational and media discourses of the society we live in. Moreover, the possibilities and choices we see on offer, or as Leslie Johnson (1993: 9) puts it, 'the space made available . . . for young women to grow up in', will vary from culture to culture. Nevertheless, across the differences between cultures and histories, there is common ground to be found in the experience of growing up female rather than male, in a world that still distributes power and freedom on the basis of gender. In her novel *Sula* Toni Morrison (1983) writes of the friendship between two black women.

> Because each had discovered years before that they were neither white nor male, and that all freedom and triumph was forbidden to them, they had set about creating something else to be . . . Their meeting was fortunate, for it let them use each other to grow on . . . (Morrison, 1983: 51–2)

By 'meeting with' and studying the lives and experiences of women in other cultures and times we can perhaps begin to discover new ways in which to grow – in order to create 'something else to be'.

REFERENCES

Abel, E., Hirsch, M. and Langland, E. 1983: *The Voyage In: Fictions of Female Development*. Hanover, NH: University Press of New England.

Ardener, S. (ed.) 1981: *Women and Space: Ground Rules and Social Maps*. London: Croom Helm in association with the Oxford University Women's Studies Committee.

Arnold, A. 1969: *Pictures and Stories from Forgotten Children's Books*. New York: Dover.

Atwood, M. 1989: *Cat's Eye*. London: Virago.

Beauvoir, S. 1949: *The Second Sex*. (1972 edn tr. H. M. Parshley.) Harmondsworth: Penguin (1972).

Berger, J. 1972: *Ways of Seeing*. London and Harmondsworth: British Broadcasting Corporation and Penguin Books.

Butler, J. 1990: *Gender Trouble: Feminism and the Subversion of Identity*. London: Routledge.

Chang, J. 1991: *Wild Swans: Three Daughters of China*. London: HarperCollins.

Chodorow, N. 1978: *The Reproduction of Mothering: Psychoanalysis and the Sociology of Gender*. Berkeley: University of California Press.

Douglas, M. 1978: *Purity and Danger*. London: Routledge & Kegan Paul.

Eliot, George 1979: *The Mill on the Floss* (ed. A. S. Byatt). Harmondsworth: Penguin. [First published 1859.]

Firestone, S. 1971: *The Dialectic of Sex: The Case for Feminist Revolution*. London: Jonathan Cape.

Frame, J. 1983: *To the Is-Land*. London: The Women's Press.

Gilligan, C. 1986: Remapping the moral domain: new images of the self in relationship. In T. Heller et al. (eds), *Reconstructing Individualism: Autonomy, Individuality and the Self in Western Thought*, Stanford: Stanford University Press.

Humm, M. 1989: Subjects in English: autobiography, women and education. In A. Thompson and H. Wilcox (eds), *Teaching Women: Feminism and English Studies*, Manchester: Manchester University Press.

Jackson, S. 1993: Love and romance as objects of feminist knowledge. In M. Kennedy, C. Lubelska and V. Walsh (eds), *Making Connections: Women's Studies, Women's Movements, Women's Lives*, London and Washington, DC: Taylor & Francis.

Johnson, L. 1993: *The Modern Girl: Girlhood and Growing Up*. Buckingham and Philadelphia: Open University Press.

Katz, C. 1993: Growing girls/closing circles: limits in the spaces of knowing in rural Sudan and US cities. In C. Katz and J. Monk (eds), *Full Circles: Geographies of Women over the Life Course*, London: Routledge.

Kincaid, J. (1986) Girl [written in 1978]. In A. Carter (ed.), *Wayward Girls and Wicked Women: An Anthology*, London: Virago.

Kingston, M. H. 1977: *The Woman Warrior: Memoirs of a Girlhood Among Ghosts*. London: Allen Lane.

Lees, S. 1993: *Sugar and Spice: Sexuality and Adolescent Girls*. Harmondsworth: Penguin.

Lesage, J. 1988: Women's rage. In C. Nelson and L. Grossberg (eds), *Marxism and the Interpretation of Cultures*, Urbana, IL: University of Illinois Press.

Mirza, H. 1992: *Young, Female and Black*. London: Routledge & Kegan Paul.

Moretti, F, 1987: *The Way of the World: The Bildungsroman in Europe Culture*. London: Verso.

Morrison, T. 1983: *Sula*. London: Triad Grafton. [First published 1973.]

Rich, Adrienne 1977: *Of Woman Born*. London: Virago.

Rose, J. 1983: Femininity and its discontents. *Feminist Review*, 14, 5–21.

Stone, L. 1979: *The Family, Sex and Marriage in England 1500–1800*. Harmondsworth: Penguin.

Thiam, Awa 1986: *Speak out Black Sisters: Feminism and Oppression in Black Africa*. London: Pluto.

Walker, A. 1983: *The Color Purple*. London: The Women's Press.

Walker, A. and Parmar, P. 1993: *Warrior Marks: Female Genital Mutilation and the Sexual Blinding of Women*. London: Jonathan Cape.

Walkerdine, V. 1984: Some day my prince will come. In A. McRobbie and M. Nava (eds), *Gender and Generation*. Basingstoke: Macmillan.

Winterson, J. 1985: *Oranges Are Not the Only Fruit*. London: Pandora.

Young, I. 1989: Throwing like a girl: a phenomenology of feminine body comportment, motility and spatiality. In J. Allen and I. Young (eds), *The Thinking Muse: Feminism and French Philosophy*, Bloomington: Indiana University Press.

CHAPTER
3 Mothers

Kimberley Reynolds

Plate 2 Mary Cassatt, *The Bath*, 1891, colour print with drypoint, soft-ground etching, and aquatint,
$10\frac{3}{8} \times 10\frac{5}{8}$ in. The Art Institute of Chicago; photograph: The Women's Art Slide Library, London.

This chapter is about the way women learn to think about and become mothers, and particularly about the ways women have written about their experiences as mothers, daughters and mothers of daughters. When you have finished reading it, you will be familiar with a range of contemporary and historical theories about mothering. You will also have encountered questions about the social, political and psychological meaning of mothering and been required to consider mothering as a construct rather than a biological fact. Through examining the literary representation of mothering, you will look at mothers' contribution to socialization, strategies of power, and the relationship between femininity, sexuality, and mothering. Lastly, the chapter requires you to think about yourself as and in relation to mothers.

Motherhood

My daughter was also my first child. When the midwife put her in my arms and I looked into her face I had a sudden shock of recognition: I knew her face intimately already, for my baby daughter looked exactly like my mother. The understanding that in giving birth I had both become my mother and mother to my mother was an epiphany – a moment in which previously disparate ideas came together – which has informed all my subsequent thinking about motherhood. In fictional writing by women about mothering I found my preoccupations were common, but in the institutionalized literature about mothering – from parents' guides through psychology textbooks – this sense of continuity and shared experience between generations was clearly not important. Motherhood represented something else in these studies, and one of the aims of this chapter will be to ask questions about what mothering is, and how it comes to have different meanings and functions in different times and cultures.

EXERCISE

Without using any reference sources (including dictionaries), devise your own definition of 'a mother'.

Next, list up to six attributes you associate with mothering (these can be both qualities and activities). When you have done this, ask yourself some questions about the kinds of things you have emphasized. Some questions you might like to think about are suggested below.

1. Did you emphasize the biological and physical aspects of being a mother (bearing and caring), or do relational and emotional interactions feature more prominently?
2. On the basis of your list, do you think mothering is best done by the infant's biological mother or can anyone fill the mother's role? Does this mean that mothering is essentially a series of tasks? Could men be mothers?
3. What are the most important 'jobs' a mother does? Do you think these have always been considered important, or have ideas about mothering changed? Who decides what mothers should do? Are expectations about mothering the same for different classes?

EXERCISE RESPONSE

There are no 'right' answers to the questions grouped together as numbers 1 and 2; however, your own responses can be very informative. For instance, if, like me, you found yourself starting with emotional and relational words such as 'love', 'patience' and 'being there', but found your list being taken over by ideas associated with the work of mothering ('organization' and 'having no time'), it is worth thinking about why this shift occurred. Were you thinking about your own mother, yourself as mother, a mother you know, or perhaps images of mothers such as those you see on television or in advertisements? Do any of the aspects and images of mothers/mothering that come easily to mind include men?

You may have found it more difficult to give a detailed answer to question number 3, but you are probably aware that the job of the mother varies considerably from period to period and culture to culture. Throughout this chapter you will find information about the way in which the idea of the mother has been shaped and changed in response to social needs and pressures. When you have finished the chapter, try to remember to go back and look at question 3 again to see how your answer has changed.

Mothering

Mothering is both the simplest and the most complex of relationships. At its most basic, a woman becomes a mother through the physical act of having one of her eggs fertilized, carrying it in her womb, and giving birth to a child. That this process is essentially physical and chemical has been repeatedly demonstrated by the range of activities intended to increase fertility in women, including the phenomenon of the 'test-tube baby' and, most recently, plans to remove ovaries and eggs from aborted foetuses for implantation in barren women. In most societies, however, mothering is much more than a biological process.

Particularly in the post-Freudian Western world, mothering has become entwined with social, psychological and ideological issues, and in the process been transformed from simple procreation and basic caring to profession, obsession, perversion, phenomenon and paradox. In Britain, the complexity of contemporary attitudes to mothering was encapsulated in the media coverage given to two 'mothering scandals' of 1993 – the case of an actress who was believed to have left her daughter 'home alone' while she went on holiday, and that of a fifty-eight year old woman who gave birth to twins after undergoing treatment for infertility in Rome. The tabloid press in particular mounted scathing campaigns against these 'irresponsible' mothers who (it was claimed) put their own pleasures and interests ahead of their children's and so had 'no right' to have children.

The degree and extent of anger at these women is deep-seated and largely derived from our contemporary fantasy of ideal or perfect motherhood. Just as the ideology of femininity is disseminated at all levels of society (see the discussion in chapter 2), this fantasy of the ideal mother is endlessly fuelled through sources as diverse as advertising campaigns, paintings (for instance, the one which is reproduced on page 38), literature, health information booklets, schools and government legislation (see Dally, 1982). The 'good' mother is endlessly patient, forgiving, nurturing and, most important of all, unfailing in her love. She meets her children's needs and fulfils their desires. This image of the good mother is not timeless or universal. Where cultural sentimentalization of mothering does prevail it is relatively recent and class specific. For instance, in Britain there has always been a tradition of paid 'mothering' – from wet nurses through governesses, nannies, and boarding schools.

The problems created by the fantasy of the good mother – problems of living with, separating from, and eventually becoming mothers – preoccupy many women. Because the ideal is a fantasy, one of the most effective ways of exploring it is through literature, for as Freud (1972) points out in 'Creative writers and daydreaming' (first published in 1908), the writer is essentially engaging in acts of fantasy or daydreaming which s/he subjects to conscious revision to make them both acceptable and interesting to others. As with the interpretation of dreams and fantasies, reading stories involves making meanings by discovering material which is disguised or otherwise concealed. This means that the extent to which writers succeed in making their texts appealing depends largely on how far the situations and emotions described correspond to those experienced and felt by the reader. Since, at least until technology supersedes biology, each of us has a mother (even an absent mother is a significant other), texts which explore what it is like to be mothered and to be a mother are likely to be highly meaningful to all women.

The figure of the mother is simultaneously a reality, an archetype and an historical construct. For feminists, the role of the mother is particularly problematic. Some see motherhood as the *modus operandi* of female oppression: 'the heart of women's oppression is her child bearing and child rearing role' (Firestone, 1971). For others, the problem lies not in motherhood, but in its social construction, which currently makes mothering synonymous with subjugation. The following pages consider some of the most influential theories about mothering, and examine ways in which a wide range of women writers have explored the nature of motherhood, and in the process tried to rethink and reshape its meaning.

EXERCISE

Make a list of some literary examples of mothering you have found important. Books from your childhood and popular fiction (for instance, Sue Miller's (1987) *The Good Mother*) are just as important as texts you have studied formally.

1. Can you identify any common characteristics in the mothers in these works? Are they predominantly strong, loving and empowering, or do they tend to be destructive and damaging?
2. How many of the texts you listed were written by women? Of these, how many contained largely positive images of mothering? Were most written from the point of view of the child? How many are preoccupied with the mother's feelings about her mothering?
3. Feminists have taken two main stances on mothering. Either it is a repressive social institution which needs to be abolished if women are to succeed, or it is a vital part of social life and women's experience which needs to be properly recognized. With which of these opinions do you agree? Can you identify any texts in your list which seem to support either attitude?

Whatever texts you listed, it is likely that several of them are about the relationships between mothers and daughters. In the relatively brief history of the novel, mother-daughter sagas have been widespread, many of them being written by women who have struggled to reconcile their needs to create both books and children. One area which has preoccupied women writers for much of the last century and a half is maternal culpability: how far are a daughter's problems the fault of the mother? Florence Nightingale encapsulates the dilemma faced by mothers in her essay 'Cassandra' (1852–9), where she begins by pointing out the falsity of the images of domestic bliss in which they 'cradle' themselves and rails at them because they 'teach their daughters to conform', but then adds, 'what else can they say to their daughters without giving the lie to themselves?' (in Strachey, 1978: 396).

The Psycho-Dynamics of Mothering

Among the most important changes in attitudes to mothering have originated in work done by developmental psychologists and psychoanalysts (Urwin, 1985). While this is not the place for detailed debates about the merits and abuses of these approaches (ideas for further reading are provided in the References section at the end of this chapter), it is important to be familiar with some of their most influential practitioners and concepts, for many women have felt it necessary to use literature to explore their feelings about theories and experiences of mothering which have affected them.

You will notice as you read through the next section that many of the theorists referred to are men. This is because in the field of mothering, as in most professional and intellectual arenas, before the middle of the twentieth century it was rare for women be in positions which made it possible for their ideas to be published and debated. One consequence of this was that in order to attain positions of power and influence, women had to negotiate the largely man-made history of the subject. Inevitably women's reactions have been shaped in response to the thinking and literature produced by their male predecessors. It is with some of the most influential of these that the next section begins.

Mothering and the State

In the 1950s attitudes to mothering took on new significance, largely through the influence of Dr John Bowlby, whose *Child Care and the Growth of Love* was published in 1953. In this highly popular book, Bowlby emphasized the importance of the mother-figure as provider of affection and security in the healthy development of the child. Children who were denied the close and constant relationship provided by the mother at home were, according to Bowlby, in emotional and psychic, if not physical, danger. They also, he argued, posed a threat to society, since Bowlby posited a relationship between juvenile delinquency and lack (or loss) of mothering through the breakdown of the family. Additional information about the influence of Bowlby's theories and the state's preoccupation with traditional families is found in boxes 3.2 and 3.3 at the end of this chapter.

In many ways, Bowlby's ideas can be seen to be closely related to ideological constructions of the family and women's place in post-war society. The preoccupation with producing well-adjusted, stable, healthy and well-educated children was widespread following the disruption and disturbances of the war years. Children, who represented society's investment in the future, took on increasing significance throughout the post-war period, and it was largely the mother's job to make sure that they grew up able to function in the modern world. (Bowlby maintained that nature destined women to be mothers, and accordingly it was women, whether or not they were actually mothers, who needed to be at home to look after society's children.) It was no longer sufficient for a mother simply to make sure that her children were physically healthy and understood social manners and mores; they had to be psychologically sound too.

As a consequence of this social shift in expectations and the new institution-alized hierarchies for reinforcing and regulating it, mothering became less 'instinctive' and 'natural'. Women no longer felt it was adequate simply to do what their mothers and/or the women around them had done, but began to turn to 'experts' such as Truby King or Dr Spock, to ensure that they were the right kind of mothers producing the right kind of children (for a discussion of the way in which mothers became isolated from other women from whom they could learn and with whom they could share anxieties and problems, see Dally, 1982).

The idea that there is a 'right' way to mother which can be learned and evaluated, both by what the mother does and how the child develops, imme-diately sets up **norms** (meaning expectations/standards) which can operate in many ways and at many levels in society. Once such norms exist, most women find it difficult to ignore them, and do everything they can to provide the best environment for their children, even if what they are asked to do violates their feelings and bodily urges. Perhaps the best example of women's determination to listen to medical authorities rather than their bodies is provided by the work of Dr Truby King.

Truby King's theories came to prominence in the 1920s and were underpinned by the belief that since the goal of childhood is to become an autonomous adult, the child needed to be helped towards independence and separation from the moment s/he was born. King warned mothers against the dangers of spoiling their children – especially by displaying their affection or failing to be entirely firm and consistent in their behaviour. It was Truby King who demanded that mothers establish strict routines and policies covering feeding, sleeping, crying, and so on. To this end, mothers bound their breasts to stop the milk from flowing, turned to bottles and charts, routinely parked the baby in the pram at the bottom of the garden to avoid hearing its crying, and set up rigid regimes for each day.

While for some mothers and babies the Truby King method certainly worked, for others it occasioned misery and guilt. The sense of frustration and failure such an overtly institutionalized method of mothering could evoke is poignantly explored by Doris Lessing (1993) in the second of her 'Martha Quest' books, *A Proper Marriage* (written in 1954), and also in Mary McCarthy's (1964) *The Group*. Both women drew on their own experiences and wrote openly about the physical and emotional upheavals which are part of mothering. Lessing in particular explored the anxiety and unhappiness which could beset the Truby King mother.

EXERCISE

This section has been looking at the kinds of institutionalized pressures experienced by new mothers in the middle years of the twentieth century, and the ways in which mothers became increasingly isolated as they tried to live out the routines prescribed by childcare experts. The following questions are designed to encourage you to think about mothering today.

1. What kinds of norms have been established at the end of the twentieth century (think of health, physical and mental development and behavioural norms)? List some of the mechanisms which exist to monitor whether or not a child conforms to these norms.
2. What is the impact on the mother of such norms? Are they likely to make her feel more confident or more vulnerable? What role do you think her relationship with other mothers may play in helping her negotiate externally imposed norms?

EXERCISE RESPONSE

It is easy to think of the benefits which result from sound childcare regimes. A good example from the past is provided by the impact of Truby King's work on infant mortality. Part of the thinking which lay behind his decree that mothers should not cuddle and kiss babies was a concern for hygiene. When Truby King first began practising in New Zealand, one baby in every forty died of infant diarrhoea each year. His emphasis on cleanliness and minimal contact helped to change this figure to one in every thousand babies.

Less clear are the ways in which mothers can become isolated and discouraged by markers which show them to be 'failing' because their children are not the right weight or height, don't sort their toys quickly enough, can't balance on one foot, or won't share. It has been argued, notably by Ann Dally (1982), that the system of monitoring babies is just as much a way of controlling mothers as it is a way of ensuring that children are well cared for. Dally argues that by constantly reinforcing the need for mothers to be present and to be helping their children to succeed, the state manipulates mothers into being cheap labour and providing environments and activities which would otherwise be its responsibility. It is important to remember that it is not only officials of 'the state' who reinforce the ideological imperatives attached to mothering. As Florence Nightingale realized in the last century (see page 42), the previous generation of mothers also has a vested interest in making sure that their daughters are 'good' mothers. Some of the ways in which mothers do this are explored in the discussion of Jamaica Kincaid's 'Girl' in Chapter 2.

The Influence of Freud

Each of the theories and theorists outlined above has been substantially influenced by the work of Sigmund Freud. Chronologically, of course, Freud precedes them all, but since feminists' understanding of mothering has largely resulted from revisiting and reworking what Freud had to say, in some senses his is also the most recent and relevant material for this study. For that reason I would like you now to read, or reread, box 2.1 on 'Theories of identity formation' (pages 18–20).

Feminist rereadings of Freud's theories have identified different patterns in the dynamics of parent–child conflict. For instance, the sociologist, Nancy Chodorow (1978), argues that the pattern of the Oedipal drama is the same whatever the sex of the child. All children, she says, are in love with their primary carer, who is usually the mother. Therefore it is the relationship with the mother, and the way in which separation from her is achieved, that is primarily responsible for whether a child grows up to be masculine or feminine. (Before going on to read the rest of this chapter, please stop and look at box 9.1, 'Connection and separateness', pages 199–200).

According to Chodorow, it is more difficult for a boy to become masculine than it is for a girl to become feminine; indeed, she argues, boys must *learn* to be masculine in opposition to the mother and the mother's body, while girls have only to realize that they are like their mothers. Chodorow's understanding of gender construction is very much coloured by her thesis that in order to break the cycle by which the existing patriarchal society reproduces itself it is necessary to change the infant's relationship with its primary caretaker – usually the mother or a mother figure. The result of typical mothering is, she says, to produce girls whose destiny is likely to be domestic, and who will generally find themselves allocated to (and accepting) social positions which are inferior to males. At the same time, this kind of mothering tends to result in boys who are socially confident and successful, but who find it extremely difficult to form affective caring relationships and who are virtually incapable of nurturing. If Chodorow is right, mothers are central to the continuation of male dominance because they foster masculinity in their sons and collude in the repression of the next generation of women through promoting femininity in their daughters. (For further discussion of Chodorow's work, see chapter 2, pages 19–20 and chapter 9, pages 199–200.)

EXERCISE

1. Compare your experiences of being mothered (and if you have children, with being a mother) with those described by Chodorow. Would you say that you have success-

fully separated from your mother? If you have brothers, how does your behaviour compare to theirs (for instance, if you are all living away from home, do you contact your mother more frequently than they do)?

2. What kinds of tensions are/were most prominent in your relationship with your mother? Could some of these be due to the problem of trying to separate from someone with whom you identify?

EXERCISE RESPONSE

The emphasis in Chodorow's analysis is on the social pressure to separate from the mother and to become an individual; however, many feminists fundamentally disagree that this is a necessary stage in personal development. In answering these questions, you may have found yourself in a 'Catch 22' – reluctant to be classified as weak because you have not successfully separated from your mother, and also reluctant implicitly to reject your mother by agreeing that it is necessary to be separate from her. If this is how you felt, there are many other women like you who find there are a number of positive aspects which result from being connected to their mothers.

One of the benefits which can result from a good and enduring relationship with your mother is the sense of connection and continuity discussed at the beginning of this chapter. This recognition of the way women are linked through a chain of mothers can be a source of strength and meaning; particularly in modern Western-style societies where mothers often feel isolated (Dally, 1982; Urwin, 1985). A more politically radical benefit for mothers and daughters who value being connected has been identified by some lesbian mothers (see box 3.1). Baba Copper (1987) argues that the emphasis on separating mothers and daughters is a goal of what she calls 'heteropatriarchal mothering':

> A tight mother/adult daughter bonding may be the ultimate patriarchal no-no. Therapists reinforce the definition of female maturity as a woman who has separated from, not bonded with her mother. There are the oft-repeated mother-in-law jokes which pressure married women to discard their mother as ally. Although loving relationships between traditional mothers and their heterosexual daughters are not unknown, most daughters value the distances which their lives have generated away from their mothers. (Copper, 1987: 234)

Kimberley Reynolds

<table><tr><td>BOX 3.1</td><td>

Attitudes to Lesbian Mothers

Lesbian mothering has been attacked on a number of fronts. Women who openly declare themselves to be lesbians are discriminated against by the courts (in divorce cases, that a mother is a lesbian is one of the rare factors which causes custody of her children to be given to the father), largely on the advice of social workers and psychiatrists. Prejudice (conscious or unconscious) against all forms of homosexuality cannot be discounted in such decisions, as evidenced by the comments made in response to the 1993 White Paper on adoption by a number of prominent figures. Lady Olga Maitland, MP, told the press that adoption by gay couples 'would be morally very dangerous. . . . a child would be open to sexual abuse' (Welford, 1994).

Despite the fact that no reliable evidence exists to support any of the claims made against lesbian mothers, powerful opposition has grown up around 'expert' testimony that they represent a threat to their children. Many feminists argue that this is because the separation of motherhood, sexual pleasure, and a heterosexual lifestyle threatens social organization; it is the quintessential example of women's capacity to be sexually independent of men.

Some Misconceptions about Lesbian Mothers

It is said that lesbian mothers may damage their children in the following ways:

- The absence of a male partner could adversely affect psychological development by impeding the Oedipal phase.
- Gender identity could be confused through lack of a male partner; also lesbian women (it is said) make confusing role models by not behaving in gender-typical ways.
- Exposure to lesbian behaviour might prevent the child from developing a 'normal' sexual orientation and/or promote homosexual preferences.
- Lesbian relationships are unstable, possibly leading to harmful disruption and tensions.

The evidence

No reliable evidence has been produced to show that lesbian mothering results in any of the problems listed above. A study specifically concerned with the effects on children of being mothered by a lesbian concluded, 'rearing in a lesbian household *per se* did not lead to atypical psychosexual development or constitute a psychiatric risk factor' (Golombok, Spencer and Rutter, 1983: 565).

</td></tr></table>

One book which explores some of the levels on which mothers and daughters are connected is Toni Morrison's (1988) powerful and disturbing novel, *Beloved*. *Beloved* tells the story of Sethe, a runaway slave living in America in the period shortly before and during Reconstruction (the post-Civil War period when the institutions of slavery were officially ended). The complex plot revolves around Sethe's role as mother; specifically the shocking moment when she decapitates one of her daughters and tries to kill her other children to prevent them from being captured by slavers hunting for Sethe.

Sethe's goal is to live as a 'proper' family (by which she means mother, father and children living together in a home of their own) free from the separations and substitutions which characterized the family lives of slaves. Like most slaves, Sethe was raised by a surrogate mother and had to be told her own mother's history; her determination to mother her own children and to keep them from slavery at any cost is thus made more poignant. The strength of Sethe's desire comes from the collective memories of the mothers and daughters in her family, and through them the racial memories of all those who died during the 'middle passage' or journey between Africa and America. Sethe does not know she has these memories, however, until they are released by the return of the daughter she has killed in the form of the ghostly Beloved.

Beloved is an enigmatic character, capable of meaning many things at once. For Sethe she represents not just the return of the lost daughter, but the return of memory. When Beloved comes into the unhappy house Sethe starts to relive and deal with the many horrific events in her life. For the purposes of this chapter, the most important of these is the severing of the bond between mother and daughter caused by the killing of the child. Beloved's presence demands that this bond be restored, and though she comes back as a grown daughter, the level of her need is infantile. The consequences of this are complex, for Sethe not only regains her child, but she also discovers her own childish self for the first time. Morrison makes the reader conscious of the mingling of mother and daughter by using language which constantly blurs the boundaries between the subjective (or internal and personal) experiences of the two. Look, for instance, at the following passage, which Rebecca Ferguson (1991) usefully compares to the interaction described as 'the mother's role of giving back to the baby the baby's own self' (p. 118), which means that when the baby looks at the mother, what s/he sees is a reflection of her/himself:

> I AM BELOVED and she is mine . . . how can I say things that are pictures I am not separate from her there is no place where I stop her face is my own and I want to be there in the place where her face is and to be looking at it too a hot thing

When thinking about the mother/daughter links in *Beloved*, it is important to remember that Sethe has two daughters: Beloved, the baby she killed, and Denvir, the child who survived. In this novel, the renewed connection between Sethe and

Beloved is shown to be unnatural because it is locked into infantile patterns. By contrast, Denvir, who has lived with only her mother and grandmother since her brothers left home, learns to leave her mother and go into the world precisely because her own bond with Sethe is broken by the return of Beloved. Before her dead sister's return, Denvir too had been in an overly intense grandmother/ mother/daughter triad. Breaking this bond between generations of mothers and daughters is seen as a liberation, for Denvir learns to hear, to speak, to interact, and to form new relationships.

Beloved tells the story of generations of slave mothers, and the version of history it provides – which is a psychological history as well as one based in historical reality (Ferguson, 1991: 113) – places particular emphasis on these women's efforts to keep their families and their culture alive through their roles as mothers (chapter 1 considers what may be considered as a positive legacy – high self-esteem and minimal conflict between work and mothering – for African American women and other women from slave-based economies). A very different kind of text which shares many of the same concerns is Louisa May Alcott's (1868) *Little Women*. What is interesting about comparing these two works is that although written under very different social and historical circumstances, both are interested in simultaneously celebrating and criticizing the images of motherhood they create.

Louisa May Alcott wrote *Little Women* when the Victorian ideological construction of the mother maintained that she should be the 'angel of the house'. In practice what this meant was that the mother was to be unfailingly self-sacrificing, devoted to the care and service of others, and only able to see her fulfilment through marriage and its desired end, motherhood. The domestic angel was always described as beautiful, loyal, compassionate and giving; she was also sexually passionless.

Alcott's novel, which achieved immediate and sustained popularity and has been continuously in print, influenced generations of women, including many who are today firmly committed feminists. To early readers uneasy with the position of women under patriarchy, and particularly the powerfully repressive, institutionalized patriarchy which characterized mid-Victorian Britain, the attraction of the book seems to be obvious. *Little Women*'s central character, Jo March, appears to be determined to reject its tenets and provide an enduring, attractive, and profoundly rebellious role model. She whistles, shoves her hands in her pockets, ejaculates 'Christopher Columbus!' and wishes to be the 'man of the family' in her father's absence.

More careful scrutiny of the text, however, raises problems about its attitude to femininity, and most of these problems stem from the relationship between Jo and her mother, 'Marmee'. (Remember, *Little Women* was written in the pre-Freudian era; moreover, Marmee is portrayed as a 'natural' mother who has no recourse to mothering manuals, though they did exist at this time.) The book can, in fact, be read both as a reactionary treatise, which condemns Jo's dissatisfaction with and rejection of the female role, and as a text which subverts the values and goals of Victorian femininity (Murphy, 1990).

The repressive reading concentrates on the ways in which the text subtly undermines Jo's actions and ambitions. It suggests that the book shows Jo's values to be inferior to Marmee's, and that no good can come of Jo's talents and energies until, like her mother, she finds a man able to help her control herself. The crisis of the book comes in the conversation between Marmee and Jo following the episode in which Jo's sister Amy nearly drowns because Jo is so angry with her that she chooses not to look after the younger girl when they are ice skating. Amy falls through some thin ice and has to be rescued by Laurie (Jo's boy-companion from next door).

Jo's great anger is the result of Amy's having burned a book on which she had been working for many weeks. Jo hopes that her writing will eventually allow her to become independent and even to assume the role of 'man of the house' by supporting her family. The near catastrophe with Amy serves to make Jo value family and relationships over imagination, independence, and a career. It also elicits her mother's confession that she too was once an angry young woman. From this moment on Jo gradually learns to identify with her mother and so to rethink her attitude to femininity and womanhood. As a consequence, Jo begins to acquire the domestic skills and self-control which win her father's approbation when he returns from the battlefields of the American Civil War.

There is a great deal of evidence for this reading. It is a book which undoubtedly examines the consequences which must be faced by the girl who fights against becoming 'properly' feminized, and which shows as necessary and legitimate the processes by which women collude in repressing each other; especially through mother-daughter relationships.

Plausible and coherent as this repressive reading may be, Alcott's well-documented ambivalence towards both her creativity and her femininity (Reynolds and Humble, 1993) suggest that it is worth looking at the text from different perspectives to see whether this ambivalence found expression. This is the strategy adopted by those who believe that Alcott's is a subversive text which doesn't advocate the repression of women, but rather points out the mechanisms and costs that such repression entails. As part of this process, *Little Women* offers comfort for those who want(ed) to make femininity and creativity compatible.

The subversive reading concentrates on identifying beneath the manifest plot another which gives voice to the problems inherent in being creative, ambitious, and female. While this reading acknowledges Jo's final acceptance of femininity, it emphasizes the *cost* of this process, and in doing so shows negative aspects of the feminine ideal embodied in the good mother.

The most condemning attack on femininity is provided by the character of Beth, the acme of self-sacrificing Victorian womanhood. As for so many Victorian women (and indeed for anorectic young women today), Beth's determination to repress herself becomes obsessive and self-destructive. Unable to venture beyond the confines of the house because of her shyness, and too passive to attempt to overcome it, Beth is unable completely to fulfil her feminine destiny by ministering to others, finding a husband, and becoming a mother.

Thus far both readings have constructed a picture of Marmee as the 'villain' of the piece who both provides an ever-present and powerful role model of mother-as-feminine-ideal and actively works to repress her daughters by encouraging them to accept and imitate her behaviour. However, the book also offers an equally important and very different way of understanding Marmee's role. *Little Women* constantly explores the tension between the needs of the community and the individual's search for identity. If individuality is associated with masculinity, it could be argued that Alcott is suggesting that the problems of society (here the book's Civil War background becomes very important) are associated with the drive to construct the self as autonomous. By contrast, what is visible in the book is the power derived from collaboration and mutual dependence, as represented by Marmee and her daughters. Mrs March and the girls are respected and effective agents in the town, relieving the distressed and maintaining the community so that life can go on when the war is over. They are shown to be capable of action precisely because they reject autonomy and individual achievement in favour of communal activities and complementary relationships (compare this idea to Gilligan's concept of the 'self in relationship' and 'interdependence of attachment' discussed in box 2.1 on 'Theories of identity formation', pages 18–20). Though this collective way of constructing the text is associated with women in the text – and specifically with Marmee – it is advocated for all. The only way to resolve the war is through reconstruction; the nation must become the grand model of collective activity. The subversive potential of this reading is clear, for if the female, collective model of society is to dominate, patriarchy must be replaced by matriarchy, and women's sphere of influence to move from the home to the community.

EXERCISE

1. If you read *Little Women* when you were younger, try to remember what you felt about it then. With which characters did you identify? Did you want Jo to become a 'little woman' and marry Laurie? How closely did your hopes for Jo correspond with those expressed by Marmee?
2. Which of the readings described above do you find most convincing? Is it possible to agree with the reactionary and the conservative readings at the same time? How far is the mother in this text implicated in the reproduction of patriarchy?
3. Chodorow talks about the need for the individual to become autonomous in order to be socially successful. Do you think the image of mothering provided by Marmee challenges this assumption?

Returning to Chodorow's thesis, if a more equable power relationship between the sexes is to prevail, then mothering behaviour which reproduces the imbalances characteristic of patriarchy must be changed. This is not as straightforward as it may at first appear, however, since over the centuries women have developed complex strategies for functioning in male-dominated societies. Paradoxically, many of these strategies involve exaggerating the restrictions and norms of society and using them to gain power (see the discussions of footbinding and female circumcision in chapter 2). One consequence of this may be, as Florence Nightingale pointed out, resentment on the part of daughters as they realize that their mothers have coerced them into accepting the lies they tell themselves about their lives as wives and mothers. This kind of manipulation and deception, together with the pressure for daughters to separate from their mothers as part of the process of growing up, can transform the way the mother is perceived from benign and angelic ideal to deforming embodiment of evil.

'Bad' Mothers and the Poetry of Olga Broumas

The idea of the bad mother – one who refuses to nurture and even seeks to destroy her children – is an ancient one, probably most familiar from the wicked step-mother of fairy tales. The psycho-dynamics of the bad mother have most famously been explored by Melanie Klein (1975), who theorized that the baby thinks of the mother in terms of the good breast and the bad breast. The good breast is that which provides food and comfort; the bad that which withholds food and disciplines the infant. Even when the baby learns that both breasts represent the same mother, it is helpful mentally to separate them as the anger felt against the bad mother is frightening to the child, who depends entirely on her.

Bruno Bettelheim (1976) identifies precisely this pattern in the representation of mothers in fairy tales. The good mother (who may be the natural mother or a symbolic substitute such as the fairy godmother) and the bad mother (since the last century usually stylized as the step-mother) are depicted as separate, which means that the child reading or listening to the story is able to express hostility for the bad mother without contaminating the good. According to Bettelheim, one reason why a girl is inclined to construct the mother as 'bad' is that she believes them to be rivals for the father's affections.

For Bettelheim, the bad mother is a product of the child's Oedipal attachment to the father, but in a large number of contemporary texts by women the bad mother is one who damages her daughter in a variety of more complex ways. Nevertheless, many women writers have used well-known tales – 'Snow White' 'Cinderella' and 'Sleeping Beauty' – as the basis of their explorations of mother–daughter relationships, for in them we see archetypal bad mothers who seek to negate or destroy their daughters. 'Snow White' provides a particularly powerful example, for each method the wicked mother uses to destroy her daughter is a perversion of good mothering skills (grooming, dressing and feeding).

Perhaps because of their symbolic qualities, and because, at least in Europe and North America, virtually all children are acquainted with the most famous fairy tales, they have proved particularly attractive to many women writers who are attempting to explore their attitudes to mothering (both how they were mothered and how they mother). Greek-born Olga Broumas (1949–) has used 'Little Red Riding Hood' for this purpose, and in her retelling, the tale takes on a wide range of themes, issues, experiences and problems arising from the dynamics involved in mothering and being mothered.

EXERCISE

If it has been some time since you last read this fairy tale, first read a traditional version of it (look for one by the Grimm brothers or Perrault). As you read the following poem, try to identify how Broumas (1977) uses the Red Riding Hood story to explore her attitudes to mothering – both being mothered and being a mother. Then answer the questions following.

> Little Red Riding Hood
> I grow old, old
> without you, Mother, landscape
> of my heart. No child, no daughter between my bones
> has moved and passed
> out screaming, dressed in her mantle of blood
> as I did
> once through your pelvic scaffold, stretching it
> like a wishbone, your tenderest skin
> strung on its bow and tightened
> against the pain. I slipped out like an arrow, but not before
> the midwife
> plunged to her wrist and guided
> my baffled head to its first mark. High forceps
> might, in that one instant, have accomplished
> what you and that good woman failed
> in all these years to do: cramp
> me between the temples, hobble
> my baby feet. Dressed in my red hood, howling, I went –
> evading
> the white-clad doctor and his fancy claims: microscope,
> stethoscope, scalpel, all

the better to see with, to hear,
and to eat – straight from your hollowed basket
into the midwife's skirts. I grew up
good at evading, and when you said
'Stick to the road and forget the flowers, there's
wolves in those bushes, mind
where you got to go, mind
you get there,' I
minded. I kept
to the road, kept
the hood secret, kept what it sheathed more
secret still. I opened
it only at night, and with other women
who might be walking the same road to their own
grandma's house, each with her basket of gifts, her small hood
safe in the same part. I minded well. I have no daughter
to trace that road, back to your lap with my laden
basket of love. I'm growing
old, old
without you. Mother, landscape
of my heart, architect of my body, what other gesture
can I conceive
to make with it
that would reach you, alone
in your house and waiting, across this improbable forest
peopled with wolves and our lost, flower-gathering
sisters they feed on.
(Broumas, 1977)

1. Highlight any images, vocabulary, or other influences you find from the original story. Try to decide why they have been used, and how they affect your understanding of the poem.

2. Compare the ways in which Broumas's poem deals with some of the issues discussed in relation to the other texts we have considered. For instance, the problem of separation between mother and daughter; female sexuality, and gender? Is the mother in the poem 'good' or 'bad'? If 'bad', in what ways does the poem suggest she has failed? Is there a sense of collective female experience?

3. Olga Broumas is a lesbian feminist. Can you find ways in which her politics seem to affect how she thinks about mothering? (Use the information in box 3.1 on 'Attitudes to lesbian mothers' on page 48 to help you.) What aspects of the relationship between biology, maternity, and feminism does the poem explore?

EXERCISE RESPONSE

As you answered the questions in this exercise, I hope you found yourself able to make connections between some of the other texts discussed here, and also others you have read. This poem invites you to think about all the versions of and illustrations for 'Little Red Riding Hood' you have encountered at different times in your life – from picture books to explicitly adult versions such as Angela Carter's (1983) short story, 'The company of wolves' and the film made of it. Texts calling attention to their dependence on and interaction with other texts in this way are said to be demonstrating **inter-textuality**. This term is used to make readers aware of a process which is usually unconscious: each time we read something new, we bring with us all the other reading that we have done. When a text makes us aware of this and directs our attention to the original(s), both texts are transformed for the reader. In Olga Broumas's poem, for instance, we are immediately asked to think about the red cloak and hood as a 'mantle of blood'. This idea in itself is not new: many critics have suggested that the red hood or red cap represents the onset of menstruation. However, in the poem, it is not menstrual blood which is evoked, but the blood which accompanies birth. Thus in this image alone the reader is asked to bring together a reading of the story in which nothing is known about the symbolism of the red outfit, a later reading in which it is thought to represent the girl's entry into puberty, and another in which it is birth-blood. All these possible readings (and there are others) are used to make sense of the rest of the poem.

For me, Broumas succeeds well in evoking the sense of connection between mother and daughter, and thus in raising a question which is of importance to many feminists. If, by rejecting traditional power relations and sexual roles we also refuse to become mothers, are we not in danger of severing an important link in the chain of connection between women?

Conclusion

I hope that this chapter has helped you to think about mothers and mothering in new ways. It is easy to focus on the tensions and problems which are associated with the role of 'Mother' – indeed, as Copper (1987), Dally (1982) and Urwin (1985) point out, Western society creates conditions in which mothers seem bound to 'fail' and which encourage us to separate from and even to turn against our mothers as part of becoming mature. Therefore I want to end by thinking again about the fact that the role of the mother in society is socially constructed, which means that it can be changed. What can we do to highlight and nurture positive images and conditions for mothers? One of the first things we need to do is to take mothers seriously. This means both to provide balanced ideas about mothering rather than to idealize the role and image of the mother, and also to ensure that women have the conditions and support necessary for them to mother effectively. Equally important is the need to unpack some of the psychological baggage with which mothering is laden – is it possible for mother/child relationships not to become difficult when so much of the emotional and physical well-being of the child(ren) is invested in the mother, and so much of the mother's sense of self-esteem and purpose rests on her child(ren)? (This situation becomes particularly problematic when, after insisting on the need for mother–child dependency, we also insist on the need for separation?) As an ever-increasing body of women learn to question their circumstances and the ideologies which underpin them, and make their way into positions of public influence, there will be opportunities to rethink and redefine the image and role of mothers. It is difficult to underestimate the possibilities for change which could accompany such revisions to the construction of motherhood.

Non-traditional Mothering

BOX 3.2

The 'traditional' nuclear family – mother, father and child(ren) – is regarded by many as the linchpin of society. It underpins economic, social and political structures, and accordingly is defended (or controlled) by legislation, financial incentives, and moral pronouncements. Effective contraception, feminist reconstructions of the female role, changes in the economy and labour force, and equal opportunities legislation have all contributed to the decline of the stereotypical 'ideal' family group. This has resulted in strong reactions from both ends of the political spectrum. Those on the right take a line which can readily be traced to the work of Dr John Bowlby. They claim that the problems of society are caused precisely by the breakdown of family life, and that the remedy is to go 'back to basics'. For families this means reaffirming the primacy of the two-parent, heterosexual model, with mother at home looking after the children and father working to support the family. For those on the left, these changes to the family are understood as democratic. Social practices which have privileged male activities, power and property have been challenged, and largely readjusted.

Some Facts

- The 'traditional' nuclear family is a relatively recent phenomenon, bound up with the needs of industrial capitalism.

- In other countries and in different historical periods, it is/was normal practice for those other than the parents to have the primary care and responsibility for children.
- In Britain today families that are 'non-traditional' in the sense of departing from the stereotype may have become the norm. (Golombok, Spencer and Rutter, 1983: 551)

Although much evidence exists to show that the traditional nuclear family need not be crucial to either the well-being of the child or that of the state, those who openly flout or otherwise seek to challenge this model frequently find themselves demonized. Two groups which have received considerable attention, much of it hostile, are single mothers and lesbian mothers (see boxes 3.1 and 3.3).

BOX 3.3

Single Mothers in the 1990s

For much of the last 150 years the single mother was widely regarded as a 'fallen woman', and her offspring were illegitimate. Today many of the traditional stigma associated with women who have children outside of marriage have gone, only to be replaced by a new, equally censorious discourse. There are many ways of becoming a single mother, ranging from planned or accidental pregnancy through desertion, death, divorce, adoption and artificial insemination. Women who have children on their own come from all economic and educational backgrounds, age groups, races and religions. Some are supported by loving families and partners, others are required to look after themselves and their children on their own. Whatever the actual situation, single mothers often find themselves accused of anti-social behaviour.

Common Accusations made against Single Mothers

- Single mothers are said to be irresponsible scroungers, manipulating the social security system by having babies in order to obtain housing and support.
- Single mothers are said to be incapable of controlling their children, therefore they are blamed for increases in violence, crime, and declining social standards.
- For feminists, single mothers who replace dependence on a man with dependence on the state are problematic.
- Single mothers without male partners endanger their children's psycho-sexual development (see box 3.1 on 'Attitudes to lesbian mothers').

Points for Consideration

- While the number of unmarried mothers has steadily increased over recent decades, this does not mean that all technically 'single' mothers are bringing up children on their own. Many women now have long-term relationships outside marriage.
- There is evidence that the children of single (non-lesbian) mothers are more often referred for psychiatric counselling than those of two-parent (including lesbian) families (see Golombok, Spencer and Rutter, 1983). The reasons for this are as likely to be caused by such things as domestic tension (perhaps relating to the breakdown of the parental relationship), financial hardship, and relocation as to be attributable to parenting by a single mother *per se*.
- Institutionalized anxiety about single mothers may be related to social power structures, which largely depend on the traditional father-dominated family for their reproduction.

REFERENCES

Alcott, Louisa May 1868: *Little Women*. (London: Frederick Warne & Co, no date.)

Bettelheim, Bruno 1976: *The Uses of Enchantment: The Meaning and Importance of Fairy Tales*. London: Thames & Hudson.

Bowlby, John 1953: *Child Care and the Growth of Love*. Harmondsworth: Penguin.

Broumas, Olga 1977: *Beginning with O*. London: Yale University Press.

Carter, Angela 1983: The company of wolves. In Jack Zipes (ed.), *The Trials and Tribulations of Little Red Riding Hood: Versions of the Tale in Sociocultural Context*. London: Heinemann.

Chodorow, Nancy 1978: *The Reproduction of Mothering*. Berkeley and Los Angeles: University of California Press.

Copper, Baba 1987: The radical potential in lesbian mothering. In Sandra Pollack and Jean Vaughn (eds), *Politics of the Heart: A Lesbian Parenting Anthology*, Ithaca, NY: Firebrand Books.

Dally, Ann 1982: *Inventing Motherhood: The Consequences of an Ideal*. London: Burnett Books.

Ferguson, Rebecca 1991: History, memory and language in Toni Morrison's *Beloved*. In Susan Sellers (ed.), *Feminist Criticism: Theory and Practice*, Hemel Hempstead: Harvester.

Firestone, Shulamith 1971: *The Dialectic of Sex: The Case For Feminist Revolutions*. London: Jonathan Cape.

Freud, S. 1972: Creative writers and daydreaming. In D. Lodge (ed.), *C20th Literary Criticism*, London: Longman. [First published 1908.]

Golombok, Susan, Spencer, Ann and Rutter, Michael 1983: Children in lesbian and single-parent households: psychosexual and psychiatric appraisal. *Journal of Child Psychology and Psychiatry*, 24, 551–72.

Kincaid, Jamaica 1986: Girl. In Angela Carter (ed.), *Wayward Girls and Wicked Women*. London: Virago.

Klein, Melanie 1975: *Envy and Gratitude and Other Works*, 1946–1963. London: Hogarth Press.

Lessing, Doris 1993: *A Proper Marriage*. London: HarperCollins. [First published in 1964.]

McCarthy, Mary 1964: *The Group*. Harmondsworth: Penguin.

Miller, Sue 1987: *The Good Mother*. Boston: G. K. Hall.

Morrison, Toni 1987: *Beloved*. New York: Alfred A. Knopf.

Murphy, Anne B. 1990: The borders of ethical, erotic and artistic possibilities in *Little Women*. *Signs*, 15, 3, 562–85.

Reynolds, Kimberley and Humble, Nicola 1993: *Victorian Heroines: Representations of Femininity in Nineteenth-Century Literature and Art*. Hemel Hempstead: Harvester.

Strachey, Ray 1978: *The Cause: A Short History of the Women's Movement in Great Britain*. London: G. Bell & Sons.

Urwin, Cathy 1985: Constructing motherhood: the persuasion of normal development. In Caroline Steedman, Cathy Urwin and Valerie Walkerdine (eds), *Language, Gender and Childhood*, London: Virago.

Welford, Heather 1994: Gay pride and joy. *Guardian*, 4 January.

CHAPTER
4 Girls and Schooling

Valerie Hey

Plate 3 *Burntwood Girls' School, London.* Format Partners; photograph: Jacky Chapman.

This chapter looks at the effects of gender on the schooling of girls. One immediate way of engaging with the topic is to look at what women themselves have written about their schooling.

The material has been drawn from a variety of sources – historical, sociological, biographical – and has been organized into four sections. The first focuses on autobiographical accounts of school, and asks you to explore your own experiences of school. The second examines the history of formal schooling in Britain. The third discusses feminist theories of girls and schooling, while the fourth explores the role of the 'hidden curriculum'. These themes have been selected to provide a number of foci for thinking about how girls' school experiences are gendered.

After reading this chapter you should have a better understanding of your own educational experiences. You should have some understanding of the history of girls' education and current feminist analyses of girls and schooling. You should also be able to identify the role of the formal *and* the hidden curriculum in the reproduction of beliefs, behaviour and outcomes based on notions of normality. You should appreciate the centrality of gender in the re/production of this 'normality'.

Girls' Own Stories: Biographical Accounts of Schooling

The aim of this first section is to encourage your interest in the topic through reading and reflecting upon 'snapshots' of schooling. For nearly all of us, school was a significant early experience. For those of us who went through the 'normal' schooling process, a large proportion of our childhood and adolescence was spent in school, and thus school played a significant role in our growing up. Not surprisingly, schooling is therefore implicated in *how* we grew up.

In her autobiography, the New Zealand poet Janet Frame (1990) writes: 'I remember the delight of learning French words and songs and the names of science apparatus (bunsen burner, litmus paper); the cooking lessons, lemon sage, puff pastry, cream crackers; how to scrub a wooden table; the sewing . . .' (Frame, 1990: 72). These are memories of school in New Zealand in 1935. And they are happy memories. For some people school is a delight, for others it is torture, for many it is something in between. But however much we liked or loathed the experience, we all remember certain key things which we associate with school, such as French words, bunsen burners and puff pastry, or maybe school dinners, or hockey boots.

From very early in life, children learn that they are gendered beings, and school is one of the places that reinforces this message. Even when girls and boys do the same lessons in the same class, we need to ask the question: are they having the same experience? Consider this story from 40 years ago. Twins, a girl and a boy, go to the same local primary school together. They are both bright and both thrive in the school environment. At the end of the school year they come home with their school reports: the boy's is full of words like 'promising' and phrases such as 'a bright future'. His twin sister's says nothing about her future, but makes negative comments about her talkativeness.

Probably you will find this story shocking, but it is true: it happened to one of the contributors to this book. If you think it must have been unusual, read the extract below (from Jill Tweedie's (1993) autobiography, *Eating Children*):

> Listening to all this esoteric lore [stories of her brother's life at boarding school in the 1950s] I was torn between scorn and a niggling groundswell of envy. It was stupid, that went without saying, only idiots would think up so many pointless rules and regulations, and I was glad I didn't have to obey them but oh dear, there must be something to them, otherwise the grown-ups would laugh at them too, or say 'mmm', as they did when I told them things about my school. Instead, whenever Robbie told them his stories, they leaned forward to listen really carefully and if they laughed, they laughed as if they were giving him a prize. They were much more interested, too, when he talked about his friends, scab-kneed boys called Ingham Minor or Toadspawn or Smellysocks, than they were when I talked about mine. They never asked me what my friends' surnames were or what their fathers did. I was missing something, I knew that, but what? Why did I have a picture in my mind

of a castle being erected stone by stone? with turrets and towers and flags and high walls to keep Robbie in and me out? I don't care, I told myself under the bedclothes at night. They're only a lot of silly boys, who cares what they do? (Tweedie, 1993: 62)

EXERCISE

What messages is the young Jill Tweedie learning from her parents' response to her brother's school stories?

Why do you think 'the grown-ups' wanted to know what Robbie's friends surnames were? Or what their fathers did?

What does Jill Tweedie mean by 'a castle . . . with turrets and towers . . . to keep Robbie in and me out'?

EXERCISE RESPONSE

You will probably have decided that this experience taught Jill Tweedie that boys and girls are not equal: what boys do (and say) is treated as important, whereas what girls do (and say) is not. The questions about her brother's friends and their fathers taught Jill Tweedie that the powerful in society (well-educated, white males) are linked through the male line, and that school (that is, private boarding school) is the place where upper-middle-class boys establish the links with one another which will serve them well in later life (the so-called Old Boys' Network). Jill Tweedie's image of a castle expresses her reluctant but growing awareness that, as a girl, she is forever excluded from this privileged group.

This is, of course, not just a question of gender, but also of social class, since both girls and boys from less privileged backgrounds are excluded from this group too. One of the points we want to establish in this chapter is that gender cannot be considered in isolation from other factors such as class and race. The following extract is taken from the autobiographical writing of bell hooks (1993), a Black American woman from a working-class background. In this passage, she affirms the political necessity of maintaining an active link with her poor black family and community.

Maintaining connections with family and community across class boundaries demands more than just summary recall of where one comes from. It requires knowing, naming, and being ever-mindful of those aspects of one's past that have enabled and do enable one's self-development in the present, that sustain and support, that enrich. One must also honestly confront barriers that do exist, aspects of the past that do diminish. My parents' ambivalence about my love for reading led to intense conflict. They (especially my mother) would work to ensure that I had access to books, but would threaten to throw them away if I did not conform to other expectations. Or they would insist that reading too much would drive me insane. Their ambivalence nurtured in me uncertainty about the value and significance of intellectual endeavour that took years for me to unlearn. While this aspect of our class reality was one that wounded and diminished, their vigilant insistence that being smart did not make me a 'better' or 'superior' person (which often got on my nerves because I wanted to have that sense that it did indeed set me apart, make me better) made a profound impression. From them I learned to value and respect various skills and talents folk might have, not just to value people who read books and talk about ideas. They and my grandparents might say about somebody, 'Now he don't read nor write a lick, but he can tell a story', or as my grandmother would say, 'call out the hell in words' . . . Language is a crucial issue for folk whose movement outside the boundaries of poor and working-class background changes the nature and direction of their speech. . . . Learning to listen to different voices, hearing different speech challenges the notion that we must all assimilate – share a single, similar talk – in educational institutions. (hooks, 1993: 106–7)

In this extract, bell hooks talks about her personal experience of education. Again, the issue of language is raised. bell hooks' account demonstrates that it's not just the vocabulary of language associated with school which marks out whether we belong or not, it's also a question of whether we speak 'properly'. She argues that we should challenge the assumption that there is one 'correct' way of writing and speaking which is appropriate in the academic world, and insists upon a plurality of speaking styles which embrace rather than eliminate ways of speaking learned earlier in our lives. This extract is included to indicate the importance of recognizing that gender is experienced differently in different times and in different locations. The social experience of being black and working class has a profound impact on bell hooks' experience of education.

EXERCISE

In the above extract, bell hooks indicts the tendency of institutions to silence dissent through demanding conformity to a form of writing or speaking that is deemed 'proper'.

Can you recollect instances in your own educational experience when you were encouraged or coerced into changing your speech, writing or behaviour on grounds of it being deemed unacceptable – either in terms of race, class or gender?

In this section we have begun to think about the different ways girls experience schooling. Many commentators argue that schooling and school institutions function as the major means through which individuals come to have a particular place in society. Classic sociological explanations of schooling suggest that education works as the major sorting system in society. To put it simply, education's role is understood to be about slotting people into a workforce already divided along lines of *class*. Feminists have shifted the focus by asking questions about the ways in which schools also function to reproduce *gender* inequalities.

In the rest of this chapter we will draw on these feminist debates to discuss three further themes related to gender and education. These themes have been selected to help you to think about the ways girls' school experiences are organized. We'll start by looking at the historical development of education in the nineteenth century to see how ideologies of femininity found expression there.

Femininity Goes to School: Femininity and the Formal Curriculum

The historical development of education in England in the nineteenth century traces the role of ideologies of femininity and their contestation. Exploring policy documents from the past reveals the assumptions of policy makers, while personal and popular accounts tell us something about their effects. It is, however, more difficult to assess the intangible effects of such policies and beliefs on the aspirations and expectations of schoolchildren and their parents. Nevertheless, these Victorian themes of femininity left powerful residues. Indeed they continue to have an influence today.

Educational provision was initially restricted to the aspirant sons of the upper class. This practice confirmed the scholarly clerical tradition of Oxbridge. Despite capitalist expansion stimulating the demand for education, middle and upper-class women and their working-class sisters were variously denied access. The subsequent history of education traces numerous challenges to this exclusion. A highly condensed account of this history follows.

A class of their own: Arguments for and against education for working-class children and middle-class girls

> What is deemed to be appropriate education and schooling for girls and boys is closely tied up with prevalent notions of femininity and masculinity and with the sexual division of labour. Up until the late nineteenth century a large proportion of working-class children and the majority of working-class girls received their education in the home and in the 'family' setting. (Measor and Sikes, 1992: 36)

Intriguing documentary evidence exists showing contradictions in the arguments which were used by various groups to support a right to an education. An editorial in *The Times* in 1854 spoke of the danger of working-class subversion and advocated education as a means of keeping working-class men away from political organizing and the contaminating influence of:

> cheap publications containing the wildest and the most anarchical doctrines [which] are scattered, broadcast over the land, in which religion and morality are perverted and scoffed at, and every rule of conduct which experience has sanctioned broken, and on which the very existence of society depends, openly assailed. . . . The middle classes who pass their lives in the steady and unrepining duties of life may find it hard to believe in such atrocities. Unfortunately they know little of the working classes . . . (*The Times*, 1854)

This backcloth of class-based fear establishes a context in which we need to set the struggle which (middle-class) women waged to gain entry to formal schooling. While the 1870 Elementary Education Act was meant to lay the foundation of a universal regime of education, the necessary provision and attendance regulations were not in place for many decades. The Act did, however, stimulate the demand for education but responses to this were predictably differentiated by both class and gender.

Fee paying schools developed and these varied in terms of quality, curricula, size and prestige. Some were little more than 'domestic boarding establishments, where a small number of girls and young women lived "en famille" and were taught to be "young ladies" – and very little else' (Measor and Sikes, 1992: 37).

Molly Hughes (1934) was a pupil at such a school and later commentated critically on her experience:

> In my twelfth year my mother decided to send me to an Establishment for Young Ladies about a mile from my home. It must have been to give me some companionship, for I can conceive of no other rational motive for the step. Indeed I have come to think that the main value of school life is to prevent one's getting on too fast in the natural surroundings of home. (Hughes, 1934, quoted in Measor and Sikes, 1992: 38)

Pauline Marks (1976) cites figures to suggest that in 1898, approximately 70 per cent of middle-class girls aged eleven and over were similarly being 'domesticated' at such schools.

For those parents, girls and radical educators dissatisfied with the narrowness of the provision, there was formidable opposition. Ideologies of femininity were deeply implicated in how policy makers, government officials and others thought about the right means through which middle-class girls should be schooled:

... boys are sent out into the world to buffet with its temptations to mingle with bad and good, to govern and direct. ... girls are to dwell in quiet homes, amongst a few friends, to exercise a noiseless influence, to be submissive and retiring ... to educate girls in crowds is wrong. (Sewell, 1865: 219)

These assertions were stimulated by so called 'scientific' theories about womens'/girls' bodies. The study of science and mathematics was thought to be particularly damaging to girls' reproductive organs:

... in its full sense, the reproductive power means the power to bear a well-developed infant, and to supply the infant with the natural food for the natural period. Most of the flat-chested girls who survive their high-pressure education are incompetent to do this. (Spencer, 1867: 486)

Notions of a fragile femininity preoccupied policy makers:

... as regards mental work, great care should be taken to avoid any undue strain. Lessons requiring much concentration, and therefore using up a great deal of brain energy, Mathematics, for instance, should not be pushed. With some girls it is well to discontinue one or more subjects for a time if they begin to show signs of fatigue ... such subjects as cookery, embroidery or the handicrafts may well be introduced into the curriculum as they cause comparatively little mental strain. (Campbell, 1908)

The ideological oppositions at play here are key to interpreting the ways in which a middle-class concept of femininity and masculinity took shape. These oppositions are: mind against body, male against female, action against passivity/tranquillity, brain against womb. Femininity was thus associated with the 'natural' bodily facts of reproduction, while masculinity itself was by implication viewed as more 'rational', stemming from the identification of masculinity with the mind. By extension, bodies needed 'protecting', while minds needed 'educating'.

We need to remind ourselves that at the time these educational ideas had currency, vast numbers of working-class young women and girls were employed in regimes of the hardest physical labour. Such girls and women worked in coal mines; in cotton and woollen mills; in the sweated clothes trades and in all levels of commerce, domestic labour and manufacturing. Black girls and women also, nominally emancipated as free labour, worked in the homes of the aristocracy as super-subordinated and exploited peoples. However, few members of the leisured classes bothered to extend their notions of 'fragility' to encompass the black women and white working-class girls and women who laboured for them either directly as domestic labour or indirectly to provide the cheap labour from which they drew their profits. Land and property owners indulged their desires about domestic harmony solely in terms of 'their' fragrant white wives and daughters. Pioneers of women's and girls' education like Dorothy Beale of Cheltenham Ladies

College and Frances Buss (founder of the North London Collegiate School), who along with other reformers set up The Girls Public Day Trust, were keen to establish a stake for middle-class girls in the new expansion of education. They did so through a variety of tactical accommodations with the powerful normative model of femininity. Some based their schools on similar lines to the competitive and sport-centred ethos found in the male public schools, while others encouraged a feminine ethos through regulating dress and teaching deportment. Eventually these class manners of deportment and 'proper dress' were exported to all schools. You can trace this recurrent influence in Mary Evans' (1991) account of the almost surreal school uniform regulations described in her autobiographical exploration.

If privileged women found access to education difficult, how much more tenacity was required by working-class people, especially daughters. A complex mix of historical factors led to numerous legislative concessions. These provided a framework which reflected these interconnecting political developments. The consequent impact of these overlapping, and in some cases contradictory, concerns increased the pressure for working-class girls' education. Again the emphasis was upon producing competent home-makers. The actual content of education for working-class children did not touch upon the harsh and exploitative material conditions in which they lived. The earned poverty of the working class – represented in poor housing, health and life expectancy – remained, despite ideological exhortations about 'cleanliness and hygiene'.

The bourgeois desire to produce in working-class girls, domestic rectitude, produced its own ironies – the absence of working-class girls from school caused by their detention at home, in the very tasks which their elders and betters deemed most improving for them!

This Victorian self-serving and deeply quirky fascination with the 'domestic' was not so much dislodged as further institutionalized, along with the establishment of a more systematized state education regimen. The 1926 Hadow Report laid the basis for the famous tripartite distinction between grammar, technical and secondary modern. In 'modern' schools the curricula was biased towards 'practical work and realistic studies' preparatory for adult life and the 'realistic' studies strongly embedded stereotypical ideas of gender, with girls given 'housecraft' in order to: 'render girls fit for leaving school to undertake intelligently the various household duties which devolve on most women' (Board of Education, 1926: 232).

Schools were eventually reorganized along the lines recommended by Hadow in the statutory requirements of the 1944 Act which importantly structured education as the responsibility of local education authorities (LEAs) in three main stages primary/secondary/further education. The school-leaving age was raised to fifteen. Educational inequalities were supposedly addressed by rational means – that is, by standardized IQ test of the eleven plus. Curricular patterns were laid down and justified with recourse to arguments about nature and femininity. John Newsom (1948), an important educational thinker expressed it thus:

> Women possess certain particular needs based on their *psychology, physiology, and their social and economic position* . . . The fundamental common experience is the fact that the vast majority of them will become makers of homes, and that to do this successfully requires the proper development of many talents. (Newsom, 1948: 110, my italics)

I can recollect a housecraft lesson about washing men's handkerchiefs in the late 1950s, at one such secondary modern school!

The larger number of girls who left school earlier than boys, a social outcome which should have generated questions, merely worked to confirm the assumption that females were to be viewed as economically dependent on males.

Notions of femininity continue to structure girls' experience of schooling. These notions reflect a *white and middle-class* femininity. This poses problems for girls from working-class homes. Girls from different race and ethnic origins are even more outside of this ideology of white femininity than working-class white girls. Black – and here I am referencing African Caribbean and Asian girls – do not share this history. Indeed they do not share a common history with each other either.

Black girls' femininity is assumed to take different forms and they are constructed quite differently. If the model for white working-class girls' sexuality was domestic dependency in monogamous marriage, the strongest form of servitude – slavery continues to provide the ideological concepts through which the social management of black African Caribbean girls takes place. (For further discussion of black girls' sexuality, see chapter 2, page 24; also chapter 7, pages 138–9.)

Amina Mama has argued that we need to understand the powerful ideological messages given by the work which black women are directed to. Work such as nursing, cleaning and other service jobs are classified as 'feminine' thus masking their physically demanding (and at times demeaning) nature (Mama, 1984). Michele Barrett claims that 'the ideological model of [black women's] work, is not that of the wife, but of the servant' (Barrett and McIntosh, 1985: 39).

Heidi Mirza (1992) makes the point that modes of black African Caribbean femininity have never been conceptualized within the specific terms of female passivity. However, racist and racially divisive notions of female sexuality have been assigned to different groups of black girls on the ground of their 'race'. These identifications have drawn from British colonial history. Asian girls are thus described as super-passive and compliant and dominated by 'their' men (Parmar and Mirza, 1981). African Caribbean girls are said to be hyper-feminine, sexually provocative and 'larrupy' (Hey, 1988). Racist beliefs about rapacious African or conversely dormant Asian sexuality, which abounded in white colonialist histories, persist in these attributions.

Groups of black girls have fought and continue to fight to retain and practice accounts of femininity which did not presume female economic and psychological dependency:

> What the young black women in the study were expressing was essentially an ideology that emphasised the relative autonomy of both the male and female roles. Ironically, the dynamic that has produced this equality between the sexes within the black social structure has been the external imposition of oppression and brutality. (Mirza, 1992: 164)

Despite these crucial differences (which form part of a much wider argument than can be attempted here), the ideology of femininity which defines for girls a future dominated by their *potential* capacity as child bearers and as *dependants* is dominant and *all* girls come under its influence. I want now to consider how gendered subject preferences and assessment continue to be manifested in schools today.

Gendered subjects

What is learned at school is an outcome of a gendered curriculum. Subjects which constitute the formal curriculum have become strongly associated with girls/boys, one gender rather than the other. This can be illustrated by looking at the subjects girls and boys enrol in for GCSE examinations (see table 4.1).

You can see from table 4.1 that several patterns emerge showing a distinct gender effect in the distribution of pupils within subject specialisms. There is a marked preference for boys to be entered for science courses and for girls to be entered for language examinations. Biology is predominantly claimed by girls as

Table 4.1 All GCSE groups entries 1990

Subject	Male % of entries 1990	Female % of entries 1990
Biology	38.9	61.1
Chemistry	55.1	44.9
Economics	61.4	38.6
English	49.7	50.3
English Literature	45.9	54.1
French	41.8	58.2
Geography	57.9	42.1
History	48.3	51.2
Mathematics*	48.3	51.7
Physics	70.8	29.2

* These are figures for the coursework option.
Source: 1990 *Inter-Group Statistics* cited and adapted from Stobbart, Elwood and Quinlan, 1992

a 'female' science. Boys outnumber girls in economics and chemistry, the reverse is the case in English literature and history.

These patterns reflect the sense pupils have that such subjects are either more or less feminine or masculine. Few compulsory subjects escape such designation. There are gendered disparities in exam outcomes as well:

> The two 'compulsory' subjects, English and mathematics produced very different outcomes. During 1988–1990 on average 54.6% of girls gained Grades A–C in English compared with 41.5% of boys. In mathematics this pattern was reversed with girls gaining 34.6% grades A–C and boys 38.9%. These constitute dramatic differences given that it is much the same cohort taking both. (Stobbart, Elwood and Quinlan, 1992: 265)

Patricia Murphy (1991) offers some insights into how assessment works at all times within the context of gender. Thus how well or poorly individual pupils perform on say particular science tasks is related to the absence or presence of a gender inflexion in how the questions are asked. Questions which carry distinctive gendered narratives cue pupils into seeing that it is a question which is or is not, aimed at them:

> If we are assessing pupils' ability to interpret pie charts, for example, and set a question which looks at the varying proportion of different fibres in girls' school blouses, girls achieve higher scores than boys. If, on the other hand, the focus is on the proportions of different types of cars produced by a factory at different times of the year the situation is reversed. *Pupils' experience outside of school lead them unconsciously, to define areas of the curriculum where they expect to be successful, or conversely unsuccessful.* (Murphy, 1991: 206, my italics)

Patricia Murphy's research into how gendered expectations mark a subject or a subject content as 'appropriate', reminds us of the ways in which gender permeates our ways of thinking and feeling. Girls or boys are not simply pushed into specific parts of the curriculum – they appear to jump and in that sense could be said to 'choose'.

Different feminist analyses suggest that there are different causes of girls' position, though all of them reject biological explanations. The ways in which some subjects are seen to be less available to girls has been the subject of complex questioning and detailed research. Alison Kelly (1981) has identified the 'masculine' image of science as a case in point. Valerie Walkerdine (1985, 1989) has drawn attention to wider and denser arguments about the ways in which reason itself is seen as 'masculine' so that femininity, and by implication girls, are placed outside of it. Such arguments return us to the same themes which preoccupied the gatekeepers of education.

'Feminists go to School': Feminist Theories of Girls and Schooling

There is no consensus about the causes of girls' position in school and their subsequent position in the labour market. There are instead a number of different accounts. Some of these emphasize structural factors, stressing the role and function of schooling as a mechanism of social and economic control.

Alternatively other theories concentrate upon the social experiences of girls at school and focus on aspects of gender socialization. Yet other writers take issue with the concept of socialization, claiming that it denies individual **agency** (a concept that recognizes the potential and actual power of the individual to influence the course of their lives). Recent theorizations seek to understand how girls' own behaviours and identities are made through their gendered interactions rather than imposed on them from outside. For the sake of clarity and brevity I want to propose that there are four main feminist schools or positions about girls and schooling. These are outlined in box 4.1.

BOX 4.1

Feminist Approaches to Girls and Schooling

The liberal feminist tradition locates the problem of gender difference in educational experience in the apparent reluctance of girls themselves to identify with *all* aspects of the curriculum. Interest has focused in particular on the hostility of girls to studying science. The general approach is to identify *blocks* said to prevent girls from reaching their potential. These blocks lead to resistance which depresses girls' aspirations, ambitions and confidence. Socialization is a key term in this model and it is accorded a great deal of explanatory power. The solution is in resocialization or changing attitudes of girls, parents and teachers. One strategy to facilitate this change would be to create a more *girl-friendly* classroom.

A second perspective is drawn from socialist/Marxist accounts. Here, the State is seen as using schools to inculcate a set of ideas/values believed to be important for the perpetuation of the industrial and social organization known as capitalist (see box 6.1, pages 113–13). Madeleine MacDonald's (1980) notion of gender codes exemplifies the approach:

> . . . it is possible to investigate the ways in which schooling transmits a specific gender code whereby individuals' gender identity and gender roles are constructed under the school's classification

---

system. The boundaries between the appropriate activities, inter- ests, and expectations of future work for the two sexes is main- tained, and the relations between the two are determined by such a gender code.

> ... In traditional schools one may find a strong boundary between the definitions of masculinity and femininity, which will be reinforced by the application of this principle to the spatial organization of the school, school uniform, classroom activities and curriculum subjects . . . The child's behaviour will be evaluated according to sex-appropriate criteria (eg., 'that is quite good for a girl', 'little girls don't do that'). (MacDonald, 1980: 22)

Schooling functions to inculcate children into their respective class and gender destinies within the sexual and social division of labour. Other com- mentators, using a related cultural studies approach, emphasize girls' agency and have shown how girls become gendered in various social practices like reading romance, following fashion, television viewing and listening to pop music. Ethnographic studies of girls at school have shown working-class girls' pleasure in their 'culture of femininity' (McRobbie, 1978: 108). This fascination with 'romance' has been interpreted as a resistant strategy. Resistance is an important theme within such analysis. Mirza, among other black feminist commentators, has noted that white working-class practices such as romance are inapplicable to black African Caribbean girls (Mirza, 1992).

The approach, known as radical feminist, has proved very influential in showing how schools provide opportunities for boys and men to display their subordinating of girls and women:

> Comments made by boys seem to fall into two broad categories. The first kind are a form of insult having a non-sexual content, the second contain overt sexual meanings. In as much as both are directed predominantly at girls by boys in a mixed school, both constitute sexual harassment. (Mahony, 1985: 44)

Patriarchy as both a power source and social resource is a key concept in this narrative. Boys and men are said to exercise patriarchal control directly through socially sanctioned forms of verbal and physical vio- lence.

Fourthly, post-structuralist and post-modern approaches offer a way of thinking through the relations between agency and **structure** in alter- native ways. (Structure has been used to refer to the ways in which individuals are linked to society through networks of social relationships like the family or school. These have been understood to have a powerful constraint, setting limits to the choices that people make.) Post-structuralists use psychoanalytically informed concepts such as desire, fantasy and forms of identity, to argue for an understanding of the ways in which we come to take up positions as correctly male or female. The concept of discourse introduced in chapter 2 is central to this form of thinking.

Writers adopting a post-structuralist methodology seek to understand ways in which the 'outside' of society is said to end up on the 'inside' in the form of human desires, aspirations and structures of feeling, without resorting to the concept of socialization. They argue that subjects' behaviours are the result of complexes of unconscious and conscious processes. Put simply, post-structuralist accounts theorize the ways in which the individual takes up her/his place within a society already coded through its language as a sexist, racist and class divided set of social relations. Writers such as Jones (1993), offer explanations which look at the sort of investments girls and boys have in maintaining or challenging gender relations:

> . . . [because there are] the various and contradictory discourses on femininity operating within schooling and family sites; there are several possibilities for a feminine subject – there are a range of ways (albeit limited) in which girls can be.
> Being/becoming a girl in educational settings, then takes on various possible meanings, which *shift* within discursive contexts, or within different taken-for-granted meanings. Thus the possibilities for 'girls' are both limited by the dominant conceptions of femaleness but also variable – in so far as those conceptions differ. (Jones, 1993: 159, my italics)

All of the theories presented in box 4.1, 'Feminist approaches to girls and schooling', and their associated empirical work confirm that gender is significantly implicated in how girls and boys come to understand their place within schooling. We have noted the stamp of gender on: examination distributions; outcomes; talk in classrooms; ethos; and various practices of students, staff and parents. The documentation of how the social facts of gender are woven into the fabric, texture and systems of the school is enormous. We have seen only snapshots of the evidence.

Gender, class and race ideologies and practices become embedded and enmeshed each within each other and within the hidden and unconscious dimensions of the school. The next and last section asks questions about how different groups of girls become agents within schools. We will briefly explore how the informal (hidden) curriculum can work both to reinforce or contradict the intentions of the school.

'Now You See It, Now You Don't' – Femininity and the Hidden Curriculum

Barrie Thorne (1993) defines the 'hidden curriculum' as:

> Social biases (of which school staff may or may not be consciously aware). These may infuse various practices of schooling such as stereotypes in books, graphics, and the content of classroom talk, expectations that help shape: processes of academic tracking; differential attention given to boys compared with girls, or white compared with African-American or Chicano students. Far from muting pre-existing forms of stratification, schools may help reproduce class, racial and gender inequalities that are fundamental to larger society. (Thorne, 1993: 51)

Although the definition derives from American experience (tracking means streaming), it applies in principle to the social experiences of schooling under discussion in this chapter. The hidden curriculum has been the subject of interesting and imaginative research. There is a wide-ranging and powerful critique of the role of the informal curriculum in perpetuating gender subordination. In this section I will consider three main aspects of the hidden curriculum: the role of teacher expectation in the presentation of lessons and how this impacts on teacher–pupil interactions; the influential effects of children's own peer group relations; and the examination of the gendered use of space in schools.

Clarricoates' (1987) work 'Dinosaurs in the classroom' is one influential study of the ways in which the social messages of teachers contribute towards the ethos of schooling as heavily gender stereotyped. She shows how gender is spoken within classrooms:

> The education media did an extensive television project on dinosaurs for top infant classes (6–7 year-olds). The teacher encouraged the children to participate fully in the venture by painting pictures and writing short essays on them, examples of which were hung around the walls of the classroom. The impact of recognizing that a project is either boys' 'things' or girls' 'things' was apparent to pupils and teachers alike. During such a lesson a teacher (again in a top infant class) stated: 'Get your books out on dinosaurs please.'
>
> 'Oh no,' cried the girls, 'Not again, we're always doing boys' topics, Miss.'
>
> 'Well perhaps later on in the term we'll do something on houses and flowers', compromises the teacher. (Clarricoates, 1987: 157)

Clarricoates' study reveals the ways teachers unwittingly endorse children's traditional views on gender through a failure to challenge the associations the girls made between 'dinosaurs' and 'boys' things'. However, many feminists teachers and writers have tried to challenge such assumptions through providing alternative representations. One compelling account of a feminist intervention into classroom life is provided by Bronwyn Davies (1989). Her study focused on the daily school lives of preschool children and the role of gender in their behaviour, play and understandings. In particular she examines their reactions to a humorous re-write of a classic fairy tale, 'The Paper Bag Princess' (Munsch and Martchenko, 1980).

The story inverts the usual pattern of a male hero-passive female heroine to show a resourceful Princess Elizabeth and a rather wimpish and petulant Prince called Ronald. Both characters are threatened by a marauding dragon who burns down the Princess's castle, burns her clothes off and steals the Prince. Undaunted, Princess Elizabeth fights the dragon and gets the Prince back. He is appalled by her dirty demeanour and is not grateful for her fortitude in rescuing him.

> Elizabeth walked right over to the dragon and opened the door to the cave.
> There was Prince Ronald.
> He looked at her and said, 'Elizabeth, you are a mess! You smell like ashes, your hair is all tangled and you are wearing a dirty old paper bag. Come back when you are dressed like a real princess.' (Munsch and Martchenko, 1980)

Princess Elizabeth consequently rejects his criticism in independent defiance.

> 'Ronald,' said Elizabeth, 'your clothes are really pretty and your hair is very neat. You look like a real prince, but you are a toad.'
> They didn't get married after all. (Munsch and Martchenko, 1980)

Bronwyn Davies (1989) summarizes how various girls attempt to make sense of the text:

> Most of the girls demonstrate a clear understanding of Elizabeth's plan to save Ronald, seeing her as brave and nice, though for some she is still yukky. During the part of the story where she is still tricking the dragon there is for the girls, unlike the boys, an awareness of her anger, though only one mentions she is clever and one says she is stupid. More girls than boys see her as saving Ronald and only two see her 'getting him back', but some see her as having fun with the dragon, or being angry with the dragon because of her clothes, and some have no idea what she is doing and why. At the end some totally reject her for her nakedness. Some mention that they would have liked a happy ending, either marriage or friendship. Only a few think she was right to walk away, and one thinks she shouldn't have bothered to save him in the first place. Of those who think Ronald was right to reject her, the major focus is on her dirtiness, but she is also a 'bum', naughty, bad and a bitch, again evoking the feeling that she is being judged in sexual terms. (Davies, 1989: 67)

Most children found the 'dirty' princess unsympathetic, and only a few girls were able to appreciate the 'feminist' message. The majority simply inverted the intention of the text and understood the ending as showing a rejection of Princess Elizabeth by Prince Ronald – not the other way around! Children's commitment to traditional narrative structure, from which they have gained familiar gender identification and much pleasure is not easily eradicated.

Recent ethnographies of classroom and playground life provide other opportunities to see 'gender work'. These richly textured accounts of children at school and at play allow us access to the strategies which children use among their peers, and teachers use within school settings in a variety of gendered transactions (Davies, 1989; Thorne, 1993). These ethnographies provide evidence of a range of possible and potential outcomes which *do* show variability and locate for us specific instances of girls (and boys) challenging stereotyped behaviour.

Here is Thorne describing a powerful inter-racial group of five girls – two white girls and three black girls. Several members of the troupe were tall and physically powerful. Collectively they constituted a powerful presence in the 'Oceanside' playground:

> One day this troupe came near three white boys, one of the Black girls leaned over and said tauntingly, 'It's not nice to talk about Mother Nature'. The boys ran, she chased them for a short distance and then returned to the striding troupe. Then one of the white girls stuck out her foot, threatening to trip two white boys who stood at the fringes. She broke into a run, one of the boys chased after her. Another white girl said 'I won't let him touch you', and ran after him. He grabbed at her hands; she kicked her leg out got him down and sat on him. (Thorne, 1993: 73)

Here is an unusual example of girls taking up a position as dominant – subverting the pressures boys place upon girls to concede territory within the borders of appropriate femininity. Girls in this troupe resisted, making it possible for girls to temporarily cross the gender divide.

Other feminist research has also pointed out that schools as physical spaces are used by the different genders in different ways. Pat Mahony's (1985) study *Schools for the Boys* argues that boys monopolize physical space:

> Although I have not checked with a tape measure, it does seem that the space assumed by boys to be theirs is far greater than the space assumed by girls. Boys not only 'spread' into gangways and spaces around their own desks (which are often the ones most central to the teacher), but they also appear not to notice that space is already occupied by a girl. It is not uncommon to find a boy leaning across a girl's desk in order to 'flick' another boy, crumpling her work in the process. Neither is it uncommon, when this behaviour is challenged to encounter amazement and incomprehension from the boys. (Mahony, 1985: 28)

An important and under-researched dimension in schools' informal cultures relates to the ways in which girls' and boys' friendship patterns emerge as social expressions of gender. Evidence from researchers interested in the relations between masculinity and femininity and schooling, reveal stark differences in how girls and boys 'do' friendship. These peer relations carry crucial gender messages and identifications for children:

> A vignette: among a peer group of South London boys in a particular club [where a youth worker interested in the issue of how masculinity works], the mark of friendship is hitting each other – playfully but hard. No one who is not a friend is admitted to this intimacy. (Connell, 1987: 85)

Girls' intimacy takes quite different forms. Girls' friendship behaviour includes: seat saving, information and clothes swopping; sweet sharing; secret and problem sharing. The emphasis is on the getting and practising of the social skills of emotional labour (Hey, 1988). Schools may not be sensitive to these interpersonal aspects of the hidden curriculum and may denigrate the emphasis girls place upon making and managing friends. Crude interventions by teachers into the territory of girls' friendships risk providing negative messages to girls. One such message is that the social issues which they deem very important to self-esteem and social support are seen as either trivial or dangerous. The teacher quoted below exemplifies both attitudes:

> A teacher in the school where this research was conducted . . . [said about a girl with whom he was spending a considerable time counselling] 'I'm convinced it's not her, though, it's the company she keeps, particularly that – Do you remember her? That's where the trouble lies.' (Meyenn, 1980: 108)

Either way these critical or dismissive accounts can work to undermine girls' confidence because it appears to the girls that adults confirm boys' generally hostile attitude to girls' peer relationships. One important dimension to boys' hostility relates to their reading of girls intimacy as 'inappropriate'. It seems that even quite young boys have absorbed messages that girls' 'proper' destiny is to attend to them. Girls' friendship groups are uniformly given the label 'lesbians' (Lees, 1986). This is a form of social control which some girls seem to have taken up: 'I was meant to go to a girls' school right and I changed it to [a mixed school] in case I came out a lesbian . . . [giggles]' ('Gabbie' quoted in Hey, 1988).

Social practices such as name-calling carry forward an all-pervasive and important hidden agenda about 'normal' masculinity and femininity. These messages provide other sources of social learning – lessons of life – for girls and boys which in many respects, comprise a social curriculum which has a more powerful hold upon school subjects, precisely because it is made by themselves.

EXERCISE

Work out how extensive the 'hidden curriculum' is. To help you build up an audit of the 'hidden curriculum' choose either your current educational institution or a past one. A useful framework through which you can examine the gendered nature of your educational institution is to consider the following factors: what is the nature of the images presented in the prospectus? What use do females and males make of the building and its surrounds? What are the respective statuses of women and men in the organization? It is important to record the extent to which the gendered divisions you identify are also differentiated by race.

Conclusions: Unfinished Schools

In this chapter we have surveyed a (brief) history of girls' schooling and looked at some current debates about how schools work to secure the placing of girls in feminine subjects. We have attempted to explore how gender expectations work in and through schools' organization and practices. There has been an attempt to indicate the ways that girls' experiences are also determined by their class and race. It should not be forgotten that schooling plays a key role in the transmission of ideas about sexuality, endorsing heterosexuality as the norm. The assumption of heterosexuality as the norm was after all the principal notion underpinning the equation of girls' education as an education in domesticity.

Do you consider capital, boys, patriarchy, or our own desires and subjective sense of self – our identity to 'blame' for the way we are 'schooled'? Do we need: 'assertiveness training', separate schools, or a set of new 'discourses' which permit us a wider range of ways to be 'feminine'? Given the gendering of school subjects there is some case to be made for insisting that girls do science and boys do domestic subjects. Yet if this is the case, and this is in part addressed through the imposition of the National Curriculum, then how can we still prevent the derogation of 'girls'' subjects as 'soft options' and the over-valuing of 'male' science? These are all open, if daunting, questions which I hope will not intimidate you to the point of disengagement. The text has tried to make the case for a continuing critical reflection upon our past, present and future involvement with both formal and informal education.

REFERENCES

Barrett, M. and McIntosh, M. 1985: Ethnocentrism and socialist feminist theory. *Feminist Review*, 20, 21–47.

Board Of Education 1926: *The Education of the Adolescent: The Hadow Report*. London, HMSO.

Campbell, J. M. 1908: The effects of adolescence on the brain of the girl. Paper Presented to the AUWT meeting, 23 May.

Clarricoates, K. 1987: Dinosaurs in the classroom – the 'hidden' curriculum in primary schools. In: M. Arnot and G. Weiner (eds), *Gender and the Politics of Schooling*. London: Hutchinson for The Open University Press.

Connell, R. W. 1987: *Gender and Power: Society, the Person and Sexual Politics*. Cambridge: Polity Press.

Davies, B. 1989: *Frogs and Snails and Feminist Tails: Preschool Children and Gender*. Boston, MA: Allen & Unwin.

Evans, M. 1991: *A Good School: Life at a Girls' Grammar School in the 1950s*. London: The Women's Press.

Frame, Janet 1990: *An Autobiography*. London: The Women's Press.

Hey, V. 1988: 'The company she keeps': the social and interpersonal construction of girls' same sex friendships. Unpublished Ph.D. Dissertation, University of Kent, Canterbury.

hooks, b. 1993: Keeping close to home: class and education. In M. M. Tokarczyk and E. A. Fay (eds), *Working Class Women in the Academy: Labourers in the Knowledge Factory*. Amherst: University of Massachusetts Press.

Hughes, M. 1934: *A London Child of the Eighteen Seventies*. Oxford: Oxford University Press.

Jones, A. 1993: Becoming a 'girl': post-structuralist suggestions for educational research. *Gender and Education*, 5, 2, 157–66.

Kelly, A. (ed.) 1981: *The Missing Half*. Manchester: Manchester University Press.

Lees, Sue 1986: *Losing Out: Sexuality and Adolescent Girls*. London: Hutchinson.

MacDonald, M. 1980: Socio-cultural reproduction and women's education. In Rosemary Deem (ed.), *Schooling for Women's Work*, London: Routledge & Kegan Paul.

McRobbie, A. 1978: Working class girls and the culture of femininity. In Women's Studies' Group (eds), *Women Take Issue: Aspects of Women's Subordination*, London: Hutchinson.

Mahony, P. 1985: *Schools for the Boys*. London: Hutchinson.

Mama, A. 1984: Black women, the economic crisis and the British State. Special issue – Many Voices One Chant: Black Feminist Perspectives, *Feminist Review*, 17, 21–35.

Marks, P. 1976: 'Femininity in the classroom': an account of changing attitudes. In J. Mitchell and A. Oakley (eds), *The Rights and Wrongs of Women*, London: Penguin.

Measor, L. and Sikes, P. 1992: *Gender and Schools*. London: Cassell.

Meyenn, R. J. 1980: School girls' peer groups. In P. Woods (ed.) *Pupil Strategies*, London: Croom Helm.

Mirza, H. S. 1992: *Young, Female and Black*. London: Routledge.

Munsch, R. and Martchenko, M. 1980: *The Paper Bag Princess*. Toronto: Annick Press.

Murphy, P. 1991: Assessment and gender. *Cambridge Journal of Education*, 21, 2, 203–14.

Newson, J. 1948: *The Education of Girls*. London: Faber & Faber.

Parmar, P. and Mirza, N. 1981: Growing angry: growing strong. *Spare Rib*, 111, October, 18–21.

Sewell, E. M. 1865: *Principles of Education Drawn From Revelation and Applied to Female Education in the Upper Classes* Vol. 11. London: Longman, Roberts & Green.

Spencer, H. 1867: *The Principles of Biology 2* Vol. 2, Part 1V, 'The laws of multiplication'. London and Edinburgh: Williams & Norgate.

Stobbart, G., Elwood, J. and Quinlan, M. 1992: Gender bias in examinations: how equal are the opportunities? *British Educational Research Journal*, 18, 3, 261–76.

Thorne, B. 1993: *Gender Play: Girls and Boys in School*. Buckingham: Open University Press.

The Times 1854: Editorial. 2 September.

Tweedie, Jill 1993: *Eating Children*. London: Viking.

Walkerdine, V. 1985: On the regulation of speaking and silence. In C. Steedman, C. Urwin and V. Walkerdine, *Language, Gender and Childhood*, London: Routledge & Kegan Paul.

Walkerdine, V. 1989: *Counting Girls Out*. London, Virago.

CHAPTER
5 Jobs

Christine Zmroczek and
Beryl Madoc-Jones

Plate 4 *Nurses Station, South London Hospital for Women.*
Format Partners, London; photograph: Joanne O'Brien.

This chapter is about women's work. We shall be looking at the broad range of tasks which come under the heading of women's work, focusing particularly on paid jobs. But it is impossible to consider women's paid work without also taking into account the other work women do – unpaid work of various kinds, but most of all in the household.

You will be introduced to theoretical ideas about women's work, as well as accounts of women's experiences. We will use Britain as a case study and the experiences of Black women as an important focus. In this chapter we use Black with a capital 'B' to indicate a political category, within which very different groups and individuals come together as they share the unwelcome experience of racism in British society and elsewhere. Wherever appropriate we will be referring to specific women who may be in the category Black, such as Asian women, African women, Caribbean women, or Chinese women. At the end of this chapter you will have a general idea of the broad patterns of women's paid jobs and their relationship to women's unpaid work in the home. You will be able to appraise some of the difficulties encountered by women in paid jobs and some of the ways in which women have successfully overcome them.

First of all let's get clear what we mean by 'jobs' and what we mean by 'work' in this chapter. The most common understanding of a job is that it is an activity for which we are paid. Another important concept is 'work'. Work may be used as an alternative to jobs meaning paid work, but there is also a great deal of work done which is unpaid work, such as housework and voluntary work, for example raising money for local groups, or serving on their committees, or making the tea at meetings. It is often argued that most unpaid work is done by women (Witz, 1993). In this chapter we will concentrate on paid jobs and women's work in the household.

As we have already mentioned, it is really difficult to talk about women's jobs, meaning our paid employment, without also considering all the other tasks we do, as carers in the family. For many women this also includes work in the family business, for example the wife or daughter of a small shopkeeper may also work in the shop, often for little or no pay. The wife or partner of a man who is self-employed as a car mechanic or plumber might be essential to the success of the business, needed at home to answer the phone for his business calls, keep his appointments diary and do the accounts. A woman may also do paid work (jobs) at home, called 'homeworking', ranging from highly paid computer programming and analysis to poorly paid sewing or envelope stuffing. Homeworking of all kinds is frequently an attempt by women to manage their multiple responsibilities in the home with the need or desire to earn money.

Women's Unpaid Work

Most women have responsibility for a broad range of unpaid tasks related to the home and family as well as having paid jobs for much of their adult lives. The unpaid tasks will probably include many of the following:

Housework: This includes cooking, cleaning, washing, and other work to maintain the house and those in it in a physical sense.

Caring: Looking after children, husbands, other relatives and kin, other household members, often also neighbours and friends. Most women provide a substantial amount of emotional support, stress relief and advice services – in an informal way – to their loved ones in addition to caring for their physical well-being.

Consuming: Women are largely responsible for shopping and purchasing of goods used by the household. This is a task which, as you probably know yourself, takes up a good deal of women's time and energy. It also requires considerable skills in making the choices about what to buy, knowing what is available, and it often involves sophisticated budget management to make ends meet.

Social life: Women are also usually the ones who organize and maintain much of the social life for family members – for example: chauffeuring children and others in the household, providing opportunities for children to meet with their friends at home and at outside activities; arranging family get togethers, for birthday or holiday festivities at Christmas, rammadan, sabbath etc.; dinners for husband's friends or colleagues; communications with relatives; visits to and from family and friends; washing football shirts; providing food for various social occasions at home; for fund-raising for schools and other organizations – the list of tasks women do is almost endless.

EXERCISE

1. Make a list of what you did yesterday from the time you got up until you went to bed.
2. How many of the activities on your list are related to your paid job and how many to other kinds of work? How many were entirely for your own leisure or pleasure?

3. How many activities on your list were a combination of unpaid work and leisure, such as watching television but doing the ironing at the same time, or taking the children to the park?
4. Is there anything significant missing from the examples given earlier of women's unpaid work in the household which appears on your list?
5. How many different kinds of work activities have you included?
6. Are you surprised at the variety and quantity of work you do in an average kind of day, or was it what you expected?

Now that you have completed this exercise you will have a clearer idea about the range of women's work. Of course much of women's work in the home can be satisfying and pleasurable. Caring for those we love has many rewards. But it is also the case that many of the tasks involved are repetitious and can be boring and thankless. One of the problems is the assumption that work that needs to be done to maintain the household and its members is mainly women's work. Women frequently find there simply isn't enough time in the day! Women's unpaid work, a relentless daily routine, can have a significant effect on women's paid employment in the labour market. We will explore this later in the chapter.

In the next section, we will look at how work in Western society came to be separated into paid jobs and other work. We will use the British experience for our main examples.

The Separation of Home and Work

Have women always been expected to be 'Jill of all trades', undertaking so many different tasks inside and outside the household? Certainly it was expected in the past, according to historian Alice Clark (1993), who wrote her book about seventeenth-century women's work just after the First World War. She says:

> The ordinary domestic occupations of Englishwomen consist in tending babies and young children, either as mothers or servants, in preparing household meals, and in keeping the house clean, while laundry work, preserving fruit, and the making of children's clothes are still often included in the domestic category. In the seventeenth century it embraced a much wider range of production; for brewing, dairy-work, the care of poultry and pigs, the production of vegetables and fruit, spinning flax and wool, nursing and doctoring, all formed part of domestic industry. (Clark, 1993: 5)

She goes on to tell us that the household production of goods both for domestic use and for sale or exchange 'existed side by side during the Middle Ages; for example brewing, baking, spinning, cheese and butter making were conducted both as domestic arts and for industrial purposes' (Clark, 1993: 8).

Women also worked alongside their husbands as their assistants in the trades, and were often able to take over in his absence or on his death. At the same time they might have been running a business of their own, for example brewing. So women were expected to turn their hands to many kinds of work and the difference between paid jobs and unpaid work was less marked. The home was where work of all kinds was carried out.

The development of capitalism and the Industrial Revolution in the late seventeenth and early eighteenth centuries (see box 6.1 on capitalism, page 113) saw the separation of paid jobs from the home into factories and other workshops where goods were produced for sale, leaving most of the domestic tasks of feeding, clothing and caring for the members of the household as unpaid work. In a capitalist economy this work has increasingly been given less value than paid jobs, because it does not directly produce goods for sale and profit.

Domestic tasks, whether paid or unpaid, have almost invariably been seen as women's work. You may have noticed that at the beginning of the extract above Alice Clark mentions that women do caring jobs for others 'either as mothers or servants'. The work of domestic servants was usually arduous, with long hours, often very poor conditions and low pay, yet it has been one of the only choices for working-class girls until recently. They needed to have jobs to support themselves and contribute to their households as soon as they were old enough, as the following extract shows:

> A girl born in 1900 would expect to leave school at from 12–14 and start work immediately unless she was needed to help at home. Her choice of job would depend on her family's situation but also the opportunities in the area where she lived. For most girls this meant factory work if it was available, otherwise domestic service except for those few from middle class or the most prosperous working-class backgrounds who might aspire to shop, clerical work or teaching. (Davidoff and Westover, 1986: 1)

So really there was not a lot of choice, for most girls and women. Now read a couple of extracts which will give you some insight into some of the tasks assigned to domestic servants, described in the words of the women themselves. The first, Molly, worked as an under-housemaid during the First World War in the large household of an Edinburgh advocate, where there were seven household servants besides herself:

> I had quite a lot of work to do because I had to help in the laundry as well as (doing the work of) an under-[housemaid]. I had to carry the coal from the basement right

up to the drawing room flat and the under-table maid, she had the dining room. I was right at the top flat too because I had the nursery as well. I had all that carrying and I was up early in the morning because of course the head maid she didn't do anything like that. And then in the afternoon I had to go and help in the laundry and it was all the sheets. I had to fold the sheets and then they were all mangled. That was my afternoon work . . . I had to do the hall tea for all the staff. . . . I had to do the hall tea on my evening off and I hadn't to go out till that tea was finished and washed up which meant I wasn't out till after five o'clock. And that was only once a week. (Quoted in Jamieson, 1990: 147)

In the second extract we hear from Jane Fitz who was a live-in domestic servant in the 1930s in a small guest house:

I earned about 10/- a week and food of course. And it was a very cold room I had in the guest house, it was a kind of storeroom, it had everything stacked in there and a bed along side and it was bitter cold. It was a husband and wife who owned it and run it. They had long staying people, they didn't have people coming and going. They let out furnished rooms and gave them meals. I didn't see much of anyone except to give them their trays. She did all the cooking and I cleaned the rooms, the stairs and sitting room and the owners' quarters. . . . I only had one afternoon off a week. I started in the morning at 7 and finished about 9 in the evening. I had a little break after I'd washed up the dinner, before I helped with the evening meal. Maids worked hard in those days, but they were kind enough to me. (Jane Fitz, unpublished interview)

Molly and Jane tell us about the various tasks they had to do as domestic servants, in their paid jobs. As we observed earlier, domestic service was one of the few jobs open to working-class girls at the turn of the century. Few women today are full-time paid domestic servants but a lot of women earn money part time as cleaners, or home helps, for example. But most women, unless they are rich enough to pay others to do it all for them, do a lot of *unpaid* domestic work. In other words they do their own housework. It can require considerable organization and management skills but because it is unpaid it is undervalued, in British society and even by ourselves. In 1987 the Legal and General Assurance Company estimated a wife's work in the home at £423 per week (Holdsworth, 1988: 34). Remember this is an insurance company who might be called upon to pay out such sums in the event, say, of an insured wife's death, so this may not be a particularly generous estimate. Even so, when wives themselves were surveyed, they estimated their own replacement value at only £150 a week.

In other parts of the world the differentiation between paid jobs and other work is often not so marked, but an even larger range of tasks may well be included in a woman's working day. For example, in many countries in Africa and Asia women are responsible for most of the agricultural work, growing crops for food, to sell or to exchange, and also tending cattle. Gathering and preparing food such as grinding corn or rice to enable it to be made into the day's food are almost exclusively women's tasks in many cultures. This work can take many hours each day before cooking can begin. Cooking is almost universally seen as women's work. Fuel for cooking may have to be found and carried back home. In many regions another essential daily task is collecting water for household use and for crops and cattle. This sometimes involves considerable journeys to the local source of water. (An account of a typical day in the life of an African woman can be read in chapter 6, page 124.)

You can see now that women's workload is extremely extensive, whether differentiated between paid jobs and unpaid work or more undifferentiated as, for example, in some of the countries referred to as 'the Third World'. The following quote from the United Nations illustrates this very well and shows the imbalance between women and men.

> Women are one half of the adult population and one third of the official labour force, performing two thirds of the world's working hours, earning one tenth of the income and owning one per cent of the world's property. (United Nations, 1980 in French, 1992)

There are two factors particularly important for understanding this extraordinary imbalance. The first is the **sexual division of labour**. This means that work is allocated on the basis of gender and this seems to operate in most countries and cultures (see box 5.1). Although the sexual division of labour takes different forms and has different consequences depending on the particular location, generally women appear to be disadvantaged in relation to men by it and especially in terms of jobs and pay. The second factor and very much linked to the first is **power**, the relationship of men as a group to women as a group is usually one of disadvantage to women (see box 5.2). We'll look at these ideas in more detail with the help of some statistics drawn from British examples.

Women's Employment in Britain

In this section we will be building up a profile of the positioning of women through paid jobs in the labour market. The main characteristics to be considered are the following:

1. Women's participation in paid jobs, known as the paid labour force, as full-time and part-time workers.
2. Pay.
3. Segregation in particular types of employment and particular jobs.
4. Job satisfaction.

5. Discrimination at work.
6. Unemployment.

Sexual Division of Labour

BOX
5.1

All societies have a division of labour based on sex – work that is seen as women's work and work that is seen as men's work. However, the nature of the work that is done by men or women varies from society to society and has changed historically in our own society. In almost all societies the care of babies and young children is seen as women's work, but in many societies men take on the task of caring for young boys, in others older children generally look after younger ones, and in others again the older women care for the children. Cooking is mainly seen as women's work, except the preparation of feasts and ceremonial meals which is frequently seen as men's work. In many, but not all, societies hunting and fishing is regarded as men's work, but planting and harvesting is frequently undertaken by women either alone or alongside men. Women, in many societies, are responsible for the care of livestock. On the basis of this evidence Ann Oakley (1982) has suggested that the sexual division of labour is socially constructed and not based on natural sex differences. Jobs become identified as men's jobs or as women's jobs. (Abbott and Wallace, 1990: 121–2)

Power

BOX
5.2

The exercise of male power over women may vary in different classes and racial groups and may reveal itself in different ways. But it is a feature of all relationships between men and women in a society in which men as a group have power over women as a group, and have a vested interest in keeping it that way. Power is not just to do with access to money – although that's a big part of it. It's also about access to paid work and to the political process. Working men in trade unions have colluded with their employers since at least the Industrial Revolution to deny women craft skills, to fix the rates of pay for jobs that men do at a higher rate, to prevent women from competing for men's jobs, to confine women to low paid, insecure employment and to claim for themselves a family wage with which to ensure women's economic dependency at home. (Taking Liberties Collective, 1989: 4)

Jobs: full and part-time paid work

Nearly half of all paid workers in Britain are women. The official figure in 1993 for women in employment and self-employed stood at 49 per cent (*Social Trends 24*, 1994) but it is likely that this was an underestimate as many of women's paid jobs may not appear in official statistics. Women who work as homeworkers in textiles, for example, or who work in a family business may have been counted only as 'housewives'. The usual age limits for women in official statistics are 16–60. Yet some women under and many over these ages certainly are doing paid work. In 1991, 53 per cent of all women of working age in Britain were 'economically active' (*Social Trends 24*, 1994). This means they are either in paid employment or registered as unemployed, that is looking for a job. This compares with 75 per cent of men. This indicates how important women's paid jobs have become in the economy generally. It should also be noted that many women who do not fall into the official categories required to register as unemployed may still be looking for work and so again this estimate of women's economic activity is probably an underestimate. Another important point to note is that many women, particularly in Britain, have part-time jobs, combining household responsibilities with paid work. Far fewer men have part-time jobs. In fact in 1990, four out of five of the 5 million part-time workers were women (Equal Opportunities Commission 1990, in Witz, 1993).

As you would expect, there are differences between women in different groups. For example, in Spring 1993 almost seven out of ten African Caribbean and white women were economically active and six out of ten Indian women, but only two out of ten Bangladeshi and Pakistani women (*Social Trends 24*, 1994). Research suggests that this last group of women are particularly likely to be homeworkers combining a job with looking after children, and as such their jobs are more likely to be under-recorded (Bhachu, 1988, cited in Graham, 1993). Black women are more likely to be in full-time jobs than white women. Forty-four per cent of white women work part time, compared with 29 per cent of African Caribbean women and 16 per cent of Asian women (*Employment Gazette*, 1991). Although Black women work longer hours in paid employment than white women, their average earnings are still at just about the same level (Bruegel, 1989). In other words, on average, hour by hour Black women are paid less than white women.

Pay

Taking an average of the earnings of Black and white women manual workers, hour by hour women earn about 70p for every £1 a man earns. Non-manual women workers are even worse off earning only 62p for every male £1 (Coyle and Skinner, 1988; Rees, 1992). It is clear that some women are paid more, and sometimes substantially more, than some men – these figures are an average, but they do indicate that there is a significant imbalance between the pay of women and men. Nearly half of women in paid employment (45 per cent) have part-time jobs, while only 5 per cent of men do. Mr average is paid for 43 hours per week, whilse Ms average is paid for only 30 hours per week (Cockburn, 1991). Obviously many part-time jobs are far less than 30 hours a week. The average is 18.5 hours per week and many women have jobs with fewer hours than that (Martin and Roberts, 1984).

To summarize so far, women workers on average are paid less per hour than men, and work fewer hours than men. So women's weekly earnings can be considerably less than those of men.

Job segregation

The third point in our profile of women's jobs is occupational or job segregation. Although in Britain today women can be found in most occupations from nuclear physicist to truck driver, managing director to home help, jobs continue to be segregated in much the same way as they have been since the turn of the century (Hakim, 1979, in Coyle and Skinner, 1988). Occupational segregation means that some jobs are regarded as men's jobs and others as women's. Women's jobs are most often those which are low paid, low in status and categorized as low skilled (see box 5.3).

BOX 5.3

Skill

While skill sounds as if it is something which can be measured in some objective way, in practice it is not. Workers and management effectively negotiate about skill descriptions just as they negotiate about wages. Many of our modern trade unions have their roots in earlier guilds, which had of course been substantially taken over by men in the late seventeenth century. Male workers were therefore in a stronger position to project their craft skills then were women. Even where women were also organized their 'brothers' tended to claim higher status and pay for the tasks they themselves performed. Skills increasingly became a masculine prerogative, and many skilled occupations became exclusively male. . . . Capitalist assaults on such monopolies of skill therefore represented a threat not only to the economic power of their holders but also to their masculinity. . . . Women's paid work was increasingly devalued, just as other things female were devalued, and in many instances this has resulted in women's work being deemed unskilled when equivalent work done by men is described as semi-skilled or even skilled. (Faulkner and Arnold, 1985: 45–6)

Women workers as a whole are segregated in particular occupations and industries. Over three-quarters of all women workers (80 per cent) work in occupations where 50 per cent or more of the other employees are women (Equal Opportunities Commission, 1987; Rees 1992). That means that women are more likely to be working alongside other women in particular areas designated as women's work than with men. For example more than half of all employed women, full-time and part-time, work in just two groups of jobs: the first is clerical, secretarial and other related types of office work, and the second is in catering, cleaning, hairdressing and other sorts of personal services. These groups of jobs are all likely to be low paid and often low in status, with few benefits, and frequently with poor working conditions such as long hours and shift work. In addition, low priority may be given to health and safety precautions. Women also predominate in education, health and welfare jobs, particularly at the lower end of the scale.

Our discussion so far has been about **horizontal segregation**. There is also another kind of segregation – **vertical segregation**. This means that the higher we look up the ladders of pay and status the fewer women we see. Top jobs usually go to men with women clustered at the lower end of the job hierarchies. This holds true even for those occupations in which the majority of employees are women such as in nursing and teaching. Research from the Equal Opportunities Commission (1990) shows us that at the top levels of management only 1–2 per cent are women. In other words, only one or two at most of every 100 top managers are women.

Let's take another example, computing, which as a relatively new area of work, is generally reckoned to be more open to women than many of the more traditional and long-established professions. Yet, even here, only 3 per cent of women reach the top as data processing managers and only 14 per cent as project managers, while 64 per cent of help desk analysts, who answer telephone enquiries, are women (*Computer Economics*, May 1991, quoted in *Computing*, 30 January 1992).

Job satisfaction

The next aspect of women's workplace experience we will consider is job satisfaction. When asked, women do certainly state that they seek and gain satisfaction from paid work, but as you might imagine it does vary according to the types of work women do, where they work, with whom they work and importantly a woman's own image of her job. This means that a woman stacking shelves in a supermarket can say she gets satisfaction from her job because she enjoys meeting her colleagues, getting out of the house and sustaining an identity as a worker rather than as the undervalued 'housewife', while for another woman, the same job does not satisfy her on any level other than being able to earn some money. Studies show that a majority of women give the need to earn money as a primary reason for doing paid jobs (Graham, 1993) although other factors such as satisfaction are also important. In general, women's earnings are crucial to the household, for example 'four times as many households would be in poverty if married women stopped going out to work' (Morris, 1991, quoted in Graham, 1993: 113).

The following extract is taken from a novel *The Rector's Wife* written by Joanna Trollope (1991). The heroine, Anna, finds herself in a situation in which she desperately needs to earn to supplement the family income. She is a graduate and has worked in a language school. However, the family has been relocated in a village as a result of her husband's work as a clergyman. Employment opportunities for Anna are very restricted. When we enter the narrative, the only employment she has is 'homework' as a translator. Her response to her situation represents some important issues which confront mothers who need to find paid work. Anna applies for a job in a supermarket:

'May I take your name and address?' Mr Mulgrove said. Anna gave it. He did not flinch when she said 'the Rectory'. Perhaps he didn't even realize what the implication of living in a rectory was.

'I don't mind what I do,' Anna said.

He said delicately, 'Stock involves quite a lot of ladder work, in the warehouse . . .' as if Anna might be not up to such physical strenuousness.

'I think I'd rather climb ladders than sit at a checkout.'

Mr Mulgrove rather wanted to say that her voice and appearance would be an asset on the checkout, good for Pricewell's public image (a cause dear to his heart), but he was uncertain how to put this. 'I wouldn't like you to be in the wrong situation . . .'

Anna, emboldened by the energy of taking action, said, 'Would I be paid more for one than the other?'

He shook his head.

'What would I be paid?'

As Anna was the sort of person Mr Mulgrove associated with being a customer rather than a member of staff, he was suddenly embarrassed. He flicked, with much throat-clearing, through a plastic-sheeted folder.

'Three twenty-one an hour.'

'Three pounds and twenty-one pence –'

'Yes.'

'Heavens' Anna said. 'You see, I need to make at least fifty pounds a week for thirty-six weeks a year.'

He could not look at her: he was overcome by her. He said, 'That would mean twenty hours a week as a part-time assistant. Four hours a day for five days'. There was a little pause.

'You're on,' Anna said. She held her hand out to him. He took it doubtingly.

'You're sure?'

'Yes.' She smiled at him. 'Yes. It also means no Church and no village for twenty hours a week.'

He did not understand. He wondered if he were making a mistake. He said, 'Of course, there has to be a three-month trial –.'

'Oh, of course.'

'And you will have to work under supervision for the length of that period –.'

'Why, do you think I might be difficult?'

Mr Mulgrove went scarlet. Give him a school leaver any day, or a nice, motherly woman going back to work once her children were grown up, or an obliging pensioner, prepared to collect trolleys from the car parks . . .

'I won't be difficult,' Anna said gently, to comfort him. 'I need a job and I'd be really grateful if you would let me have one.'

He looked at her for the first time. Why on earth did she need a job? What was she doing? Bravely he said, 'You're not having me on?'

'No,' Anna said, 'no. My youngest child is being bullied at school and I want to send her to St Saviour's.' (Trollope, 1992: 56–8).

Anna's motivation for job-hunting and her interest in the supermarket opening is clear: to meet an unexpected and pressing need for her child.

EXERCISE

1. Can you suggest another reason, other than solving her daughter's problem, which would contribute to job satisfaction for Anna?
2. What does Anna's experience represent which would help you to understand difficulties faced by a professionally qualified wife and mother urgently seeking a return to employment?

EXERCISE RESPONSE

In addition to acknowledging the obvious satisfaction Anna felt from providing funds for a specific family need, you will probably have sensed that she had a feeling of 'escape'. Anna hints at the opportunity to get away from the everyday demands of her role as a clergyman's wife.

Anna's predicament when faced with an extremely limited jobs market highlights the experience of many women looking to return to work. She is contained geographically by a location determined by her husband's work. Although well qualified, she has to consider jobs for which little or no skill is required. This is a common experience for women. Martin and Roberts in their 1984 survey found that 37 per cent of women returning to work after the birth of their first child took a lower level job than they had had before becoming a mother – and furthermore such a job is likely to be worse paid.

> The work Anna considers is a job viewed as *women's work*. It is associated with housewives' tasks as consumers, providers and shoppers. This may be one reason why women's work in supermarkets is low paid and predominantly part time.

The next point in our profile concerns discrimination which is a considerable barrier facing many women in the jobs market.

Discrimination

Discriminations based on sex, 'race', class, disablement, sexuality, religious beliefs and age can prevent women from gaining education, training, jobs, promotions and career opportunities. In this section we want first of all to focus on discriminations encountered by Black women due to racism. Racism has been and continues to be a major problem in the workplace for women and men. One illustration of this is described in the next extract. The woman in the extract is typical of many women and men who came to Britain soon after the end of the Second World War from the Caribbean islands. They came to find jobs in response to invitations, advertising and propaganda from the government designed to attract cheap labour from the 'colonies' to help rebuild the shattered economy. Many came intending to stay only a short time to save money to take home. Others came out of curiosity, leaving behind good jobs.

> At home in Trinidad my husband had a good job and our life was okay . . . I didn't even have to work when we were at home, but once we got here I had to find a job. It was hard, especially when you would go for a job and they would always say it had gone. Eventually I found a cleaning job in a hospital, which I have had for 22 years . . . All those stories you heard about people coming here and saving a lot of money weren't true. (Quoted in Bryan, Scafe and Dadzie, 1985: 23–4)

Another woman recalls:

> I've had a lot of jobs since I've been in this country. My first job when I arrived in 1958 was as a finisher, doing hems, buttons and so on. I didn't like the work because it was tedious but I stayed there 3 months . . . [Then she asked for a rise, but was sacked without an explanation.] . . . My next job was as a chamber maid at the United University Club in Trafalgar square. . . . The residents were openly prejudiced and I was scared because I didn't know what they would do. [She eventually found another job in a hotel.] I stayed there a year. I got on well with the other workers. I think this was because we were all foreigners. The chef was Polish and the other girls were Irish. I lost the job because I was pregnant. (Bryan, Scafe and Dadzie, 1985: 30–1)

After the birth of her first child, she tried to find other suitable jobs, but it was even more difficult because of her family commitments. This is a problem shared by many women.

> After my son was born in 1964, I gave up full time work and went back to working part time in the evenings. When my husband got home from work, he would look after the children while I went to work, When they were a bit older I took up shift work. I started at 9 am and finished at 3.30 pm, then I went back at 5 pm and worked through until 8 pm. I found it a great strain but I wasn't thinking about myself. (Bryan, Scafe and Dadzie, 1985: 31)

How are these experiences of racial discrimination related to Black women and jobs today? Many of the same patterns of discrimination are still discernible, despite equal opportunities legislation. But they are often hidden within discussions and statistics dealing with 'women' in an undifferentiated way. They are more likely to be overqualified for the jobs they do. For example, 16 per cent of Black women have qualifications beyond A level, compared with 12 per cent of white women, and 14 per cent of white men (Labour Force Survey, 1987–89 cited in the *Guardian* 12.6.91). Job segregation patterns are somewhat different, too. Black women are similarly clustered in manual and lower clerical jobs, but they are more likely to be in manufacturing and considerably less likely to be in banking and finance (Bhavnani, 1994).

Black women's pay is likely to suffer through a range of discriminations. We have already noted that Black women are likely to be paid less by the hour than white women and that many women, Black and white, have low paid jobs. However, because of racism Black women are even more likely to find it hard to obtain well paid jobs. They are likely to remain in the same sorts of jobs their mothers had thirty years ago, such as those described at the beginning of this section. It is worth remembering, though, that in the last thirty years changes have been taking place, a new professional generation has grown up in Black British communities. A new generation of Black women entrepreneurs are starting their own businesses (Westwood and Bhachu, 1988). These developments are reflected in statistics gathered for the government's Labour Force Survey for 1990. In the category professional/manager/employer – the 'top' jobs – only 11 per cent of women in the workplace hold these posts, compared with 27 per cent of men. However, if we break this down for different groups of women we find that 16 per cent of Chinese women hold top jobs; 11 per cent African; 11 per cent white; 10 per cent Indian; 8 per cent African Caribbean women; 7 per cent African Asian; 4 per cent Pakistani. No Bangladeshi women hold top jobs according to this survey (Bhavnani, 1994).

Women with disabilities, Black and white, also suffer from discrimination. They find it difficult to obtain suitable employment and they are more likely to be in low skilled jobs or unemployed than either men with disabilities or women without disabilities (Graham, 1993; Witz, 1993).

Another area of discrimination encountered by Black and white women alike is sexual discrimination. According to the law, this occurs (in relation to women) when 'an employer treats a woman less favourably than a man because she is a woman' (Read, 1988: 26). Sex discrimination legislation (in place since 1975) recognizes direct and indirect discrimination. The latter type is more common. It occurs when an employer applies a condition to workplace practice which applies to all employees but is such that the proportion of women who can comply is very much lower than that of men and it is to the detriment of a woman so affected. The main areas of workplace practice in which discrimination commonly happens are pay, interviewing/selection procedures and promotion practices. In professional occupations, women are typically found to be working at lower levels than men, indicated by seniority and pay. For example, although women now represent 42 per cent of those qualifying as barristers in the legal profession, they are grossly under-represented at the highest levels. In 1992, out of a total of eighty-three High Court Judges only three were women (The General Council of the Bar, 1992: 22). Research into women's experiences in the professional workplace draws attention to the problems of dual careers, lack of childcare facilities and employers' prejudices (Brannen and Moss, 1988, 1990). This is a further example of vertical segregation already discussed in this chapter.

One of the barriers many women encounter is at the point of negotiating promotion opportunities. Consider the following case of a woman employee who brought an action against her employer for discrimination after failing to gain promotion. She took her case to an industrial tribunal, the procedure for gaining redress in the form of compensation. Her employer was a major energy supply industry:

> The application to the tribunal was made after the applicant had failed for the second time to be appointed to the position of manager of one of the company's retail outlets. The applicant had worked with the company for some 14 years prior to the application and during that period she had gained promotion from sales assistant to deputy manager and had acted as manager of a shop during a 12 month period when the manager was absent due to illness. There had been no criticisms of the applicant's performance as acting manager and in fact she had been nominated by the sales manager for the company's Star Award in recognition of her managerial potential and motivation.
>
> When it became clear that the manager for whom she had been deputising would not be returning to employment with the company, the post of manager was advertised and the applicant was one of the candidates interviewed. She was unsuccessful at interview and a man was appointed to the job. Five men and two women in addition to the applicant had been interviewed. After the interview a piece of paper

was found on the floor of the interview room on which had been written the words 'Good screw', and when this was investigated by the company it was discovered to have been written by one of those on the interviewing panel ... no immediate disciplinary action was taken against the officer who admitted writing the remark, and neither was it proven at that stage that the remark had been specifically directed against the applicant rather than against either of the two other female candidates. The applicant continued to be employed by the company at the same outlet but under the new manager appointed by the interviewing panel.

Just over a year later the job of manager at the same outlet again became vacant and the applicant once more took up the position of acting manager during the interregnum prior to the new appointment. She was interviewed again for the post of manager but a male candidate with less experience than herself was appointed. The applicant was considered by the interviewing panel to have been a good number two for the job. However, when the person appointed decided that he could not take up the job after all, rather than offer the post to the applicant, the company decided to readvertise the post. Of the two candidates, a 24 year old male and a 40 year old female, the man was appointed. (Chambers with Horton, 1990: 54–5)

This case demonstrates some important issues that hold women back in their career progression. The woman applicant for the managerial post had proved her capability. Nevertheless, she was overlooked repeatedly. Each time she was passed over in favour of a man whose capabilities could only be estimated as he was an external candidate. Furthermore, she was passed over on the second occasion for a man known to have less experience. The incident of the note indicates that at interview there is a tendency for women candidates to be assessed by criteria other than those required for the job. Men's propensity to weigh up a woman's sexual attractiveness (and potential availability) can be one of the most insidious forms of sex discrimination to be found in the workplace. Women workers are also sub-jected to sexual harassment. Camilla Palmer (1992: 215) tells us that harassment at work 'is alarmingly common' and refers to a study by Alfred Marks (a nation-wide employment agency) in 1990/91 which suggested that about two-thirds of employees have experienced some form of harassment on several occasions. Sexual harassment has been defined as 'unwanted conduct of a sexual nature, or other conduct based on sex affecting the dignity of women and men at work' (Palmer, 1992: 215). It includes not only suggestive physical behaviour but also suggestive comments, jokes and even innuendo. As with all kinds of sexual discrimination the onus is on the individual to prove it as far as the law is concerned. This can be extremely difficult as there are rarely any witnesses. It is also often a situation in which many women will balk at 'going public'. Nevertheless, in recent years there has been a noticeable trend for those working on tribunals to take a more serious view of harassment. This is reflected in higher damages being awarded to claimants.

Unemployment

The last point in our profile of women's jobs must be a brief mention of unemployment. Employment and unemployment go hand in hand. Traditional assumptions about women's 'real' place being in the home, about women's jobs just being for 'pin money' mask the importance of women's incomes for very many households in which women are the sole or main earner. In many households, two incomes are needed to maintain even a basic standard of living. Unemployment also has consequences for women's independence or power within the household, and for women's ability to support their children. It is known that unemployment has adverse effects on men, damaging self-image and inducing stress and apathy. Little thought and discussion has been given to the implications for women. In the current climate of a shrinking jobs market in Britain, women's unemployment must be considered seriously. Women's jobs at the low skill end of the market are likely to be automated in the search for greater profitability through the continued introduction of technologies, while women's segregation in particular types of jobs will often prevent women from taking up the newly created more technical types of jobs. However, the concentration of women in services, where a high level of human input and interaction is required, protects women's jobs to some extent. Women's reputation as low paid and flexible workers can often work positively in our favour. Employers may actively create jobs and businesses based on women workers. In some parts of Britain previously known for high male employment in traditional industries such as coal mining, new factories employing mainly women on low level production line work are moving in. None the less women's unemployment remains high despite, as we noted earlier, a tendency for women not to be included in official figures. Anne Witz (1993) refers to research estimating that over 40 per cent of unemployed women do not register as unemployed and are therefore missing from the statistics.

Before you go on to the next section, working through the following exercise will enable you to summarize what you have learnt so far.

EXERCISE

1. Reflect on the profile of women at home and in the labour market which has been established in the previous sections and make a list of some of the main factors about women's work. Which of them connect with your experiences?
2. What connections do you think there are between the two areas of women's work: paid jobs and unpaid tasks?

EXERCISE RESPONSE

We can summarize some of the points you may have made in response to the two questions above. Women's work can be divided into two main areas:

1. *In the household*: Women usually have the main responsibility for the household, doing the housework, and providing food and care for the family and/or other members of the household.
2. *In jobs*: Women are clustered in low paid jobs which are low skilled, bearing resemblance to the kinds of work which is said to come naturally to women in the domestic sphere, that is cleaning, catering, sewing, serving and servicing others in various ways. Women are far more likely than men to be in part-time employment.

As we have seen many of the jobs women do are not paid at all, so if you are making links between women's paid jobs and women's unpaid domestic responsibilities, then research shows that you are right to do so. Studies show, for example, that women with children under five are very much more likely not to take full-time paid jobs than those with older children or with no children at all, and even the part-time hours worked by women with children are constrained by childcare needs. It is calculated that approximately 222,000 women may be unable to seek paid work as they are caring for elderly or infirm relatives, and a further 146,000 are limited in what hours and jobs they can do (Rees, 1992). Research also shows that mothers are likely to take up paid work for which they are overqualified to fit in with their childcare commitments (Martin and Roberts, 1984; Dex, 1987).

In the next section we will look at the constraints on women's paid jobs in more detail.

Further Issues for Women with Jobs

A lack of suitable childcare and community care for other dependants can present problems for women with regard to jobs. We might ask why men do not seem to face the same problems as a rule, or why government seems reluctant to recognize the problems? One of the reasons relates to the sexual division of labour which allocates to women rather than men childcare tasks. The issue of childcare has been widely discussed in the media in recent years. It is not, however, a new issue, but one with a long history.

In the extract below, Rose Kerrigan, a Jewish working-class woman living in London (Jewish Women In London Group, 1989) describes some of her experiences during the Second World War. Women were needed then to fill the places in industry left by men joining the forces, as well as enrolling in the services themselves. To encourage married women's participation the government provided some assistance with domestic responsibilities, including nurseries, canteens and restaurants, and other services such as extra laundries. Rose Kerrigan comments:

When Jean was nine months old I got myself a job. At that time women could do some kind of war work. When they need you they can provide the means. During the war the government opened up nurseries for the women because they had to get the women to come and work. I went to the post office but soon they said they didn't really need me. Because it was war work I had got Jean into a nursery, and having got her in, I had to have a job or I wouldn't have been able to keep her there. I was very disappointed, so I went to the local tailor and asked him whether he could do with a hand, and he gave me a start. (Jewish Women In London Group, 1989: 68–9)

Rose worked in clothing manufacture for the rest of the war, with her daughter cared for in the government nursery during working hours. When the war ended, the government no longer saw the need to encourage women's participation in paid jobs. Rose goes on to say:

They gradually did away with nurseries, and how did they do it? They charged so much that women couldn't afford to pay. They also made out there was no need for them. They wanted women back in the home so that when the men came out of the army they could get jobs. We had a lot of fights over them doing away with the nurseries. After that I worked in a clothing factory. I organized a union. There were different rates of pay for women and men and one thing the unions did, they raised the wages. (Jewish Women In London Group, 1989: 69)

Childcare is a continual problem for women who want to have paid jobs. Government continues to be reluctant today, as it was at the end of the war, to provide nurseries or other facilities for childcare, or to enact legislation requiring other employers to do so. Women frequently have to take whatever jobs they can to fit in with their children's needs, and these jobs are often at the lowest end of the pay scale, involving shift work and poor conditions. The dilemma facing women is described vividly below:

I work from 5 p.m. to 10 p.m. every evening. I took this job eight years ago because the hours suited me. I would be with the kids all day and go to work when my husband got home. Now they're at school, I'm still there to meet them, so in that way the job is good. But what satisfaction is there as a punch card operator? The job doesn't offer me any scope for promotion and getting training is impossible. There's no way they are going to send someone like me, a part time worker and a Black woman at that, for in-service training. So, although I'm lucky to have a job when so many people are unemployed, I still wish I could go to college and improve my prospects. (Quoted in Bryan, Scafe and Dadzie, 1985: 51–2)

Altogether domestic and caring commitments can place women at a disadvantage in terms of paid jobs and curtail their opportunities. Women may well decide to take part-time work to deal with their dual responsibilities, as it offers an opportunity to earn some money and to gain a measure of independence. But we also need to recognize the advantages for employers in having a large part-time workforce of women to draw on. Part-time jobs in Britain often do not have the same status or benefits as full-time work, despite recent changes in legislation concerning rights to benefits. They are often casual jobs, without proper contracts, so that employees can be taken on as required, and then sacked, often without notice, when no longer needed. Today this is often known as a flexible labour market. Other characteristics of this kind of working include the ability to switch from one kind of task to another, on an assembly line for example with little or no additional training. Part-time jobs for women, designated low skill at low rates of pay, often replace full-time skilled work for men. This is called the **feminization of labour**. The lack of a statutory minimum wage in Great Britain further erodes women's chances of getting paid a good rate for the job they do.

Another point which needs to be considered is the failure by many employers to take women's employment seriously. Employers often assume that women are committed first and foremost to their home responsibilities. *All* women are subject to these assumptions. This leads to constraints on opportunities for well paying, satisfying careers and poorly paid part-time jobs alike.

The work women do in the household is largely servicing and caring for others. This carries over into women's paid work. In office work of all kinds women are expected to perform 'housewifely' tasks, such as making coffee, welcoming visitors or organizing other people. These skills are certainly always in demand, but they are currently very much undervalued in terms of paid employment. This could change with a re-evaluation of women's communication and management skills, acquired at home. Whether this would mean improvements for women in the paid job market remains to be seen. The sex-typing of jobs and occupations severely restricts women's opportunities as a group, but it is also important to remember the gains that women have made since the turn of the century in the range of jobs we do now, and in the realization of our potential as paid workers.

Success in Jobs: Workplace Achievements

We know that one of the most remarkable transitions in women's lives since the Second World War has been the fact that most women can expect to spend a great deal of their adult lives doing a paid job. This chapter has discussed in detail the obstacles which women have had to face in the marketplace. While all these issues are extremely important, it would be misleading not to present another side of the picture. In many ways women have been remarkably successful in constructing space in the workplace. Women's educational performance has improved dramatically in recent years and we are now well represented in higher education. These changes have helped set the agenda for job success. Women's progress in occupations previously the territory of men has been described as slow but steady (Hansard Society Commission, 1990). Women are learning to develop strategies which allow them to hold their own with male colleagues. The following extract shows how one woman doctor in the United States tackled her frustration stemming from lack of promotion:

> I began to complain loudly. I went to the department chairman and said, 'Here's what I'm working on.' He said, 'Well, everybody does that.' My answer was, 'Everybody else has been promoted to associate attending and associate professor, but I have not.' Well, lo and behold, six months later, I got promoted! (Lorber, 1984: 78)

Science has been notoriously difficult for women to break into as professionals. Yet even here women are beginning to develop their own strategies to locate themselves in the foreground of scientific research. An example is Dr Heather Giles, a senior pharmacologist at the Wellcome laboratories, Beckenham, Kent. A quick look at her biography reveals that she reached her senior position without tramping the traditional male pathway:

> Dr Giles' unusual career history is an indication of the different expectations of men and women in science, and the strange route that women sometimes have to take to reach the top. She has been in charge of the analytical pharmacology team at Wellcome's receptor group for six months – a role which she took over from a man and which had always been previously filled by men – but for the first eight years of her professional life her only contact with drugs was when she injected them into patients as a nurse at Kings College Hospital in London. (*The Times*, 14.11.94)

Earlier, we noted the common phenomenon that professionally qualified women can find themselves in a position of having to take jobs which do not match their qualifications. Other women have been able to upgrade their training as adults and move into prestigious and well paid jobs. This was the experience of Dr Giles.

Another workplace arena in which women have had notable success over the last two decades has been the world of small business development. We will end this section on successful women with the profile of a young Black woman, Yolande Beckles, whose success has been documented by Carol Dix (1991). After leaving school she worked for Sainsbury's where she had the opportunity to gain some managerial training. She developed an interest in training for women, specifically Black women, going on to set up as a freelance trainer. Within two years she set up two companies, 3 Circles, a company which marketed training packages for women, and a dance school called Moving Parts Performing Arts School. She describes herself in the following way:

> What am I? I'm a woman who doesn't just talk about what she wants to do, but who does it. Until 1987, I was an employee. Then overnight I became a business woman. I went into that without any market research, with no business plan. I just made it work. My confidence and luck have pushed me through. So far, I feel I am exploiting the two areas in which I know I excel. (Dix, 1991: 146)

Future developments in jobs for women cannot be predicted. Women have shown their strength, flexibility and tenacity in juggling their responsibilities at home and in paid jobs, and deserve to have an increasing range of satisfying, well paid job choices available.

EXERCISE

For the final exercise in this chapter we are going to ask you to reflect on your own experiences. Now that you have read the chapter carefully and done the exercises, you will be able to identify more clearly the structures which surround women's experiences of paid jobs and work in the home. These structures (job segregation, discrimination, lack of childcare facilities) can hinder our opportunities to make the most of our aspirations. Consider the following questions:

1. Think back over your *own* experience and note achievements in both paid and other work.
2. There will have been choices to make, barriers to surmount and success to be acknowledged. How would you tackle similar situations, should you meet them now?

We hope that what you have learned in this chapter will enable you to understand some of the issues which women meet at work. Increasing awareness of theoretical ideas, combined with women's own accounts of work experiences help all of us to assess our lives in a wider social context. This analytic process contributes to identifying choices which we see as appropriate for us. This knowledge in itself can be empowering.

REFERENCES

Abbott, Pamela and Wallace, Claire 1990: *An Introduction to Sociology: Feminist Perspectives.* London: Routledge.

Bhachu, P. 1988: Apni Maezi Kards. Home and work: Sikh women in Britain. In S. Westwood and P. Bhachu (eds), *Enterprising Women: Ethnicity, Economy and Gender Relations*, London: Routledge.

Bhavnani, Reena 1994: *Black Women into the Labour Market, A Research Review.* Manchester: Equal Opportunities Commission.

Brannen, Judith and Moss, Peter 1988: *New Mothers at Work: Employment and Childcare.* London: Unwin Hyman.

Brannen, Judith and Moss, Peter 1990: *Managing Mothers: Dual Earner Households after Maternity Leave.* London: Unwin Hyman.

Bruegel, Irene 1989: Sex and race in the labour market. *Feminist Review*, 32, 49–68.

Bryan, Beverley, Scafe, Suzanne and Dadzie, Stella 1985: *Heart of the Race: Black Women's Lives in Britain.* London: Virago.

Chambers, Gerald with Horton, Christine 1990: *Promoting Sex Equality.* London: Policy Studies Institute.

Clark, Alice 1993: *Working Life of Women in the 17th Century.* London: Routledge. [First published 1919.]

Cockburn, Cynthia 1991: *In the Way of Women: Men's Resistance to Sex Equality in Organizations.* London: Macmillan.

Coyle, Angela and Skinner, Jane (eds) 1988: *Women and Work: Positive Action for Change.* London: Macmillan.

Davidoff, Leonore and Westover, Belinda (eds) 1986: *Our Work, Our Lives, Our Words: Women's History, Women's Work.* London: Macmillan.

Dex, Shirley 1987: *Women's Occupational Mobility: A Lifetime Perspective.* London: Macmillan.

Dix, Carol 1991: *Enterprising Women.* London: Bantam Press.

Employment Gazette 1991: Ethnic origins and the labour market. *Employment Gazette*, 99, 2, February 59–72.

Equal Opportunities Commission 1987: *Women and Men in Britain.* Manchester: EOC.

Equal Opportunites Commission 1990: *Women and Men in Great Britain.* London: HMSO.

Faulkner, Wendy and Arnold, Erik (eds) 1985: *Smothered by Invention: Technology in Women's Lives*, London: Pluto Press.

French, Marilyn 1992: *The War Against Women.* London: Hamish Hamilton.

General Council of the Bar 1992: *Without Prejudice?* London: The General Council of the Bar.

Graham, Hilary 1993: *Hardship and Health in Women's Lives.* Hemel Hempstead: Harvester Wheatsheaf.

Hakim, C. 1979: Occupational segregations. Research paper no. 9, Department of Employment. London: HMSO.

Hansard Society Commission 1990: *Women at the Top.* London: The Hansard Society.

Holdsworth, Angela 1988: *Out of the Doll's House: The Story of Women in the Twentieth Century.* London: BBC Books.

Jamieson, Lynn 1990: Rural and urban women in domestic service. In Eleanor Gordon and Esther Brietenbach (eds), *The World is Ill Divided: Women's Work in Scotland in the Nineteenth and Early Twentieth Centuries,* Edinburgh: Edinburgh University Press.

Jewish Women In London Group 1989: *Generations of Memories: Voices of Jewish Women.* London: The Women's Press.

Lorber, Judith 1984: *Women Physicians.* London and New York: Tavistock Publications.

Martin, Jean and Roberts, Ceridwyn 1984: *Women and Employment.* London: Department of Employment and OPCS Report HMSO.

Morris, J. 1991: *Pride Against Prejudice: Transforming Attitudes to Disability.* London: Women's Press.

Oakley, Ann 1982: *Subject Women.* London: Fontana.

Palmer, Camilla 1992: *Discrimination at Work.* London: Legal Action Group Education and Service Trust Ltd.

Read, Jim 1988: *Equal Opportunities.* London: Interchange Books.

Rees, Teresa 1992: *Women and the Labour Market.* London: Routledge.

Social Trends 24 1994: London: HMSO.

Taking Liberties Collective 1989: *Learning the Hard Way.* Basingstoke: Macmillan.

Trollope, Joanna 1992: *The Rector's Wife.* London: Black Swan.

Westwood, Sallie and Bhachu, Parminder 1988: *Enterprising Women: Ethnicity, Economy and Gender Relations.* London: Routledge.

Witz, Anne 1993: Women at work. In Diane Richardson and Victoria Robinson (eds), *Introducing Women's Studies,* London: Macmillan.

CHAPTER
6 Leisure

Beryl Madoc-Jones

Plate 5 *Dancing at Eastgate WI.* © Hulton Deutsch Collection; photograph: Startup.

The idea of 'leisure' has become familiar to us in the twentieth century, at least in Western societies. We are likely to come across it most frequently in phrases such as leisure pursuits, leisure centre, leisure wear, etc., in contexts which stress the contrast between leisure and work. Despite its everyday familiarity, leisure is a complex concept to get to grips with. This is because it has different meanings for us depending on our own position in society: leisure is encountered and constructed in different ways by women (and men), according to age, class, race, physical ability (disability) and religion. Moreover, in British society in the past, leisure was not always experienced as it is now.

In this chapter I will look first at some of the ways in which leisure has been shaped by historical context. Then I will consider the manner in which those studying leisure have developed a conventional understanding of leisure as a category to use in the analysis of individual and social life. Following that is an examination of the relevance of these received wisdoms for acknowledging the significance of leisure in women's lives. Lastly I endeavour to explore ways in which feminist perspectives have been made use of to extend our knowledge of women's engagement with leisure. They have begun to unmask a previously unacknowledged area of women's oppression and, most importantly, to make known women's resourcefulness in reaching out for and claiming leisure as an area of autonomous action and fulfilment.

After reading this chapter, you should have a grasp of gender issues in conceptualizing leisure. In particular you will understand that women's social position as partners (generally of men) and mothers profoundly influences meanings of leisure. In addition, you will have some appreciation of the tensions between constraints of society (in the West patriarchal and capitalist) and the autonomy of women to make leisure. At the same time you will recognize that we can empower ourselves to establish distinctive ways of enjoying leisure.

EXERCISE

Before we go any further stop and think about your life and leisure.
Write down all the words that immediately come to mind when you think about leisure.

When you have done this reorder your words in two ways:

1. Put them in order of most importance to you.
2. Put them in order of different stages of your life (childhood, adolescence, young motherhood, retirement).

Put these notes aside now; we will return to them.

Women/Work, Ladies/Leisure

Social historians have drawn our attention to the idea that leisure has a long history. For example, Hugh Cunningham (1986) has told us that 'except in primitive societies, people have always been aware of a separation between work and leisure, and have put a high value on leisure' (p. 57). Modern meanings and practices associated with leisure have their origins in past centuries that witnessed the development of industrial society. From the seventeenth century on, a society based on the social and economic principles of capitalism has developed. The social changes associated with the rise of capitalism involved massive shifts in the organization of people's lives. (See box 6.1.)

There are three points that are particularly important to consider in relation to changing notions of leisure. First is the idea that work was dramatically reorganized through the separation of home and workplace. (See discussion in chapter 5.) Secondly, the logic of capitalism and a drive towards rationalization of work processes was associated with the growth of changing notions of time. Rosemary Deem (1986) using E. P. Thompson's (1967) famous essay on work and capitalism, has highlighted the process by which an irregular notion of time gave way to a precise measure. It was to become a mechanism by which the beginning and ending of a work unit could be demarcated, whether by the day, week or working lifetime. The recognition of a working day triggered a separation in time of work and non-work arenas in individual lives. Leisure by the eighteenth century began to mean free non-obligated time (Cunningham, 1986: 12). It was increasingly associated with what people did when not at work.

The third point concerns the importance of class for understanding the changing experience of life in a capitalist society. The way in which the space created by the separation of work and non-work time could be incorporated into lifestyle depended very much on class position. Social control of the working classes, including women was understood very much in terms of limiting opportunity for

| Social Implications of Capitalism | BOX 6.1 |

An economic system is a way of organizing resources, including natural ones such as land, sea, oil. Capitalism is associated with a particular kind of economic system characterized by capital (money), the market (free), profits (surplus money), and owners/non-owners (of the capital accumulated). Nineteenth-century thinkers (including Marx) saw that capitalism was not only an economic system but also a social system since social relations between people stem from a specific economic organization. Capitalism leads to unequal distribution of wealth and this leads to the emergence of classes. (Marx identified the Bourgeoisie and the Proletariat as classes based on property ownership.) Nowadays we are familiar with the broad categories of working class and middle class. These divisions are associated with economic advantage and disadvantage and clearly influence social position.

Capitalism in the nineteenth century became associated with changing ideas about women's and men's relationship to work and family. It became accepted that it was desirable for men to take sole responsibility for their families through their wage. This social pattern located women firmly in the home and made them dependent on men. As a result, a woman's class position has tended to be derived from her husband/father, placing her in a subordinate position in which she is dependent on men for both economic and social status.

leisure. As the classes generated by industrial capitalism took shape, the relationship between class, gender and leisure was fashioned. For many women, leisure as distinct from work would not have been a relevant concept. For very many working-class women never-ending hard work had to be endured. From childhood on, they were confronted by a relentless round of strenuous work, inside and outside the home.

To illustrate this here is an account of one woman's life written when she was seventy years old (Llewelyn Davies, 1977). Mrs Layton, as she was to become, grew up in nineteenth century Bethnal Green. As a child (under ten years old) she tried to get a job as a 'step girl' on Saturdays. At ten years old childhood was left behind and she was properly initiated into adult life and work.

> When I was ten years old I began to earn my own living. I went to mind the baby of a person who kept a small general shop. My wages were 1/6 a week and my tea and 2d. a week for myself. I got to work at eight in the morning and left at eight at night, with the exception of two nights a week when I left at seven o'clock to

attend a night school, one of a number started by Lord Shaftesbury, called Ragged Schools. (Llewelyn Davies, 1977: 20)

After her initiation into the workplace she moved through a variety of jobs – including maternity nursing and service. Marriage and pregnancy followed. A rather desperate interlude then followed with the unemployment of her husband. Mrs Layton found herself coping with a sick husband, extreme poverty and a young child. Her response to the situation was an acceptance of the need for even more work:

> My baby grew into a strong sturdy little fellow full of mischief. It was a great treat to look after him and help earn the living. At the same time it meant taking him out in the day time and working after my husband had gone to work at night. Many times till 4 o'clock in the morning in bitter cold weather I have been washing, and have just been able to get 2 hours' sleep before the child woke up, which he did about 6 o'clock. (Llewelyn Davies, 1977: 37)

EXERCISE

Look carefully at Mrs Layton's testimony about her life. Where does her work take place? Are there any ways in which you can identify in her words, meanings that match with your concept of leisure? (Look back to the previous exercise on pages 111–12 and your ideas about work and leisure.)

EXERCISE RESPONSE

You probably noted that throughout her life Mrs Layton's day focused on childcare. Her skills were domestic and so her work (paid/unpaid) was home-based. Satisfaction came mainly from pleasing others. You may share her pleasure from doing her best for her family. You may well also empathize with the scale of her workload, the near impossibility of understanding leisure as free time, time to please oneself.

In another part of society, leisure came to symbolize very different experiences. The increasing importance of the distinction between work and non-work for some women, was signalled by the evolution of the leisure class, a concept associated with the work of Thorsten Veblen (see box 6.2). The accumulation of wealth that was at the heart of the capitalist process led to the emergence of a

BOX
6.2

Thorsten Veblen (1925)

Veblen made an important contribution to understanding the implications of capitalism for relationships between people. He used the concept of leisure in a specific way (derived from Marxist theory). He suggested that it had particular sets of meanings that concerned the Marxist idea of 'non-productive time' – referring to all time that is not spent in labour (work) resulting in producing economic goods. A second meaning was derived from the notion that human achievement in non-productive time was of greater worth than that achieved in productive time. A third aspect of the concept was that individuals who had sufficient means to live without the need for paid employment could aspire to the status of the 'gentleman' (and lady).

He coined the phrase **conspicuous consumption**. By this he was drawing our attention to the desirability for those aspiring to high status to use their wealth as a way of signalling their success. A material lifestyle of a certain standard became recognized as public evidence of success and accumulation of wealth. A necessary prerequisite to the attainment of gentlemanly status. The leisure class was made up of those who had sufficient wealth to free time for the pursuit of non-pecuniary activities. The female members of the leisure class had an important role. Their contribution to the acquisition of status was through **vicarious consumption** – the organization of consumption patterns of the household. Veblen likened the situation of the lady to that of the lackey:

> In all grades and walks of life, and at any stage of the economic development, the leisure of the lady and of the lackey differs from the leisure of the gentleman in his own right in that it is an occupation of an ostensibly laborious kind. It takes the form in large measure, of a painstaking attention to the service of the master, or the maintenance and elaboration of the household paraphernalia; so that it is leisure only in the sense that little or no productive work is performed by this class, not in the sense that all appearance of labour is avoided by them. The duties performed by the lady or by the household or domestic servants, are frequently arduous enough and they are also frequently directed toward tasks which are considered extremely necessary to the comfort of the entire household. (Veblen, 1925: 54)

A very telling concept that Veblen also coined was **vicarious leisure**. This referred to the service provided by one person to make life more comfortable for another. Thus according to this theoretical framework much of the 'work' of the lady fell into this category of vicarious leisure.

class marked out by its ownership of capital and capacity for consumption. Leisure for members of this class came to have very specific meanings. The 'lady' emerged as a role for the wives and mothers of the wealthier classes. An increasing amount of time was allocated to the management of non-work activities. The lady was responsible for controlling not only the pattern of expenditure deemed appropriate but also for maintaining a lifestyle that reflected the status accruing from the work of the husband.

The lady of leisure of the nineteenth century was free from the obligation of paid employment. She differed from her working-class sister in that her daily life was not circumscribed by hard physical toil inside or outside the home. Yet she could have a daily routine, in many ways equally limited by constraints beyond her determination. Much of her time was likely to be spent on tasks meeting the demands and needs of family members (including male) so that their opportunities for leisure were carefully protected. Leonore Davidoff's (1973) study of upper middle-class ladies has revealed to us how much effort was sustained in order to participate in the Season so that the desired lifestyle for family members could proceed with minimal disruption.

Conceptual Thinking and Leisure

Leisure has been the subject of scholarly interest in many fields including history, sociology and cultural studies. More recently, a growing interest has become evident among those who work in Women's Studies. Women studying leisure have commented that much existing literature has been characterized by 'gender-blindness' (Wimbush and Talbot, 1988; Green, Hebron and Woodward, 1990). Rosemary Deem (1986) has pointed out that sociological analysis on leisure in contemporary society has started with male as a normative position. Such perspectives have not allowed for a recognition that women's experience and understanding of leisure might be different.

How do men perceive leisure?

Women's work includes many tasks and responsibilities which are not paid and are done in domestic settings (see discussion in chapter 5). This view of women's work has implications for analysing women's leisure. Before we can think about reconceptualization of leisure to facilitate understanding of women's lives, we need to review the male position. The first point to make is that the whole notion of work/leisure sets the stage for a mode of dichotomous thinking. Leisure becomes what work is not. Another distinction is that work is paid and other activities are not. Real (men's) work is paid work (Deem, 1986; Green, Hebron and Woodward, 1990). In addition to work being normally and characteristically paid, it has been regarded as 'full-time'. From this follows the idea that life can be compartmentalized into time spent at work and time spent 'not at' work.

A third idea is the notion of leisure as some kind of commodity available outside working hours. This opens up changing ways of understanding the relation between space and place in the management of routines of daily life. Leisure becomes thought of as something a person *possesses* and *uses* in that part of life spent away from work. For those in paid employment, returning home at the end of the working day marks the transition from a work to a non-work environment. Home symbolizes the place where she/he has space to pursue non-work activities. Within the home, spatial zones become associated with different activities. For some members of families – those returning from the workplace – much of what they do at home is understood as leisure. Leisure is used conceptually to make the separation between work and non-work through the use of space. Central to this is the home as a way of distinguishing between work and leisure.

A fourth notion in the conventional understanding of a dichotomous distinction between work and leisure is to identify work time and leisure time; underpinning this distinction is the recognition of obligation and a freedom to *choose* how to spend time. According to Stanley Parker, a sociologist, time outside work is thought of as existence – time and leisure – time (in Griffin et al., 1990: 91). Existence time is a category that refers to activities needed in order to meet the demands of human physiological survival such as eating, sleeping, and washing. Leisure time is truly that which involves pursuits that are free from obligation either to oneself (as in the case of existence time) or others. Thus a key concept at the heart of ideas about leisure is the freedom to choose *how* to spend one's time.

EXERCISE

Before we go any further try the following exercise.

Write down the adult members in your household. What use of space is associated with each one? What activities are linked with these spaces? What does this tell you about the home as an arena for leisure?

Debriefing comments on this exercise will be found on page 119.

How do women perceive leisure?

Let's begin with the first set of ideas just examined, that work – as opposed to non-work (leisure) – is typically paid, full-time, and located outside the home. Leisure (non-work) becomes in juxtaposition unpaid, spare-time and located outside the workplace. This fundamental division of life into compartments of work and non-work, derived from a model of men's roles as they became differentiated in industrial society (see box 5.1 'Sexual division of labour', page 91) is problematic for studying women's lives. Margaret speaks for many women when she describes her daily life as a housewife:

Lucy is six; Kate is just four and Rebecca will be two in June: three girls. The plan was four in eight years but I chickened out last summer – four is a lot to cope with. Anyway, I'd be bound to have another girl; people say 'leave a bigger gap, and you'll change the sex!'

Peter is the director of a publishing firm. He used to be a journalist, but then he was offered the chance of a stake in this firm – it's a new company – and he'd always wanted something of his own. Journalism is such a rat race. It's only a small stake, but it was what he wanted. I don't really know that much about his job, I suppose.

I get up at seven, and I'm afraid some days the first thing I do is I have to iron a shirt for Peter and a blouse for Lucy. Then I usually run the bath for the children. If they want their breakfast first I give them their breakfast. They usually refuse a cooked breakfast; they love Weetabix, they have two or three Weetabix and then they like toast and jam afterwards. I feel a bit guilty about this; I have cooked breakfast in the past but it's just been played around with. Peter usually gets up at half past eight to leave here at half past nine, and if I'm very busy he will get himself something. If he got up when the others did, I would naturally cook for him every day. It's very busy in the morning. I have to get Lucy ready for school, take her, come back, get Kate ready for playgroup, take her, come back, and then take Peter to the station. Sometimes I walk to the school and the play group, but if Peter's in a hurry and is waiting here I have to take the car, so I can get him to the station on time.

I cook at lunchtime for Rebecca and myself and usually I do a high tea: fish fingers or sausages or spaghetti bolognese – for all the children if I've got a friend in – and if we go out we quite often have a similar sort of tea. If they want something to eat before they go to bed, they'll have it. I never mind cooking for the children because I know I love food and I never mind cooking for me! It's never any trouble cooking for them because I understand that they love food as well, I suppose.

I try to get them in bed by seven. I find it impossible to get them there any earlier. They'll all go together; Lucy is quite content to go with the other two, although she's older. There is an awful lot of clearing up to do at the end of the day, especially if I've had a friend to tea. Today I had a friend with three children, so there were six children to clear up after!

Many evenings I spend on my own, because Peter's never in before eight or nine and quite often it's eleven or twelve, and when he has to go to his club with someone it's two or three in the morning. I think this is partly because he is very enthusiastic about his work – if he does come home at eight, he brings work with him!

In the evening I read the paper, or I watch television – I watch a fair bit of television. I take time to make phone calls to friends, to my parents, to my brother– without the children rushing round screaming. I also use the time to finish off odd bits of housework I haven't done in the day.

Some evenings I've stood and I've ironed eleven shirts and it hasn't worried me at all. I like to iron in here with the television on, and when I've done them I hang them along the picture rail, and I get a great sense of satisfaction seeing them hanging all the way round the room! Silly, isn't it? (Oakley, 1976: 152–3)

Our immediate response to Margaret's account is likely to be that she works very hard indeed! But her work does not fit easily the conventional (male) concepts of work as previously outlined. The first point to note is that her woman's work stretches over a long day: at least twelve hours. It would certainly exceed the customary eight-hour day in the contemporary workplace. There is no clear distinction made by Margaret between time spent working and non-work-time. Since all her housework goes unrecognized in terms of pay, her home work (as a full-time housewife) cannot be divided into categories of paid/unpaid work.

The second point made in the preceding discussion of men's ideas about leisure concerned the concept of time. For men work is characteristically full time which leads to a concept of time which organizes space in a particular way. Men's time is spent at work or away from work. Margaret did not experience her day either as time spent working or not working or through separation in terms of space of being at work or away from work. The notion of 'full time' falls short of capturing the reality and demands of her working day while the concept of 'spare time' would have little relevance.

Although the working day at home may be long, it fails to conform to male patterns of time and use of space for locating work. The third point in our 'male model' referred to the clear demarcation of leisure as separate from work in spatial organization of daily life. During the nineteenth century, home was often talked about as a private haven for men who could flee from the harshness of the public workplace and find refuge in the sanctuary of the home. Once home, they had the privilege of freedom from the constraints and demands of the job and the opportunity to indulge in pursuits of their own choosing. Today, the separation of work and home for many men means that they, too, associate home with leisure rather than work.

Look back at the last exercise on page 117 and see how you identified space in the home with non-work activities. You may well have identified the garage or the garden shed as areas predominantly controlled by men for their proprietorial use as leisure space. Many of us will immediately think of the kitchen as women's space in the home. Preparing and supervising meals occupied a great deal of

Margaret's time. Her evenings were spent mainly in the sitting room – a house space shared by members of the family or household for leisure purposes, including television. Yet for Margaret it is space which symbolizes the interweaving of both work and leisure. Notice that she enjoys cooking and combines ironing withwatching television. We will return shortly to this use of time and space. (This issue is also discussed in chapter 10, page 216.)

The organization of work also pinpoints differences in women's experience of work and leisure compared with men. Home work is often more fragmented when undertaken in the private sphere of the home than in the public workplace (Oakley, 1974, 1976; Wimbush and Talbot, 1988).

Fragmentation comes with the opportunity to pace work as an individual. In this sense the home/house worker is in a similar position to the self-employed with the important exception that her work goes un-remunerated. At the same time as experiencing fragmentation, many women at home also find that the nature of work is routinized. This may be connected with monotony and boredom (Oakley, 1974). These are characteristics facing men (and women) in the workplace, but for the lone worker at home mitigating the effects of isolation through social contact at work is problematic. Margaret managed this aspect of her working day by regularly inviting friends round (and thus creating more work).

The fourth main point in the male conventional view of leisure referred to is the distinction between work-time and leisure-time in relation to the idea of obligation and freedom from obligation (freedom to please oneself). Obligation denotes time spent in obligatory activities – in the workplace they stem from contractual duties of employment. Although housework does not carry the conditions of contractual employment (including pay!) women nevertheless feel a strong sense of obligation to partners and other members of their households. As Ann Oakley put it, the housewife despite an autonomy located in personal control of the content and pattern of her day, does not feel 'free to choose her own activities' (Oakley, 1974: 44). The work is always present and demands attention. Demands on women, particularly mothers of younger children such as Margaret, mean that it is difficult for them to find time for themselves (time that is free from obligation).

One result of this is that women develop strategies for constructing leisure which may mean simultaneously doing work and engaging in a pursuit for their own enjoyment as Margaret did in the evenings spent ironing and watching television. Alternatively, they may adopt what has been called 'free-flowing' time management, moving in and out of work and leisure with fluid ease (Stanley, 1988). Margaret snatched moments for herself when she walked to school to fetch her child; when she read the paper in the evening, perhaps, in between spells of completing unfinished chores.

Women have been described as **time-poor** (Millar and Glendinning, 1989). For many, the opportunity to set aside time of one's own may seem very elusive. An important factor will be economic resources available. We have seen, earlier in this chapter, how difficult it was for Mrs Layton, a working-class mother in the early twentieth century to have time for herself, both as a young girl and as a married woman and mother. Margaret, a 1970's middle-class wife and mother was different from Mrs Layton in that she was not poor and belonged to a comfortable, relatively affluent world. She was able to snatch time for herself in the day and have some evening relaxation. She had a car available in the daytime which increased her choices about the allocation of time to various activities. Nevertheless, she too had a long working day with limited time to herself.

The amount of time women can make available as free-time for their own personal/private pursuits has always been related to their financial position. Women who can afford to buy in domestic help can free up time for other activities and can also make their domestic work lighter through being able to purchase a range of labour saving equipment such as washing-machines and dryers. While modern technology may have in some ways lightened women's load, other social changes have intensified their sense of being time-poor. At the present time, more women than at any other time this century have some kind of paid work (see the discussion of women and jobs in chapter 5). For many women, the years of combining domestic and paid work (often referred to as the double shift) will be a stage in life when time for themselves seems to have slipped from their grasp. One such group is black British women of Afro-Caribbean origin who have a high participation rate in full-time employment and many of whom are single parents. Personal time will be particularly elusive for the full-time working single mother.

When women, both employed and houseworkers, come to retirement (their own and/or a partner's), a new stage in the life cycle of work is reached. As with other stages, leisure experiences in retirement are gendered. Retirement for men is characteristically marked publicly, through ritual practices including 'the present' and 'the party'. As a rite de passage, it becomes a public celebration which Jennifer Mason (1988) has pointed out is often seen as a reward for a lifetime of service. For the home-based partner, rather than marking the end of work, the retirement may result in an increasing work-load. Men around the house create work. More meals have to be provided and their needs including emotional, have to be responded to. Male presence at home can curtail a woman's freedom. She is likely to have less personal space and time. Jennifer Mason reported in her Kent study on couples aged 50–70 years that women's acceptance of their role to look after a partner meant that they were reluctant to leave a man in the house alone (Mason, 1988). Women retiring from the workplace themselves may co-ordinate this change in their working patterns to coincide with partners' retirement so that they will be available to create the conditions which will facilitate *his* enjoyment of *his* free-time.

One of the main reasons for women's time-poverty stems from the caring element of much of women's work. A commitment to caring for others is regarded by some writers as central to women's identity and even the development of a femininepersonality (Gilligan, 1982; Lewis and Meredith, 1988). The power of this commitment is such that to think of caring as lodged in a time capsule in the sense of a working day that is finite, cannot be sustained. Caring is a relation bonding people as well as a work activity and cannot be held in check by time. Jean Yule (1992) found that many women indicated that looking after those closest to them was pleasurable and a major source of satisfaction. However, since the caring relationship is continuous and cannot easily be put aside, it contributes to women's feeling that it is well nigh impossible to seek out leisure as freedom to use time and space for their own personal satisfaction, particularly when this might conflict with the needs of others.

One of the consequences of women's caring work and its relational connections is that women tend to feel guilty when they slip out of their caring mode. Feelings of guilt surface when they claim time for themselves. Guilt also manifests if they dwell on what more they might have done, an outcome of the fact that caring knows no boundaries and has no markers to indicate that the task is done. Notice how Margaret felt pangs of guilt about her 'failure' to cook breakfast. A feminist approach to understanding work/leisure locates the issues in the context of a patriarchal culture. Men, as the receivers rather than the givers of care, are in a very powerful position to sustain the logic of caring as a continuous process. Acknowledging this may help us to understand the feelings of guilt we as women may experience if we allocate time to exploit our personal interests, time which then ceases to be at the disposal of others.

EXERCISE

Read the following extract from a novel called *Happy as a Dead Cat* by Jill Miller (1983), and then answer the questions following it. The heroine of the novel is a thirty-seven year old mother of five who is in the process of discovering that she is oppressed. She has a friend, Jane, also a mother, who is 'liberated' and encourages her to confront her oppression. We enter the narrative at a point when the heroine is reflecting on an early attempt to claim a right to time for herself.

How I envied Jane. Every part of her day, awake or asleep, was hers. No lying restless and worried until the early hours of the morning, thinking of his reaction about the latest shrunken item of clothing, or the trousers you haven't pressed, that you know he will want the following morning. Often I would creep out of bed in the early hours and set up the ironing board, knowing that it was the only way to avoid a scene the next day. God, no wonder I felt continually tired and lethargic.

Whatever Jane did was entirely her decision, she frequently told me. 'If I'm wrong about anything, I only have myself to blame, no one else to reinforce the guilt, and if I'm right, I just sit and gloat.'

Listening to Jane, during the day, I really began to believe that I had a life of my own, and the right to expect time to myself. But once she had left the house and he came home, the doubts would come creeping back into my mind.

I smiled as I thought of the first time she had knocked at the door for me during the evening.

'Coming for a swift half up the pub?' she had asked. I went rigid, and nearly wet myself on the doorstep.

'He's in there,' I whispered, pointing to the living room, putting a finger to my lips.

'I'm sure he can hold the fort for half an hour,' she continued.

'I'll get my coat,' I said, quick as a flash, forgetting all about the string of nappy pins dangling from the front of my jumper. I took a deep breath. Here goes!

'I'm popping out with Jane a minute,' I shout into the other room, voice trembling a little.

'What about these kids?' I hear him shout.

'Ignore him,' says Jane, at which I yell, 'Won't be long, love.'

I shook all the way to the pub. Jane was ever so sympathetic, and encouraging.

'You should have done this years ago, love. We set the pattern very early on.'

'What will you have?' she asked, striding confidently up to the bar.

'Eh, oh, same as you,' I blurted, sounding the novice I was.

'Mmm, quite nice, what is it?'

'Lager, with a drop of lime to take the bitter edge from it. Good, isn't it?'

I felt as though everyone in that pub was staring at me.

'They're not,' Jane assured me, 'but pull your coat over the nappy pins.'

By the second lager, I was beginning to feel a little less jumpy. 'How long have we been here?' I asked Jane.

'How long is he out on a darts night?' came her quick reply. 'Look, love,' she spoke reassuringly, 'you're not doing anything wrong. Just consider it a lager break instead of a coffee break.'

I was still edgy all the same. 'I ought to be thinking of going soon. Rosie might need a feed.'

Jane just raised her eyebrows, 'Scraping the barrel now, aren't you, love?'

I ran from Jane's house, making sure I saw her door close first, and arrived home breathless and hiccuping. Met with stony silence from him, 'Where have you been?' from Valerie, Wendy and Hazel, bleats from Thomas, and, thank God, sleepy silence from Rosie. (Miller, 1983: 26–8)

Now answer these questions:

1. Why do you think the writer feels 'guilty'?
2. Why do you think she felt uncomfortable in the pub?
3. What do you think lay behind the husband's ability to manipulate his wife's reluctance to take time for herself away from the family?

EXERCISE RESPONSE

In response to question 1, you are likely to have noted that the heroine felt her role as mother knew no boundaries. She should always be available, in case her children needed her. She worries about her partner's reaction to her attempt to take time off/out. The children are *her* job. Failure as 'mum' lurks around the corner if she is not always about.

In answer to question 2, she is ill at ease in male (and unfamiliar?) territory. She feels conspicuous. The nappy pins symbolize her mothering status. She is not a woman out for sexual excitement – men's view of a woman visiting a pub without a male escort.

Question 3's answer is that the husband's disapproval, expressed by 'stony silence' underlines his view of her childcare role. Implicit is his understanding that as the breadwinner, he is entitled to come home to relaxation and space for himself. The children are *her* responsibility.

Before leaving the topic of time-poverty and the difficulty many women experience in chasing leisure, I will reflect on the nineteenth century situation described earlier, in which working-class women were struggling to cope with a daily round of ceaseless toil. Similar relentless work is the lot of women today living in societies that have not yet emerged as industrial societies. An analysis of leisure from a Western perspective would have little to say to many rural women in developing countries who take the brunt of back-breaking work. An account of Rachel's day, a woman in Kenya, tells its own story:

> Rachel's day is long. She rises 'when the sky is beginning to lighten', cooks breakfast, gets the children off to school and cleans the house. Then she sets off for the holding, two miles away up and down hill, where she tethers the animals to graze and gets down to planting, digging or weeding her corn, cassava and cowpeas, eating a snack in the field. On her way home she gathers whatever firewood she finds. Then she fetches water, half an hour's walk away, with the return journey uphill. As the sun begins to set, she cooks the evening meal of ugali (maize porridge) in a pot balanced

on three stones, until it is stiff as bread dough: 'You are stirring solidly for an hour,' she complains, 'and it gets harder and harder until at the end the sweat is pouring off you.' Getting the maize ground is another chore: twice a week she must trek two miles to the nearest neighbour who possesses a handmill. (Harrison, 1984: 438–9)

In this section I have argued that conventional concepts of leisure (male), provide an inadequate framework for recognizing leisure as women know it. Central to male understanding is a dichotomous distinction between work and non-work, a public workplace and private space at the heart of which is the home, a place for oneself, free from the pressure of obligation. This compartmentalization of life experience comes from difference in women's and men's social roles. They cannot make clear separations between work and leisure. Much of women's *home-work* can be thought of as *dual* activities in two senses: first, it is perfectly possible for women to carry out work and leisure activities simultaneously, like combining chores with television watching. Second, women's activities can be dual in the sense that the same task may be work in the traditional sense of meeting obligation and leisure in the sense of being intrinsically pleasurable and rewarding in personally gratifying ways. Cleaning, cooking, knitting may be work in that they provide essential service for family. For some women, these tasks will always be laborious. Yet for others, the development of skills goes beyond what is required to meet basic obligation. The doing of the task can be transformed into pleasurable pursuit, motivated by personal desire for self-gratification and pride in accomplishment.

We have seen that women are likely to have less autonomous space in the home than men. Men's control over public space also puts limitations on the scope for women to find leisure opportunities for themselves outside the home. Nevertheless, women, like men, value leisure. Women make their own leisure, matching resourcefulness to resources. It is to women's leisure-making strategies we now turn.

What Pleasure in Leisure for Women?

The ways in which women find their leisure are influenced by multiple social factors, including age, motherhood, marital/partnership status, ethnicity and access to economic resources. Leisure, like work, is experienced both in the home- and beyond it. I want to consider the significance of leisure – time, space and interests – by posing three apparently straightforward questions:

1. *What* do women do with their leisure time?
2. *Where* do women typically go in search of leisure?
3. *With whom* do women share their leisure?

EXERCISE

Before you read on, have a go at answering these questions yourself:

1. What do you do for leisure?
2. What kind of space/place do you need to pursue your leisure activities?
3. Are your leisure activities dependent on the company of one or more other person(s)? If so, who?

Deirdre Beddoe (1989) has studied the impact of leisure on women's lives in the inter-war years in Britain. I want to use these women's experiences by connecting them with knowledge of women who went before them and women in the present day, to build a picture of aspects of leisure that are central to feminine identity. She tells us that during the 1920s and 1930s dancing was the most popular form of leisure activity – a 'dance crazy' time. The opportunity women had to participate in the craze depended on class position, ranging from the debutante dance, the tennis club social to the local dance halls, catering for working-class girls.

An excursion back into the nineteenth century also draws our attention to dancing as a most important social activity. Once more, class difference shaped specific forms of cultural activity. Jane Austen in *Northanger Abbey*, gave her readers vivid accounts of attendance at the Pump Room at Bath, the place where young middle-class women came to forge social contacts through dancing. Street dancing at fairs and festivals was much enjoyed by working women. In contemporary times, dancing remains central to leisure pastime. Gilda O'Neill (1993) reminds us that going out to a disco is a choice for women seeking a night out with female company. Dancing including the modern disco is a social contact which organizes opportunities for women to meet potential partners (heterosexual and same-sex). It also provides opportunity for women in female company to have a good time without having to conform to the dictates of male approval of our public behaviour. The togetherness of a female disco outing generates confidence to use public space for our own enjoyment.

The second major activity discussed by Deirdre Beddoe was cinema going. The screen provided a means for the working-class girl to escape from 'the daily round of drudgery' (p. 117) into the opulent world of fantasy. It was a cheap form of entertainment, accessible to the working-class girl. Films brought a chance for the younger and older viewer to flirt vicariously with romance. By the 1930s the female-going audience included increasing numbers of middle-class women. Television video culture means that films have retained their centrality in contemporary culture in the construction of leisure.

A third leisure activity accessible to women of all classes was reading. The middle-class reader could buy paperback editions of novels and could borrow hard-backed editions from the Boots Library. Women's magazines, local and national newspapers further expanded choice of reading material for a female reading public. The expansion of the newspaper industry led to competition and the emergence of daily newspapers and women's magazines with specific class affiliation. These provided the main reading material for working-class women (Beddoe, 1989). Novel reading and the magazine have been described as 'feminocentric popular form' (Ballaster et al., 1991: 169). The magazine continues to offer women relaxing reading but at the same time it can represent the use of women's forms of leisure which are empowering.

The second question to address is the matter of space and place accessible to women in search of leisure: where do women typically go to pursue leisure? At the end of the previous section I made the point that men have great control over space, both in the home and in public arenas. Men have tended to exclude women from space they have made their own. Perhaps the best example of this would be the pub. Look back to the fourth exercise in this chapter (pages 122–4) and the extract from Miller (1983) contained in it. You will recall that the heroine of the story and her friend, Jane, tried to establish a claim to leisure by visiting a pub. Their choice of location was highly symbolic. It allowed the women to confront gendered notions of leisure in a number of ways.

Valerie Hey (1986) in her study of pub culture has shown us how pub going has become a 'major site of male enjoyment' (p. 12). Attempts by women to open up this gendered space have been fraught with difficulty. At the heart of this challenge to male exclusivity has been the association of drinking with both male and female sexuality. Drinking for men has been machoistic whereas for women it has been linked with female 'impurity' and negative images of woman as temptress. Attempts to regulate women's drinking owe much to men's desire to control women's sexuality.

Women have encountered a broad range of difficulties in making claim to activities using public space in their own right. These include access to adequate income to afford to engage in leisure; challenging stereotypes about gender specific activities; the practical need at times to include children in their leisure pursuits; politicizing distinctions between work and leisure, such as the right to time off women's work (Whitehead, 1976; Deem, 1986; Hey, 1986).

Despite these difficulties, women's leisure experiences have expanded. This can be illustrated by drawing upon recent feminist writers' accounts of women's successful attempts to establish autonomous leisure activities which give colour and add pleasure to women's lives.

Women's opportunities to 'go out' with other women for fun is greater at the present time than ever before. This is an indication of the control that women have won for themselves over the meaning of leisure and pleasure in their lives. The following extract narrates an account of a women's night out on the town as it was told to Gilda O'Neill (1993). It refers to a visit by women to a nightclub performance by The Chippendales, a troupe of male strippers and dancers.

> D: He's looking at himself in the mirror. Knowing he's being watched.
>
> M: Really playing to it. It was funny to us because we were watching the girls' reaction. A lot of our fun came from watching their reactions.
>
> D: 'Quick! There's one over there.' (laughter). It wasn't just the younger women, either.
>
> M: My mum said she'd come along.
>
> Gilda: I saw two quite elderly women buying a Chippendales' video. When I talked to them they seemed to know all about them.
>
> D: That's right. The older ones who came here really enjoyed it. But I'm sure that there are older women who would be very shocked by it.
>
> M: If you could see some of the older women climbing onto the stage after the show for a photograph, you wouldn't have thought it was a photograph that was on offer.
>
> D: They're all excited though, right from the beginning, whatever age they are. August, the blond one, starts them off. He goes on and stands there and he's naked apart from a towel. That definitely starts them off.
>
> M: Absolutely. But the audience is warmed up before they even come in, maybe they'd had a drink beforehand, but they'd obviously psyched themselves up. And it's not just the show any more, there's so much atmosphere from all the publicity and things surrounding it. . . .
>
> D: I really don't think women want the same thing from stripping as men. Do you? I can't think that women see it in the same way.
>
> M: I don't know. The thing is we rarely get the chance to discuss it. You see women at a thing like this and . . .
>
> D: . . . but it wasn't like a stag night or a hen night. Not that type of thing when the women actually . . .
>
> M: There is something pretty safe about this.
>
> D: Yes. The women were just there to enjoy themselves. They shout and scream.
>
> M: Bring flowers.
>
> D: Soon as they started the music, and they said 'This is The Chippendales' they all started screaming. They *screamed*. Some of them were on their feet. And they were shouting. As I say, it was August who started them off. He got them all going. Because he does look good. He's got an excellent body. There was a Chippendales' fanclub who arrived and they were all shouting at him, 'Get 'em off!' (O'Neill, 1993: 43–5)

Note that the women who attended the show included women of all ages. This account is remarkable in its portrayal of women's capacity to shake and break male taboos and to take over male territory – the night club, the space *par excellence* for men to indulge in sexual fantasy and action. For women excitement seems to be derived from a number of stimuli. They talk about the collective pleasure from going out together; the danger injected by the challenge to convention; and a celebration of their freedom to defy convention and constraints on their sexual arousal without jeopardizing personal identity. Their relationship with space in this context signifies many of the challenges that have come with radical feminism's questioning of control of women's sexuality.

The final question I want to consider is the people with whom women typically share their leisure. A great deal of leisure time for women of all social backgrounds will be spent at home and in the company of other members of families.

Particularly important to women is the company of other women. Solidarity with women for marking mutual support and friendship is a crucial aspect of women's leisure, involving and seeking out time with others (Deem, 1986). Liz Stanley (1988) has told us how important leisure time was for Hannah Cullwick, employed as a maid in London in the late nineteenth century. She describes how Hannah spent her time off in the following way: 'Kitchen visiting' was the practice whereby servants who had often in the past worked together took their leisure together by visiting each other's places' (Stanley, 1988: 22).

The importance of social gathering for women and its centrality in their experience of leisure can be appreciated by considering the enthusiasm which many women feel about participating in bingo. Read the following extract from Gilda O'Neill about one woman's account of playing bingo. It begins with Gilda asking a woman referred to as P a question:

Gilda: Have you had a big win?

P: My biggest win was 800. Then I had another win a few weeks before that of 600, didn't I? Then I had a 70, then the 800. That was in a matter of what? Three months? But that was three years ago. All I've had since is about 30, 40 pounds. But for me it's the pleasure of going. The actual club used to be an old cinema and where the seats used to be there are tables and chairs and there's a tea bar on one side and a bar on the other. It's very nice. And the caller stands up in front of you all. There's refreshments – you have tea, beer, whatever you like. Cake, sandwich. It's a proper night out but you don't have to get all dressed up or anything like that. Just casual. And a lot of people go there, it's ever so popular. We go to our club because it's such a nice atmosphere. My daughters sometimes go to different ones – they're mainly the same, but they might play slightly different games.

Gilda: Is it usually groups like you and your daughters or do some people go alone?

P: A lot do turn up on their own but they're going to meet their friends there. It's a proper social occasion. A lot of elderly people for instance go for the company. You'll see someone come in and sit at a table by themselves, then someone'll come in and sit with her. Sit down and talk to her. But our table's usually full with us three or four – we usually take an old lady with us. But we still talk to the people on the next table or have a laugh with the people behind us. It's a way for people to get out and see people, you see. You can go there, and even if you haven't got much money you can buy just one set of books, on a Monday that'd be just one pound and five pence. On a Tuesday, only one fifty a set. (O'Neill, 1993: 61)

This extract highlights the importance of women gathering together outside domestic settings. The significance lies in the opportunity to have time together in which we are not constrained acutely by the continuous responsibility to *do* for others. The importance of the bingo hall is that women can just be themselves. Leisure, for us, wherever it is found, is a time to *be*.

In this chapter I have tried to get you to think about the meaning of leisure for women. Many of the pursuits we call leisure are ones men enjoy too. Men dance, read and watch films. However, the experience of leisure is gendered. The thrust of the analysis has been that gender difference can be understood to an important extent in terms of the social construction of roles and a social division of labour underpinning them. Delving back into the past has allowed us to see that on the one hand, there is great continuity but on the other the social world changes. The impact of change is differential and women's experience continues to differ, both from that of men and between women. Our task in Women's Studies is to extend the search for explanation.

References

Ballaster, Jo, Beetham, Margaret, Fraser, Elizabeth and Hebron, Sandra 1991: *Women's Worlds*. Basingstoke: Macmillan.

Beddoe, Deidre 1989: *Back to Home and Duty*. London: Pandora.

Cunningham, Hugh 1986: *Leisure in the Industrial Revolution*. London: Croom Helm.

Davidoff, Leonore 1973: *The Best Circles, Society, Etiquette and the Season*. London: Croom Helm.

Deem, Rosemary 1986: *All Work and No Play? The Sociology of Women and Leisure*. Milton Keynes: Open University Press.

Gilligan, Carol 1982: *In a Different Voice, Psychological Theory and Women's Development*. Cambridge, MA: Harvard University Press.

Green, Eileen, Hebron, Sandra and Woodward, Diana (eds) 1990: *Women's Leisure, What Leisure?* Basingstoke: Macmillan Education.

Griffin, Christine et al. 1990: Women and leisure. In Jennifer Hargreaves (ed.), *Sport Culture and Ideology*, London: Routledge & Kegan Paul.

Harrison, Paul 1984: *Inside the Third World* (3rd edn). Harmondsworth: Penguin.

Hey, Valerie 1986: *Patriarchy and Pub Culture*. London and New York: Tavistock Publications.

Lewis, Jane and Meredith, Barbara 1988: *Daughters Who Care*. London and New York: Routledge.

Llewelyn Davies, Margaret (ed.) 1977: *Life As We Have Known It*. London: Virago.

Mason, Jennifer 1988: No peace for the wicked: older married women and leisure. In Erica Wimbush and Margaret Talbot (eds), *Relative Freedoms*, Milton Keynes: Open University Press.

Millar, Jan and Glendenning, Caroline 1989: *Women and Poverty in Britain*. Brighton: Wheatsheaf.

Miller, Jill 1983: *Happy as a Dead Cat*. London: The Women's Press.

Oakley, Ann 1974: *The Sociology of Housework*. London: Martin Robertson.

Oakley, Ann 1976: *Housewife*. Harmondsworth: Penguin.

O'Neill, Gilda 1993: *A Night Out with the Girls*. London: The Women's Press.

Stanley, Liz 1988: Historical sources for studying work and leisure in women's lives. In Erica Wimbush and Margaret Talbot (eds), *Relative Freedoms*. Milton Keynes: Open University Press.

Thompson, E. P. 1967: Time, work-discipline and industrial capitalism. *Past and Present*, 38, 56–97.

Veblen, Thorsten 1925: *The Theory of the Leisure Class*. London: Allen & Unwin.

Whitehead, A. 1976: Sexual antagonism in Herefordshire. In D. Barker and S. Allen (eds), *Dependence and Exploitation in Work and Marriage*, London: Longman.

Wimbush, Erica and Talbot, Margaret (eds) 1988: *Relative Freedoms*. Milton Keynes: Open University Press.

Yule, Jean 1992: Gender policy and leisure policy. *Leisure Studies*, 11, 157–73.

CHAPTER
7 Understanding Sexuality

Melanie Mauthner

Plate 6 Lesbians exchanging rings at a 'blessing' of their relationship ceremony, Gay pride 1994. © Format Partners; photograph: Brenda Prince.

> Sex is supposed to be the moment when we are most honestly, nakedly ourselves. This is a myth. Often we use the mask of intimacy to perpetrate the most destructive physical and emotional bullying. We use our bodies to avoid the issue. We exchange loving confidences in fraudulent currency. We fake it – again and again. We do this to hide, to deny our fears, to avoid honesty. We all live ironic lives. (Duncker, 1992: 10)

This extract from Patricia Duncker's introduction to an anthology called *Women Talk Sex* illustrates the myth that during sex we are most ourselves. Not much has been written about women's personal experiences of sex except for sexual fantasies (Friday, 1975). *Women Talk Sex*, which is more personal than Cartledge and Ryan's (1983) *Sex and Love*, is part of the process of breaking down the silences around what we do in bed, who with, what it means and whether it matters.

In this chapter I address the complexity of what is often thought to be the most natural of activities – sex. I look at the place of sex in women's lives – their pleasurable and painful sexual experiences as well as the ones women might feel ambivalent about. I have attempted to make the experiences of black women and lesbians visible. As a white heterosexual woman I am not trying to speak for other women but I want to make their presence central. I also discuss how theories about sex can help us make sense of sexual experiences at different levels: the physical, the emotional and the intellectual.

I cover some of the debates around sexuality by exploring different women's experiences through autobiographical and fictional accounts of sex as well as by analysing various theoretical approaches to sexuality. Some of these debates are quite problematic and remain unresolved: this chapter provides no ready-made answers but seeks to ask some questions about some of our widely held ideas about sexuality. One of the things I consider is the social organization of sex and the social construction of sexuality as they affect women's lives. I draw on sociological, historical, literary and anthropological sources.

I address these issues in six sections. First, I consider a number of ways of understanding the differences between sex and gender, and sexuality. The second and third sections examine the cultural and historical construction of sexuality – the way in which meanings attributed to sexual acts vary across cultures and throughout history. Then I review theoretical explanations of sexuality and also examine how sexuality is constructed through social institutions such as heterosexuality. This is followed by an analysis of how sexuality is used as a means of social control in women's lives. Finally,

I explore the differing constructions of feminine and masculine sexuality including sexual desire. After reading this chapter, you will be able to define and distinguish between the terms, 'sex', 'gender' and 'sexuality': you will see how some of the myths about women's and men's sexuality to do with active and passive behaviour affect sexual encounters. You will also have an understanding of some of the on-going debates to do with power, desire, violence and safety.

Key Concepts: The Difference Between Sex and Gender; Understanding Sexuality

What is the difference between sex and gender? Sex refers to female and male physiology, our sex organs, whereas gender is what Catherine MacKinnon (1982) calls 'a learned quality' – in other words, gender corresponds to the roles attributed by society to women and men which we describe as feminine and masculine. Although it is common to make this polarized distinction, there is an interaction between these biological and social traits which makes the distinction problematic and difficult to sustain.

EXERCISE

The aim of this exercise is to distinguish between physiological aspects of women's and men's bodies and social ideas of femininity and masculinity. This will help you understand ways in which feminine and masculine behaviour are generally perceived.

Make two columns labelled 'Female' and 'Male'. Spend a few minutes thinking about the physiological activities that differentiate the two sexes: what can women's bodies do that men's cannot?

Next, make two columns, one marked 'Feminine' and the other 'Masculine' and write under each a short list of words that are generally associated with each type of behaviour. Now look at the differences in women's and men's bodies (menstruation; ejaculation) and compare them with feminine and masculine behaviour (passivity; activity).

After doing this exercise you should have a sense of the differences between talking about sex as a biological aspect of human behaviour and the social meanings attached to people's experiences of sex and gender. The word 'sex' is also used, in everyday language, to refer to the physical 'sex act': penetration and other sexual practices, such as anal and oral sex.

Another term used to describe sexual activity is **sexuality**. Sexuality refers to a set of *ideas* about sex. It also refers to the meanings and social practices within which 'sex' takes place. These ideas, meanings and social practices include:

- sexual behaviour or social practices such as monogamy, polygamy or having more than one wife, polyandry or having more than one husband, celibacy
- sexual orientation or identity – whether we define ourselves as heterosexual, homosexual, bisexual
- sexual desire
- sexual relations or sexual politics.

This description of sexuality is by no means fixed or complete and you might want to revise it by the end of the chapter. Its main purpose here is as a working understanding of sexuality that you can refer to in the following sections.

For most of us probably when we first think about it, 'sexuality is often considered primarily biological, and socially part of the private domain' (Hearn and Parkin, 1987). We think of sexuality as 'natural' and as belonging in the home behind closed doors: these are two of the most enduring myths. Throughout this chapter, we will see that it is more complex than this.

EXERCISE

What are the different stereotypes that exist about female and male sexuality? To help you think about this, try to answer the following questions:

1. How do the terms 'slag', 'tart' and 'lezzie' applied to women define what is acceptable about their sexuality?
2. What does 'he's a bit of a lad', a 'casanova', 'limp wristed' or 'sowing wild oats' tell us about commonly held ideas about men and sexuality?
3. What are the main differences between what is sexually acceptable for women and for men?

EXERCISE RESPONSE

You have probably thought of several stereotypes about sexuality which pervade Western industrialized countries: the notion of the 'male sex drive' as 'natural' and 'uncontrollable' and that men 'need' sex, whereas women's sexuality is believed to be passive, modest, non-existent and shameful. Another assumption is that 'normal' sexuality is heterosexual and that other forms of sexuality are 'deviant', taboo and unacceptable.

These myths can be challenged in several ways. One way is to consider sexuality as more than a solely biological or private phenomenon and to examine the way that sexuality is also a product of the social forces of culture and history. From now on, we are going to use the terms feminine and masculine to refer to the social aspects of sexuality, and the terms female and male to refer to sexuality in a biological sense.

The Cultural Construction of Sexuality

While our working understanding of sexuality provides a useful starting point, it is by no means a fixed definition. In this section we will see how the terms sexuality and sex are often used interchangeably and how ideas about sexuality vary across cultures. In the next section we will look at how ideas about sexuality have changed throughout history.

When people use the words sex and sexuality interchangeably, this can be confusing. Sometimes we might use sex and sexuality to distinguish between different types of sexual experiences:

> Sexuality to me is more all-encompassing than sex and has to do with a giving of the whole being. Sex is smaller and more limited and is involved with taking. To me, sexuality is an ever-present shadow; it's a kind of feeling that surfaces. (Addison, 1992: 218)

B. J. Addison, a black woman, is writing about her feelings in different sexual encounters and about the experience of 'giving' and 'taking'. She is also comparing 'flowing' feelings with more 'focused' sensations. You might want to consider other differences between the sensual, the sexual, the genital and the emotional. All these are involved in sexuality but the meanings associated with the intensely emotional or physical, the separation between lust and love, and the place of romance in a sexual encounter will vary according to particular circumstances.

In the rest of this section we will consider some of the varied circumstances that can affect our sexual experiences. Our sexual experiences will mean something different to us and others depending on where and when we are living, whether we are men or women, able-bodied or disabled, lesbian or straight, and according to our age (see box 7.1 on sex later in life), our class and economic circumstances, our race and our ethnicity.

A Comment on Sex and Women in Later Life

BOX
7.1

Sheila Kitzinger (1985) writes that sexual desire is associated with youth and vitality in our minds, especially the notion of 'sex appeal' which is linked to the contemporary cult of youth in Western society. Change and ageing can bring about different circumstances: living alone after a death and changing feelings about our bodies. On the other hand, this stage of life can be seen as a new space for us; for some of us, growing older can bring about a new sense of freedom. Kitzinger writes:

> Whether heterosexual or lesbian, a woman may find that one aspect of this process of discovery is that she now experiences sex in a way that she enjoys, without having to attain a standard or reach a goal. Masters and Johnson showed in their research that sexual activity does not usually come to a full stop with increasing age, though the rate of intercourse is often reduced. Seven out of ten couples over 60 were sexually active. (Kitzinger, 1985: 243)

In later life, overt sexuality is seen to be more acceptable in men than in women. Yet for some women sex improves with age, sensations are less intense but much more drawn out. Emphasis on intercourse as the *sine qua non* of sex can be cruel as women live longer than men and many are single in their later years. Often masturbation tends to be considered second best: 'Yet many older women enjoy masturbation and some first discover it after they are widowed. At the same time that older women are told that they *need* sex, they are denied the right to be sexual' (Kitzinger, 1985: 245).

Here one middle-aged woman describes her fulfilment when she finds a lover her own age after a period of involvement with younger partners and the difficulty of deciding whether to talk about her past relationships:

> When that woman of my age group found me, I recognized her almost at once. With her I have entered a relationship full of pos-itive complexity, in which the struggles for honesty (first with myself and then with her), for commitment and for political engagement have become integral ... I have abandoned the image of myself as a rock, unchanging, overly responsible. Now in my fifties I have rediscovered the will to change, not *who* I am, but *how* I can be myself with greater awareness and greater effect ... (Coulson, 1992: 141)

The following examples illustrate the way that sexuality is culturally constructed. I quote from the writings of two black women on the impact of race and gender on black women's sexual experiences. In the first extract B. J. Addison continues to explore what sex and sexuality mean to her as a black woman. She examines how racist sexual stereotypes structure her experiences of sexuality:

> I think it's something that black women have but do not always acknowledge. After all, we are constantly being told how 'wanton' we are. I remember even as a child wondering why people who denigrated us publicly as loose or immoral would take advantage of us sexually in private at the first opportunity. This kind of ambivalence creates doubts deep inside about what kind of woman you will be; it's all these things that prevent your personality from having full flow. (Addison, 1992: 218)

This account of the painful legacy and impact of racist stereotypes on black women's sexuality stresses the way it has been distorted and abused. Little has been written about commonly held myths about black and Asian women's sexuality: Valerie Hey's (forthcoming) ethnography of girls' friendships documents the prevalence of myths about Afro Caribbean girls' 'hyper-sexuality' and Asian girls' 'asexuality'. Annecka Marshall's (1994) work analyses both the racist sexual imagery about black women's sexuality and its impact on black women's identities and relationships. Her aim is to challenge derogatory ideas of black women as sexual animals:

> Under enslavement Black women were defined as animalistic, evil, diseased and lascivious. The icon of the sexually denigrated Black female not only effectively legitimated the maximum exploitation of her reproductive labour but also exonerated white men who abused her from guilt. (Marshall, 1994: 107)

Annecka Marshall, a black researcher, found three types of images prevalent among the twenty-one black women who she interviewed: a few felt that the stereotypes made their sexuality invisible; others felt that images of black women defined them as 'asexual mammies'; while the majority felt that both black men and white people see them as licentious and lascivious. When she asked the women how they felt these images affected them, she received two types of replies. Compare the following responses:

> For instance, when I asked Marva, who was a 45-year-old housewife with two children, about the significance of racialized sexual images, she replied that it was not an issue that she had previously considered: 'Well, I haven't really thought about it so to me it's not really important in my life'. Fiona, a 25-year-old teacher who is single articulate and witty also said: 'Not really. I don't think so. I've never really thought about it. You know, sex is sex!' [. . .] Tracy, a 32-year-old research worker, stated:

'I certainly don't ever see myself as being a sexual temptress or a molten volcano'.
[...] Rosanne, a 22-year-old student, asserted: 'Race affects how I feel about my
sexual experiences in the sense that being a Black woman I have to compete with the
challenging myths that exist about my sexuality.' (Marshall, 1994: 117–18)

The varied views of the women who spoke to Annecka Marshall show the differences among black women, some of whom do not feel affected by dominant racist
stereotypes while most are resisting them. Though many black women have written about the links between sexuality and racism – especially in relation to racist
immigration policies and racist policing practices concerning domestic violence
(Coote and Campbell, 1982; Bryan, Dadzie and Scafe, 1985; Southall Black Sisters, 1990) personal accounts are much rarer. Both Addison's and Marshall's
accounts of the impact of racist stereotypes illustrate some of the ways that sexuality can be culturally constructed – in this case by race and ethnicity. They also
challenge the myth that we all experience sexuality in the same way.

In this section we have looked at how sexuality, attitudes towards sex and
sexual experiences are shaped and influenced by several social factors other than
biology, including race and culture.

The Historical Construction of Sexuality

Another widely held myth about sexuality is that the sexual has taken the same
form and had the same meaning throughout history. Historians of sexuality have
explored several questions: what is the link between same-sex acts and sexual
identity, how have the meanings of same-sex acts changed, and how do we know
what women in the past actually did sexually together. In this section we are
going to focus on same-sex acts in order to illustrate the historical construction of
sexuality.

The relationship between sexual activity and identity is a complex one which
has formed one of the central debates in the writing of the new history of sex.
Both in the USA (Duberman, Vicinus and Chauncey, 1991; Faderman, 1991) and
the UK (Cant and Hemmings, 1988; Lesbian History Group, 1989) this new look
at the past occurred almost simultaneously with the rise of the lesbian and gay
liberation movement's campaign for civil rights in the political arena during the
1970s; and in history scholarship during the 1980s following on from the important role played by women's history and the analysis of gender and sexuality.

Studies of sodomy laws and sodomite subcultures such as Duberman, Vicinus
and Chauncey's (1991) have explored when homosexual desire became the basis
for a gay male identity. According to historian Jeffrey Weeks (1981, 1986) the
notion of gay identity is a recent phenomenon dating from the nineteenth century
which developed as homosexuality became organized into subcultures and when

these became public. The development of a gay identity, he says, is linked not to the sexual acts but to the meanings given these activities.

One illustration of the disjunction between sexual acts, the meanings attached to these and sexual identity is the love affair between two women in Han Suyin's novel *Winter Love* (Suyin, 1994). Set in the Second World War the novel traces Bettina or 'Red's' ambivalent feelings about her sexual relationships with women. Although she knows the technical acts, when she falls in love with Mara, she eschews them in her 'pure love' – so 'lesbian without the act'. Later on, the situation is reversed: in the midst of their affair, Red rejects Mara's love and desire. *Winter Love* reflects the difficulties of 'being out' or adopting a lesbian identity in the 1940s.

If Red had lived in another century, she might not have internalized society's negative views of same-sex relationships. Evidence shows that before the twentieth century intimate relationships between women flourished and were tolerated (Faderman, 1985). Whereas at the turn of the nineteenth century a lesbian was described as 'a man trapped in a woman's body', in the seventeenth and eighteenth centuries romantic friendship implying physical contact was not regarded as sexual nor considered to be a threat – because, Faderman (1985) argues, women's lack of financial independence or political rights presented no threat to the institutions of heterosexuality and marriage.

The question of whether or not intimacy between women involved genital contact has perplexed writers who emphasize the importance of genital contact in the history of lesbianism. Both Faderman (1985) in her study of romantic friendships and Rich (1984) in her essay on 'compulsory heterosexuality' highlight the non-sexual aspects of lesbianism: this corresponds to Rich's notion of *lesbian existence*. Her other idea of the *lesbian continuum* embraces all women who are emotionally and sexually independent of men:

> I have chosen to use the terms *lesbian existence* and *lesbian continuum* because the word *lesbianism* has a clinical and limiting ring. *Lesbian existence* suggests both the fact of the historical presence of lesbians and our continuing creation of the meaning of that existence. I mean the term *lesbian continuum* to include a range – through each woman's life and throughout history – of woman-identified experience; not simply the fact that a woman has had or consciously desired genital sexual experience with another woman. If we expand it to embrace many more forms of primary intensity between and among women, including the sharing of a rich inner life, the bonding against male tyranny, the giving and receiving of practical and political support; [. . .] – we begin to grasp breadths of female history and psychology that have lain out of reach as a consequence of limited, mostly clinical, definitions of 'lesbianism'. (Rich, 1984: 227)

The issue of genital activity remains controversial. Historian Sheila Jeffreys (1989) criticizes the Faderman/Rich stance because it denies the sexual aspects of lesbianism and perpetuates its invisibility.

These changing interpretations of the meanings of sexual acts from one century to the next reflects the absence of constants regarding homosexuality and lesbianism in both the meaning of 'love' or sex and in the social and political life that is created through it. This section illustrates the claim that there is no single homosexuality but *homosexualities*, and that these are constantly changing (Weeks, 1981).

Theoretical Approaches: Biological Determinism and Social Constructionism

While there is as yet no one feminist theory of sexuality, there have been various attempts to theorize sexuality. As Caroline Ramazanoglu (1989) explains: 'Feminism still lacks an adequate theory of sexuality. There are still disputes over how far sexuality is biologically given and over what is meant by the social construction of sexuality' (p. 156).

Biological determinism and social constructionism are two of the dominant theoretical explanations of sexuality. As we saw at the start of the chapter, much conventional wisdom about sexuality is based on biologically deterministic assumptions. Most people understand sexuality as a biological force or an instinct which needs to be released. They perceive sexuality as made up of drives or urges both related to and separate from society.

Sexuality is also attributed to the private realm of the home. This view of sexuality as 'private' rather than 'public' permeates many aspects of everyday life. One example is the media and the law's understanding of rape: the focus is on the woman's provocation of the man, either by her dress or by her behaviour. There is never any questioning of oppressive forms of sexuality, which are upheld by society's institutions, such as marriage, the family, and heterosexuality. In all cases, the male sex drive is sanctioned as 'natural' and is not seen as socially and politically constituted.

This concept of a sexual drive stems from Freud's ideas about male and female sexuality (see box 7.2 on Freud's theory of female sexuality).

Focus on Freud: Brief Comment on Freud's Theory of Female Sexuality

BOX 7.2

Although Freud's work, especially his theory of female sexuality (see Freud, 1971, first published in 1933), has been challenged by a number of feminists writing in the 1960s and 1970s (Friedan, 1963; Firestone, 1971; Millett, 1977)

---

because of his notion of 'penis envy' based on male superiority, other writers have attempted to reinterpret psychoanalysis which has formed the basis for a developing 'psychoanalytic feminism' (see the work of Mitchell, 1974; Cixous, 1981; Kristeva, 1982; Irigaray, 1985).

Freud's ideas about sexuality were controversial for two reasons according to Rosemary Tong (1992: 139): first, because he wrote about what were up until then taboo subjects – homosexuality, sadism, masochism, oral and anal sex; second, because he said that what he termed these 'variations' or 'perversions' were simply stages in the development of so-called 'normal' sexuality.

In his 1933 essay on female sexuality, Freud (1971) asks 'what is a woman?': he was obviously perplexed and woman remained a mystery for him. According to Moi (1985) his theory of sexual difference is based on the *visibility* of difference, in other words anatomy: the man's penis versus the absence of a woman's visible sex organ. In his account of the development of sexual difference, there is no sexual difference in the pre-Oedipal stage between boys and girls. In his essay on 'Infantile sexuality' in *On Sexuality: Three Essays on the Theory of Sexuality* (Freud, 1977) he says that for children, these stages include the oral, anal, phallic, latency and genital stages: through the oral, anal and phallic phases the little girl is no different from the little boy.

> According to Freud, before the phallic stage, the girl has active sexual aims. Like the boy, she wants to take sexual possession of her mother with her clitoris. If the girl goes through the phallic stage successfully, however, she will enter the state of latency without this desire; and when genital sensitivity reappears at puberty, the pubescent girl will no longer long to use her clitoris actively. Instead, she will use it passively – for autoerotic masturbation or as part of foreplay preparatory to heterosexual intercourse. But because the clitoris is not easy to desensitize, there is always the possibility that the pubescent girl will either regress back into the active clitoral stage or, exhausted from suppressing her clitoris, give up on sexuality altogether. (Tong, 1992: 142)

Freud's theory of childhood female sexuality as first polysexual and then clitoral raises questions about the central place of intercourse. According to Valverde (1985: 54) 'it is never quite clear why girls give up both their happy oral sexuality and their active clitoral masturbation in order to exclusively eroticize the vagina as a passive receptacle . . .'. Freud merely states that the little girl is so overwhelmed at the sight of the large penis that her own tiny clitoris seems too pitiful to bother with. He was keen to legitimize passive, vaginal sexuality as the most mature type for a woman but could not produce a more convincing model for how this sexuality develops.

Furthermore, this so-called natural male sex drive upholds heterosexuality as the norm: most men and women are not actively aware of being heterosexual. To view heterosexuality as the norm relegates other forms of sexuality to the deviant and the abnormal. The challenge posed to biological assumptions allows feminists, lesbians and gays to view the institution of heterosexuality as compulsory and oppressive (Rich, 1984).

If we assume by contrast that human behaviour is learned and not innate, it becomes possible to study how sexual behaviour and its meanings have changed. This lies at the heart of the theory of social constructionism. In the previous section we saw how historians have studied the changing meanings of sexual activity and the changing definitions of sexual categories: the many permutations in time and place of lesbianism and homosexuality – especially the blurred line between friendship and lesbianism, between same-sex acts and defining oneself or others as gay, in other words sexual identity (Weeks, 1981, 1986; Rich, 1984; Faderman, 1985).

Another strength of social construction theory is the way that it challenges and highlights the dangers of assuming that definitions of sexuality are grounded in 'nature' or that they can be universalized, generalized or made into all-encompassing categories. Instead this theory reminds us that we need to take cultural, social and historical forces into account when we try to understand the different meanings of ideas about sex and sexual practices.

This new approach to sexuality lies at the heart of historian Michel Foucault's (1981) work. Viewing sexuality as socially constructed allowed Foucault to examine how ideas about sex have evolved over the centuries. He challenges traditional descriptions of the history of sexuality in terms of repression and prohibition and offers a way of thinking about sexuality in terms of mechanisms of power: according to him sexuality must not be seen as a drive but 'as an especially dense transfer point for relations of power' (Foucault, 1981: 103).

The focus on power in Foucault's analysis has been seized upon by feminists trying to theorize the links between sexuality and power in order to explain women's subordination. While feminists such as Caroline Ramazanoglu (1989, 1993) have drawn on Foucault, they have also criticized him for ignoring gender in his analysis, especially regarding the silencing of female sexuality:

> Foucault has influenced feminism through his argument that sexual desires are not biological essences but are constructed in historical discourses. Power and knowledge came together in sexuality. The problem with Foucault's position, though, is that it does not explain why women have so generally lost power in sexual relationships. (Ramazanoglu, 1989: 156)

In this section we have examined the theory of the social construction of sexuality, the way that the social categories of sexuality are variable rather than biologically fixed and the way that sexual behaviour is shaped by and shapes the wider social and political context. I explored the concept of sexuality as a social construct rather than as something biologically determined: in other words sexuality is a product of the times and of other factors – political, economic, historical, geographical, class and gender related – that are entirely external to the so-called 'sexual drive'.

Sexuality as a Means of Social Control

In this section we will look at the ways in which sexuality 'acts' as a mechanism of control. Often, these are not obvious because we assume that sex belongs to the private domestic sphere.

Not until February 1990, for instance, did the British government agree to reconsider outlawing marital rape which led to a change in the law in 1991 (Radford, 1992). It took 150 years to change the public view that once married, women were deemed to have given consent to sexual intercourse. Catherine MacKinnon (1982), who argues that sexuality is *the* locus of male power, asks how useful the notion of 'consent' is for distinguishing between wanted and unwanted sex:

> Few women are in a position to refuse unwanted sexual initiatives. That consent rather than non-mutuality is the line between rape and intercourse further exposes the inequality in normal social expectations. So does the substantial amount of male force allowed in the focus on the woman's resistance, which tends to be disabled by socialization to passivity. If sex is ordinarily accepted as something men do *to* women, the better question would be whether consent is a meaningful concept. Penetration (often by a penis) is also substantially more central to both the legal definition of rape and the male definition of sexual intercourse than it is to women's sexual violation or sexual pleasure. Rape in marriage expresses the male sense of entitlement to access to women they annex; incest extends it. Although most women are raped by men they know, the closer the relation, the less likely they are to claim it was rape. (MacKinnon, 1982: 532)

EXERCISE

Reread the above quote about consent and answer the following questions.

1. Think of five examples of unwanted sexual initiatives many women face.
2. Why do women find it difficult to resist unwanted sexual initiatives according to MacKinnon?

3. What do you understand by 'sex is ordinarily something men do *to* women'? Do you agree? If you disagree, can you think of some examples?
4. Think about what MacKinnon says about rape, its legal definition and the notion of consent: why does she prefer the concept of 'non-mutuality'?

EXERCISE RESPONSE

Examples of unwanted sexual initiatives other than rape might include sexual harassment; sexual violence in the home including incest and child sexual abuse (Kelly, Regan and Burton, 1991); pressure to have sex against one's will and pressure to engage in specific sexual practices. You might have thought of other types of social pressure that women experience concerning their sexuality: taboos against sex between women or masturbation (see box 7.3 on the vaginal/clitoral orgasm debate) and physical interventions such as clitoridectomy and infibulation (Thiam, 1986).

Having done this exercise you should have an understanding of the role socialization plays in women's sexuality, especially passive behaviour. Another point that MacKinnon makes is that men are more powerful both physically and in terms of their social power to define what sex is (penetration), to initiate and control sexual encounters, and to deny women any say or control about the content of sexual encounters. Some examples you might have thought of to illustrate cases where sex is not something that men do *to* women might include the idea of mutuality. Hence MacKinnon's preference for the term 'non-mutuality' to describe unacceptable sexual practices.

'The Orgasm Debate': A Summary of the Debates that have Taken Place Around the Question of Where Women's Sexual Pleasure Comes From

BOX
7.3

The question of whether a woman's orgasm originates in the vagina or the clitoris has been the source of much controversy and heated debate. While it is now generally acknowledged that the female orgasm always starts in the clitoris, it is also true that many women can also feel orgasm in the vagina as well as in the whole pelvic area including the uterus, cervix and indeed the whole body. An orgasm cannot be clitoral for many women in the world who have undergone clitoridectomy – when the clitoris is excised and or infibulated in childhood or in puberty (Thiam, 1986).

One current view is that talking about orgasm as if it were located only in the clitoris can be confusing and frustrating for many of us who have feelings which are much more widespread, intense or diffuse.

The debate developed from the Freudian belief that the healthy woman should have a vaginal orgasm. In the 1960s Masters and Johnson (1966), the sex behaviourists who conducted their research by observing couples in the laboratory, disproved this notion and asserted that orgasm originated in the clitoris. This was the main aspect of Masters and Johnson's work which appealed to feminists, that woman's orgasm was clitoral. In her re-evaluation of sexual liberation, historian Sheila Jeffreys (1990) traces the development of the vaginal/clitoral debate:

> Sexological writings had been proclaiming throughout the twentieth century that women must achieve a vaginal orgasm during sexual intercourse in order to be healthy. Some sexologists had questioned this before Masters and Johnson but they put the nail in the coffin of the vaginal orgasm through their laboratory experiments. The experiments seemed to prove that however the orgasm was experienced and wherever it appeared to come from the seat of sensation and the trigger of the mechanism lay in the clitoris and not the vagina. Feminists seized upon this with delight. The most famous valediction to the vaginal orgasm was the American feminist Anne Koedt's 1970 article 'The myth of the vaginal orgasm'.
>
> Koedt interpreted Masters and Johnson's findings on clitoral orgasm as challenging the idea that women must engage in sexual intercourse. This was not at all what the sexologists had intended. Koedt concluded that men had only maintained the myth of the vaginal orgasm and the concomitant necessity of sexual intercourse because this was the practice which gave them most convenient sexual stimulation. Men had suppressed the truth about the clitoral orgasm, she argued, because 'Men fear that they will become sexually expendable if the clitoris is substituted for the vagina as the centre of pleasure for women.' (Jeffreys, 1990: 231)

As Jeffreys points out, women traditionally remain ignorant of their sexual organs – women's genitals are regarded as disgusting or dangerous in male culture and many of us grow up feeling ashamed of them and guilty about masturbation.

I have chosen the next extract as an example of a consensual and mutual sexual encounter between two teenage girls. It is taken from Jeannette Winterson's

(1990) autobiographical novel *Oranges Are Not the Only Fruit*, set in a Christian evangelical community in a Lancashire village:

> When I reached Melanie's it was getting dark. I had to cut through the churchyard to get there, and sometimes I'd steal her a bunch of flowers from the new graves. She was always pleased, but then, I never told her where they came from. . . . We read the Bible as usual, and then told each other how glad we were that the Lord had brought us together. She stroked my head for a long time, and then we hugged and it felt like drowning. Then I was frightened but couldn't stop. There was something crawling in my belly. I had an octopus inside me.
>
> And it was evening, and it was morning; another day. After that we did everything together, and I stayed with her as often as I could. (Winterson, 1990: 88)

One of the ironies of Jeanette and Melanie's intimacy is that it is seen as a taboo in their community whereas much 'forced sex' in our society is seen as acceptable, certainly by the law. Could this be because heterosexual sex, even forced, whether in the form of incest, child abuse, rape, or other forms of unwanted sex is somehow less problematic than non-heterosexual sex?

Now read an example of coercive or unwanted sex from empirical feminist research, to contrast with the previous account of consensual and mutual but taboo sex. I want to distinguish between the 'technologies of heterosexual coercion' (Gavey, 1992) and forced sex because they can take several forms, they do not necessarily involve violence and they are common to many heterosexual encounters.

Nicola Gavey (1992) explores some of the reasons for 'women's compliance with unwanted sex and those forms of heterosexual coercion which do not involve overt force or violence' (p. 349). Some of the reasons she gives for women's compliance include: ideas about the 'normal' frequency of sexual interaction for heterosexual couples; situations where sex is required – young people living at home meeting elsewhere and people having affairs; ideas about 'real sex' (coitus); social status for teenagers gained from having a boyfriend; pragmatic reasons such as wanting some sleep or fear that saying no could lead to rape; the absence of a language of desire for women or of a language to say no; and the lack of control over sexual encounters:

> *Chloe*: I just realize the total lack of my belief in any right to say to somebody - Like if someone was standing on my foot I'd fucking tell her - Someone's got their penis in my vagina and they're grinding away and I don't feel able to ask them to stop. It's *just ridiculous*! Honestly, it's just the pits. I mean there's a hell of a lot of powerful stuff going on – (Gavey, 1992: 335)

This account of coercive sex reflects the 'compulsory' aspect of heterosexuality (Rich, 1984) as the dominant form of sexuality in Western industrialized societies in the sense that it is forced upon us and often difficult to resist. It also reflects the way that women are disciplined and their behaviour regulated while the mechanism of power remains hidden: 'this invisible operation of power is extremely efficient because it obviates the need for overt force and violence' (Gavey, 1992: 348).

Nevertheless, the threat of sexual violence is real, never far off and constitutes a form of social control difficult to challenge (Kelly, 1988). Some feminists see sexuality as a form of supremacy or power men have over women which is institutionalized by heterosexuality (MacKinnon, 1982; Hester, 1992). Others see men's sexual violence as a form of punishment, a way of 'policing' women who transgress the gendered power relations of patriarchy:

> The presence of sexual violence is . . . one of the defining features of a patriarchal society. It is used by men, and often condoned by the State, for a number of specific purposes: to punish women who are seen to be resisting male control; to police women, make them behave or not behave in particular ways; to claim rights of sexual, emotional and domestic servicing; and through all these maintain the relations of patriarchy, male dominance and female subordination. (Kelly and Radford, 1987: 238–9)

The issues of protecting women from sexual violence and policing men are difficult ones which are explored further in chapter 11 on crime. One aspect of the debate feminists have highlighted is the racist dimension of police patrolling and the difficulty faced by black women who are fighting on two fronts: on the one hand, against sexual violence and, on the other, against police racism which sees black women as a low priority (Southall Black Sisters, 1990, 1992).

In this section on sexuality as a form of social control we have addressed the issues of men's control over women's bodies and their sexuality, consent, power, mutuality and its absence in sexual encounters, coercive sex, 'compulsory heterosexuality', and protection from sexual violence.

The next section focuses on the differences between how feminine and masculine sexuality are constructed, including sexual desire. The theory of social constructionism which highlights the social dimension of sexuality enables us to question the 'natural' aspects of heterosexuality and see it as an often oppressive institution.

'I was in Lust': The Social Construction of Women's and Men's Sexuality

This section looks at how women's and men's sexuality are constructed differently and the impact this has on women's lives. Who is defining sex and for whom? What are the different definitions women and men have of sex and why? One way to understand the different experiences women and men have of sex and what these mean is to explore how their sexualities are constructed as something we achieve rather than are born with (Holland, Ramazanoglu and Sharpe, 1993).

Feminists have analysed men's sexuality as based on the power to define what 'sex' is – usually heterosexual vaginal intercourse, to define appropriate looks and actions, to sexually initiate and pursue, and the right to sex *per se*. All of these stem from and remake male power and are linked to male economic, social and cultural power (see Coveney et al., 1984; Kimmel, 1987; Seidler, 1989; Segal, 1990; Holland, Ramazanoglu and Sharpe, 1993). In addition feminists have pointed out how men are sexually serviced by women whether in marriage or in the sex industry in the form of pornography and prostitution (see Dworkin, 1981; Everywoman, 1988; Farley, 1992). As Lynn Segal (1992) explains, objections are voiced by feminists 'not to the sexual explicitness in pornography but to the sexism: to its characteristic reduction of women to passive' (p. 2).

She continues: 'porn caters to men's sexual fantasies of female availability and eagerness for sex in the context of societies which have proved unable, and until recently, unwilling, to offer women protection from widespread sex-harassment, abuse and violence, indeed, unwilling not so long ago, and for many men still today, even to acknowledge the existence of these issues' (Segal, 1992: 5). Prostitution is another aspect of the sex industry that reinforces ideas of women's sexual availability (see Roberts, 1986). The sex industry is where sex 'goes public'. Prostitution is no longer illegal in the UK; only soliciting and loitering are offences, as well as two or more women working together from a flat, a set-up deemed to be a 'brothel'. Here, sex becomes work, labour, income, powerlessness and power, exchange commodity, consumer product. Feminists' focus on the economics of sex, where sexual services are exchanged for income, is often absent from the debate about the sex industry.

Women's sexuality is often generally perceived as passive, its role to service men's 'sexual needs'. It has been unacceptable for women to take the initiative and express sexual desire (see Coward, 1984; Snitow, Stansell and Thompson, 1984). In the following painful account of intercourse, the Egyptian fiction writer Alifa Rifaat recounts a woman's sexual frustration and sorrow:

> Through half-closed eyes she looked at her husband. Lying on his right side, his body was intertwined with hers and his head bent over her right shoulder. As usual at such times she felt that he inhabited a world utterly different from hers, a world from which she had been excluded. Only half-aware of the movements of his body, she turned her head to one side and stared up at the ceiling, where she noticed a spider's web. She told herself she'd have to get out the long broom and brush it down.
>
> When they were first married she had tried to will her husband into sensing the desire that burned within her and so continuing the act longer; she had been too shy and conscious of the conventions to express such wishes openly. Later on, feeling herself sometimes to be on the brink of the experience some of her married women

friends talked of in hushed terms, she had found the courage to be explicit about what she wanted. At such moments it had seemed to her that all she needed was just one more movement and her body and soul would be quenched, that once achieved they would between them know how to repeat the experience. But on each occasion, when breathlessly imploring him to continue, he would – as though purposely to deprive her – quicken his movements and bring the act to an abrupt end. (Rifaat, 1987: 1)

Definitions of women's sexuality as passive and subordinate to men's needs in heterosexual sex contribute to the resulting subordinate position of women within sexual encounters and relationships (Holland, 1993). Men's sexuality is defined as taking, men's orgasms determine sexual encounters and sexuality becomes a coercive force where women are denied their sexual pleasure:

> One young Asian woman who preferred, and to a large extent practised, non-penetrative sex in her current relationship, signalled a certain degree of resentment at the 'male needs' focus of previous heterosexual sex she had experienced:
> 'It was like as soon as he got an erection that was alright no matter how I was feeling, whether I was aroused or not you had to do things because that was the point when things happened, when he was aroused, not when I was aroused.' (Holland, 1993: 24)

For women, desire has long been a taboo area in sexual practices and also in writings about sex (see Nestle, 1988). Kate Chopin (1993), the American writer, caused a scandal when she wrote very frankly about a woman's sexual desire in *The Awakening*, a novel published in the USA nearly a hundred years ago in 1899. In this passage, Edna muses over the pleasure and pain of her relationships with Arobin, her lover and Robert, the man she is in love with.

> Edna cried a little that night after Arobin left her. It was only one phase of the multitudinous emotions which had assailed her. There was with her an overwhelming feeling of irresponsibility. There was the shock of the unexpected and the unaccustomed. There was her husband's reproach looking at her from the external things around her which he had provided for her external existence. There was Robert's reproach making itself felt by a quicker, fiercer, more over-powering love, which had awakened within her toward him. Above all, there was understanding. She felt as if a mist had been lifted from her eyes, enabling her to look upon and comprehend the significance of life, that monster made up of beauty and brutality. But among the conflicting sensations which assailed her, there was neither shame nor remorse. There was a dull pang of regret because it was not the kiss of love which had inflamed her, because it was not love which had held this cup of life to her lips. (Chopin, 1993: 140)

Edna has defied convention not only by being in love with a man not her husband but then also taking a lover. She faces the dilemma of a married woman for whom the only legitimate form of permissive female sexual activity is marriage. The other way in which she defies convention is by transgressing norms of femininity which construct women as 'desired objects' rather than 'desiring subjects'.

EXERCISE

Reread the last three accounts of women's sexual desire by Alifa Rifaat, Janet Holland and Kate Chopin.

Compare each woman's description of her sexual desire, her ability to express it and her feelings about this (positive, negative, ambivalent).

Spend a few minutes recalling some of your own sexual experiences. Do any bear any similarities with these accounts?

Do not worry if you cannot find the 'right' language to describe your experiences: the lack of an appropriate vocabulary for talking and writing about sex, especially for women, is an unresolved issue.

EXERCISE RESPONSE

Your experiences might not have been captured by any of these extracts. Your attempts to look back on your own experience of sex should have highlighted for you the very personal and variable aspects of sexual encounters. This exercise should also show you how sexual experiences share certain elements and are a product of social forces rather than isolated incidents. You should also have an understanding of how difficult it is for women to experience their bodies and sexuality as 'desiring subjects' rather than as 'desired objects'. This issue of women as 'desiring subjects' remains one of the most controversial and unresolved issues within the feminist debate around sex and sexuality for two reasons: there are problems at both the level of experience or practice and in terms of representation.

Feminists carrying out empirical research have documented the difficulties faced by women attempting to negotiate pleasure on their own terms and trying to define what the sexual encompasses in terms of penetration, non-penetrative sex or other forms of sexual contact (Holland et al., 1991; Gavey, 1992). One study recommends the need for a positive female sexuality; for women to be recognized as sexual beings because at the moment the sexually active woman has a negative image; for men as well as women to be educated about female sexuality; and for

Melanie Mauthner

men to challenge notions of dominant masculinity so women can express their needs for sexual safety and pleasure which requires a shift to a more equal conception of sexuality (Holland, 1993).

This chapter has been difficult to write. I have had to make decisions about what 'line' to take and what voice to adopt. I wanted to avoid being dogmatic and prescriptive in the way that many writers about sexuality can be. Regarding 'voice' my decision was influenced by what would make the chapter easy to read and write.

I have also been influenced in my selection of material by what has marked me intellectually and emotionally over the years. Writing about my self in this way and about the links between the rational and the emotional is particularly relevant when it comes to sex. It is also part of the process of breaking down the barriers between reason and emotion in the realms of sexology or writings about sexual behaviour; feminist politics or writings about the women's movement; and theory or the growing academic discipline of women's studies.

In this chapter we have examined some of the most enduring myths about women's and men's sexuality. We have seen how sexuality is far more than a 'natural' biological phenomenon and instead, something that is socially constructed through culture and history. We also analysed two aspects of the debate around sexuality which continue to rage among feminists: sexual violence and the question of safety, and sexual pleasure or desire. Two themes running through the chapter concern the place of the body and power in sexuality. We addressed the issue of how sexuality acts as a means of social control in women's lives, how inequalities in structural power relations between women and men are reflected in sexual encounters and how difficult these are to resist. You might now want to revise our preliminary description of sexuality and compare it with this one:

> We take sexuality to refer to sexual practices but also to sexual identity and the varied historical and cultural forms which sexual identity can take. Sexuality, then, implies sexual beliefs and desires and the ways in which these are socially negotiated and constructed in a context of hidden power relationships. Sexuality is both public and secret, both biological and cultural, both socially constructed and the product of individual agency. (Holland, Ramazanoglu and Scott, 1990: 13)

ACKNOWLEDGEMENTS

I am indebted to my editor Beryl Madoc-Jones and to Natasha Mauthner, Fenella Morris, Adam Steinhouse and Christine Ward for reading and commenting on earlier drafts of this chapter. Their suggestions and our discussions have been invaluable for helping me clarify my thoughts.

REFERENCES

Addison, B. J. 1992: Respect. In P. McNeill, B. Freeman and J. Newman (eds), *Women Talk Sex: Autobiographical Writing on Sex, Sexuality and Sexual Identity*, London: Scarlet Press.

Bryan, B., Dadzie, S. and Scafe, S. 1985: *The Heart of the Race: Black Women's Lives in Britain*. London: Virago.

Cant, B. and Hemmings, S. 1988: *Radical Records: 30 Years of Lesbian and Gay History*. London: Routledge.

Cartledge, S. and Ryan, J. 1983: *Sex & Love: New Thoughts on Old Contradictions*. London: Women's Press.

Chopin, K. 1993: *The Awakening*. London: Women's Press. [First published 1899; 1978.]

Cixous, H. 1981: Castration or decapitation? *Signs: Journal of Women in Culture and Society*, 7, 1, 41–55.

Coote, A. and Campbell, B. 1982: *Sweet Freedom: The Struggle for Women's Liberation*. London: Picador.

Coulson, M. 1992: Taking the long way home. In P. McNeill, B. Freeman and J. Newman (eds), *Women Talk Sex: Autobiographical Writing on Sex, Sexuality and Sexual Identity*, London: Scarlet Press.

Coveney, L., Jackson, M., Jeffreys, S., Kaye, L. and Mahony, P. 1984: *The Sexuality Papers: Male Sexuality and the Social Control of Women*. London: Hutchinson.

Coward, R. 1984: *Female Desire: Women's Sexuality Today*. London: Paladin/Grafton.

Duberman, M., Vicinus, M. and Chauncey, G. 1991: *Hidden From History: Reclaiming the Gay and Lesbian Past*. Harmondsworth: Penguin.

Duncker, P. 1992: Introduction. In P. McNeill, B. Freeman and J. Newman (eds), *Women Talk Sex: Autobiographical Writing on Sex, Sexuality and Sexual Identity*. London: Scarlet Press.

Dworkin, A. 1981: *Pornography*. London: Women's Press.

Everywoman 1988: *Pornography and Sexual Violence: Evidence of the Links*. London: Everywoman.

Faderman, L. 1985: *Surpassing the Love of Men: Romantic Friendship and Love Between Women from the Renaissance to the Present*. London: Women's Press.

Faderman, L. 1991: *Odd Girls and Twilight Lovers: A History of Lesbian Life in Twentieth Century America*. London: Penguin.

Farley, M. 1992: The rampage against *Penthouse*. In J. Radford and D. E. H. Russell (eds), *Femicide: The Politics of Woman Killing*, Buckingham: Open University Press.

Firestone, S. 1971: *The Dialectic of Sex: The Case for Feminist Revolution*. London: Women's Press.

Foucault, M. 1981: *The History of Sexuality: An Introduction*. Harmondsworth: Penguin.

Freud, S. 1971: On femininity. In *New Introductory Lectures on Psychoanalysis*, Lecture 33, Pelican Freud Library, Vol. 2. Harmondsworth: Penguin. [First published 1933.]

Freud, S. 1977: *On Sexuality: Three Essays on the Theory of Sexuality* (ed. Angela Richards). Harmondsworth: Penguin.

Friday, N. 1975: *My Secret Garden: Women's Sexual Fantasies*. London: Quartet.

Friedan, B. 1963: *The Feminine Mystique*. Harmondsworth: Penguin.

Gavey, N. 1992: Technologies and effects of heterosexual coercion. *Feminism and Psychology,* 2, 3, 325–51.

Hearn, J. and Parkin, W. 1987: *'Sex' and 'Work': The Power and Paradox of Organisational Sexuality.* Brighton: Wheatsheaf.

Hester, M. 1992: *Lewd Women and Wicked Witches: A Study of the Dynamics of Male Domination.* London: Routledge.

Hey, V. forthcoming: *The Company She Keeps: An Ethnographic Study of Girls' Friendships.* Buckingham: Open University Press.

Holland, J. 1993: *Sexuality and Ethnicity: Variations in Young Women's Sexual Knowledge and Practice.* WRAP Paper 8. London: Tufnell Press.

Holland, J., Ramazanoglu, C. and Scott, S. 1990: *Sex, Risk, and Danger: AIDS Education Policy and Young Women's Sexuality.* WRAP Paper 1. London: Tufnell Press.

Holland, J., Ramazanoglu, C. and Sharpe, S. 1993: *Wimp or Gladiator: Contradictions in Acquiring Masculine Sexuality.* WRAP/MRAP Paper 9. London: Tufnell Press.

Holland, J., Ramazanoglu, C., Scott, S., Sharpe, S. and Thomson, R. 1991: *Pressure, Resistance, Empowerment: Young Women and the Negotiation of Safer Sex.* WRAP Paper 6. London: Tufnell Press.

Irigaray, L. 1985: *This Sex Which Is Not One* (trans. Catherine Porter). Ithaca, New York: Cornell University Press.

Jeffreys, S. 1989: Does it matter if they did it? In Lesbian History Group (eds), *Not a Passing Phase: Reclaiming Lesbians in History 1840–1985.* London: Women's Press.

Jeffreys, S. 1990: *Anti-Climax: A Feminist Perspective of the Sexual Revolution.* London: Women's Press.

Kelly, L. 1988: *Surviving Sexual Violence.* Cambridge: Polity Press.

Kelly, L. and Radford, J. 1987: The problem of men. In P. Scraton (ed.), *Law, Order and the Authoritarian State.* Milton Keynes: Open University Press.

Kelly, L., Regan, L. and Burton, S. 1991: An exploratory study of the prevalence of sexual abuse in a sample of 16–21 year-olds. Mimeo, Polytechnic of North London.

Kimmel, M. S. (ed.) 1987: *Changing Men: New Directions in Research on Men and Masculinity.* Newbury Park, CA: Sage.

Kitzinger, S. 1985: *Women's Experience of Sex.* Harmondsworth: Penguin.

Koedt, A. 1970: The myth of the vaginal orgasm. In L. Tanner (ed.), *Voices From Women's Liberation,* New York: Mentor.

Kristeva, J. 1982: *Desire in Language* (trans. Leon Roudiez). New York: Columbia University Press.

Lesbian History Group 1989: *Not a Passing Phase: Reclaiming Lesbians in History 1840–1985.* London: Women's Press.

MacKinnon, C. 1982: Feminism, marxism, method and the state: an agenda for theory. *Signs,* 7, 3, 515–44.

Marshall, A. 1994: Sensuous sapphires: a study of the social construction of black female sexuality. In M. Maynard and J. Purvis (eds), *Researching Women's Lives From a Feminist Perspective,* London: Taylor & Francis.

Masters, W. and Johnson, V. 1966: *Human Sexual Response.* London: Little, Brown & Co.

Millett, K. 1977: *Sexual Politics.* London: Virago.

Mitchell, J. 1974: *Psychoanalysis and Feminism.* Harmondsworth: Penguin.

Moi, T. 1985: *Sexual/Textual Politics: Feminist Literary Theory.* London: Methuen.

Nestle, J. 1988: *A Restricted Country: Essays and Short Stories.* London: Sheba.

Radford, J. 1992: Where do we go from here? In J. Radford and D. E. H. Russell (eds), *Femicide: The Politics of Woman Killing,* Buckingham: Open University Press.

Ramazanoglu, C. 1989: *Feminism and the Contradictions of Oppression.* London: Routledge.

Ramazanoglu, C. 1993: *Up Against Foucault: Explorations of Some Tensions between Foucault and Feminism.* London: Routledge.

Rich, A. 1984: Compulsory heterosexuality and lesbian existence. In A. Snitow, C. Stansell and S. Thompson (eds), *Desire: the Politics of Sexuality.* London: Virago.

Rifaat, A. 1987: *Distant View of a Minaret.* Oxford: Heinemann.

Roberts, N. 1986: *The Front Line: Women in the Sex Industry Speak.* London: Grafton.

Segal, L. 1990: *Slow Motion: Changing Masculinities, Changing Men.* London: Virago.

Segal, L. 1992: Introduction. In L. Segal and M. McIntosh (eds), *Sex Exposed: Sexuality and the Pornography Debate.* London: Virago.

Seidler, V. J. 1989: *Rediscovering Masculinity: Reason, Language and Sexuality.* London: Routledge.

Snitow, A., Stansell, C. and Thompson, S. (eds) 1984: *Desire: the Politics of Sexuality.* London: Virago.

Southall Black Sisters 1990: *Against the Grain: A Celebration of Survival and Struggle.* Southall Black Sisters, 52 Northwood Road, Southall, Middlesex.

Southall Black Sisters 1992: Two struggles: challenging male violence and the police. In J. Radford and D. E. H. Russell (eds), *Femicide: The Politics of Woman Killing,* Buckingham: Open University Press.

Suyin, H. 1994: *Winter Love.* London: Virago. [First published in 1962.]

Thiam, A. 1986: *Speak Out Black Sisters: Feminism and Oppression in Black Africa.* London: Pluto.

Tong, R. 1992: *Feminist Thought: A Comprehensive Introduction.* London: Routledge.

Valverde, M. 1985: *Sex, Power and Pleasure.* Toronto: Women's Press.

Weeks, J. 1981: *Sex, Politics and Society.* London: Longman.

Weeks, J. 1986: *Sexuality.* London: Tavistock.

Winterson, J. 1990: *Oranges are Not the Only Fruit.* London: Women's Press.

CHAPTER
8 Health

Margaret L. Arnot and
Louise Jackson

(a)

(b)

Plate 7   (a) Annie Besant. © The Mansell Collection, London.
Plate 8   (b) Nawal el Sa'adawi, Egyptian feminist author and doctor, June 1986. Format Partners;
photograph: Pam Isherwood.

In this chapter we examine a number of health issues that are particularly important for women. We highlight the importance of women having knowledge about our bodies and health in order for us to achieve and maintain good health. The chapter begins with an examination of how different women experience embodiment, how they feel being women, having a woman's body. The idea that this might vary may seem strange at first. You may think that your body just is, that it is something 'natural' and as such, unchanging, that all women's bodies are in basic respects 'the same'. Once you have studied this chapter, you may change your mind.

After encouraging you to think about these different experiences, the chapter has two more parts: 'the politics of women's health' and 'issues in the politics of women's health'. In all these sections it is crucial to think about power. After reading this chapter you will understand more about some of the particular health concerns of women. You will be encouraged to think about the relationships between women's social and economic positions, ideas about how women are supposed to be, and our health. You will also understand some of the implications for women of dominant white male control of mainstream medicine, and how women have sought to improve our access to knowledge and services. But first, to embodiment.

Embodiment: Knowledge, Menstruation and Sexuality

Can you separate your 'body' from the way society constructs the female body and the way you feel about your body? This is a difficult philosophical question that you cannot necessarily 'solve' in a week or two of thought. However it is easy to see from what follows that how we feel about our womanliness, varies greatly across both time and cultures.

Nawal El Sa'adawi, physician and at one time Egypt's Director of Public Health (until she was dismissed for her involvement in women's politics), writes from her own experiences as a young woman and as a doctor attending to the medical needs of hundreds. In the following passage from *The Hidden Face of Eve* (Sa'adawi, 1980) she gives a very personal account of growing up as a woman in the Arab world.

> Ignorance about the body and its functions in girls and women is considered a sign of honour, purity and good morals . . .
>
> It would be difficult for anyone to imagine the panic that seized hold of me one morning when I woke to find blood trickling down between my thighs. I can still

remember the deathly pallor of my face in the mirror. My arms and legs were trembling violently and it appeared to me as though the disaster which had frightened me for so long was now a fact. That somehow, in the dark of night, a man had crept into my room while I was sleeping and succeeded in causing me harm . . . the flow of blood did not stop . . . it increased from hour to hour and on the following day I was obliged to overcome the fear and shame that possessed me and speak to my mother. I asked her to take me to a doctor for treatment. To my utter surprise she was calm and cool and did not seem to be affected by her daughter's serious condition. She explained this was something that happened to all girls and that it recurs every month for a few days. On the last day when the flow ceased, I was to cleanse myself of this 'impure blood' by having a hot bath. Her words echoed in my ears; 'monthly condition', 'a hot bath' to rid me of the 'impure blood'. I was therefore to understand that in me there was something degrading which appeared regularly in the form of this impure blood, and that it was something to be ashamed of, to hide from others. So I stayed in my room for four consecutive days, unable to face anybody. When I opened the door on my way to the bathroom, I would look around to make sure that nobody was in sight, and before returning I would wash the floor carefully as though removing the marks of a recent crime, and under my arms and between my legs, several times, to make sure that no smell of this impure blood remained. (Sa'adawi, 1980: 44–6)

EXERCISE

Now answer these questions on the extract from Sa'adawi's text.

1. What qualities were most highly esteemed in Egyptian women?
2. What effect did ignorance have on Sa'adawi's reaction to her first menstrual period?
3. How did her mother explain menstruation to her, and how did this affect her perception of herself?

EXERCISE RESPONSE

The mental and physical oppression of this pubescent girl was caused by a system that required a woman to be ignorant of the way her body worked in order to be considered pure, virtuous, and honourable – and, by implication, marriageable. The young Sa'adawi was frightened when she began to menstruate and presumed that there was something dreadful wrong with her. Once she had summoned the courage to ask her mother to seek medical aid, Sa'adawi was told that this terrifying affliction would occur every month and that every month she would need to cleanse herself of the impure blood.

Present-day Arab societies are not the only ones where high value has been placed on women's ignorance. 'Innocence' and 'purity' were also esteemed in Victorian England. Annie Besant was a feminist who married the Reverend Frank Besant at the age of twenty. The marriage was very unhappy. The following passage suggests some of the reasons.

So I married in the winter of 1867 with no more idea of the marriage relation than if I had been four years old instead of twenty. My dreamy life, into which no knowledge of evil had been allowed to penetrate, in which I had been guarded from all pain, shielded from all anxiety, kept innocent of all questions of sex, was no preparation for married existence, and left me defenceless to face a rude awakening. Looking back on it all, I deliberately say that no more fatal blunder can be made than to train a girl to womanhood in ignorance of all life's duties and burdens, and then to let her face for the first time away from all the old associations, the old helps, the old refuge on the mother's breast. [sic] That 'perfect innocence' may be very beautiful, but it is a perilous possession, and Eve should have the knowledge of good and evil ere she wanders forth from the paradise of a mother's love. Many an unhappy marriage dates from its very beginning, from the terrible shock to a young girl's sensitive modesty and pride, her helpless bewilderment and fear. Men, with their public school and college education, or the knowledge that comes by living in the outside world, may find it hard to realize the possibility of such infantile ignorance in many girls. None the less, such ignorance is a fact in the case of some girls at least, and no mother should let her daughter, blindfold, slip her neck under the marriage yoke. (Besant, 1893: 70–1)

EXERCISE

Having read the extract from Besant, answer these questions.

1. What qualities were esteemed in young women in Victorian England? Look for key words related to the way in which Besant was brought up.
2. Why does Besant consider knowledge to be so important?
3. Compare Sa'adawi's response to her first menstruation with Besant's response to her first intercourse.

EXERCISE RESPONSE

Annie Besant was brought up so that she retained 'perfect innocence' regarding sexual matters, and indeed, was shielded from all affairs of the world leading to pain and anxiety. 'Sensitive modesty' and 'pride' were also qualities instilled in the young girl. She would not have had full understanding of menstruation because this in itself would have introduced her to the subject of the body's sexual functions. Besant was critical of this 'innocence'. She considered knowledge of the body's sexual functions crucial to the successful foundation of marriage. She writes here of the 'shock' and 'rude awakening' in store for a young woman after marriage if she had not been educated about sex beforehand. For both Sa'adawi and Besant, in very different cultures at different times, being kept in ignorance about their bodies led to very real psychological suffering.

Let's now compare some other understandings of menstruation. Cultural anthropologist Emily Martin (1987) conducted a study among women from all classes in the United States today and found many feelings on menstruation similar to those expressed by Sa'adawi. Yet at the same time, many women she interviewed had positive feelings about menstruation. Here are a few examples, grouped so that responses with a similar theme are together.

'I was sure I was bleeding to death'; 'saw that blood and thought I had TB'; 'thought I'd injured myself' (Martin, 1987: 93).

'made me feel like "Oh my God, I'm dirty or something!" '; 'People make you feel bad, especially men. They think that you are dirty when you have your period' (Martin, 1987: 93).

'I remember wanting it so badly. You feel like you're not a woman but you know you're starting to be a woman and it's something that sets you apart from being a little girl'; 'At times I feel it's the best thing that's happening. If I'm coming on my period it means I'm not pregnant. I'm glad to see it' (Martin, 1987: 101–3).

EXERCISE

Answer these questions about your own feelings about menstruation.

1. Were you educated about menstruation? Have you associated menstruation with debilitating illness? How has ignorance about menstruation affected you or your friends?
2. How is the view of menstruation as unclean perpetuated? Do you feel this? How can this feeling be changed? Are there any differences in attitudes to menstruation

as unclean between cultures in Western societies? Between the sexes? (These last two questions especially need to be approached in discussion groups.)

3. What are your positive feelings about menstruation? Do you think men understand women's positive feelings about menstruation?

EXERCISE RESPONSE

While some changes in attitudes to sexuality and the body have occurred in recent decades in Western societies many people remain embarrassed about discussing intimate bodily functions. Some cultures in Western societies still maintain strict taboos about the body. So some girls can still begin to menstruate without understanding what is going on.

While some information is available from anthropological and historical studies about the ways different societies have viewed menstruation, there is less published information about cultural difference within Western societies today. You might discover some in discussion with fellow students and friends. It is possible to make some observations about male understandings of menstruation.

Sophie Laws (1990) interviewed men about menstruation for her book *Issues of Blood*. She discovered that women and men understand menstruation differently and speak about it differently. However, the language of white male British culture – usually derisory, crude and sexist – serves to maintain the requirement that women remain publicly silent about menstruation. Women do not usually hear the full extent of insulting and offensive male views because these are confined to all-male culture. Yet, in Mary Daly's words, we are 'spooked from the locker room' by the male disgust and joking (Daly, 1979: 323). We know about it in a shadowy way, from playground taunting when children, and from obvious silences, sneers, and paternalistic treatment. Thus, in fear of confronting the worst of male contempt and disgust, we attempt to maintain the invisibility of menstruation.

Laws concluded that there were a number of aspects to male perceptions of menstruation, all of them based on a view of women as inferior to men. First, menstrual blood is seen as disgusting and smelly: sanitary towels are the butt of male joking, especially among school-age boys, and many men express revulsion at sexual intercourse during a woman's menses. This connection between sex and menstruation is a second key factor in male culture about the subject. Much banter and joking occurs around the topic of lack of sexual access to menstruating women. This emphasizes the way men view women as existing to serve male sexual desire: menstruating women may as well not exist. Recently, some men are beginning to understand menstrual blood as sensual: eliminating the view of menstrual blood as distasteful gives men unbroken sexual access to women. The third important aspect of male views underlined by Laws is that men see women as ruled by their hormones: moody and less reliable as a result of their menstrual cycles (Laws, 1990).

Understandings of menstruation have political implications. The view of a woman's menstrual cycle as having only one purpose – the production of babies – helps sustain a very limited understanding of women's role in society. From women's point of view, most women most of the time do not want to have a baby. The appearance of their period is a positive event, affirmation that they are not pregnant! The negative view of menstruation (and other events in women's cycles, especially menopause and pre-menstrual tension (PMT)) as failed production and as illness underpins an understanding of women as less able than men to bear the pressures of public and professional responsibilities. Historically, menstruation has been used to argue against women's entry into higher education and the professions. Today, PMT is used to put down women's ability to perform consistently in their jobs. The use of PMT as an argument against women's full responsibility for crimes such as murder also continues the view of women being by nature less responsible than men: in the past, all events associated with women's reproductive cycles – menstruation, suspension of the menses, conception, pregnancy, birth, lactation, cessation of lactation and menopause – have been used in courts to argue that women were not responsible for crimes they had committed: PMT is just the most recent addition to the list (Showalter and Showalter, 1972; Bullough and Voght, 1973; Smith-Rosenberg, 1974; Laws, Hey and Eagan, 1985; Martin, 1987).

The Politics of Women's Health: Women's Health and Women's Liberation

The previous section introduced you to the idea that how we experience our bodies is fundamentally related to how being female is constructed by the culture we live in. This understanding of women's health and illness as often socially determined is one idea at the heart of the women's health movement: if there are key social elements in women's health and illness, that means the situation can be improved.

Women in the late 1960s who formed the Western women's liberation movement quickly addressed themselves to women's health issues. In this section introducing the politics of women's health we will outline some key points before moving on to more detailed discussion of a number of specific women's health issues. First, some aspects of the treatment of women within the mainstream medical system are discussed; and second, you will find background on the women's health movement itself.

The mainstream medical system

The focus by the Western medical profession on crisis action, drugs and surgery is sometimes not suitable for women's health, where prevention of illness is frequently most important. In order to maintain good health rather than be cured once health becomes bad, knowledge is all important. The isolation of many women makes them particularly vulnerable to dependency on experts.

Furthermore, the profession itself remains dominated by men, and by white men at that. Women struggled during the later decades of the nineteenth century to be admitted to the medical profession. Male domination of the medical profession has not always benefited women's health. It is difficult to ensure that medical resources are directed in ways that meet women's interests. Concerted medical campaigns against major male killers, such as heart disease, began earlier than those against major female killers, such as female forms of cancer. It is arguable that in Britain certain preventive measures for female forms of cancer remain inadequate.

The World Health Organization (WHO) has predicted that the AIDS (Acquired Immunodeficiency Syndrome) pandemic will kill 4 million women by the year 2000; a further 13 million women will have contracted the Human Immunodeficiency Virus (HIV) (Mihill, 1993). These statistics are striking. Yet the serious threat of AIDS has, until recently, been ignored or understated in the case of women. The following passage is taken from a newspaper article 'Women and AIDS: why ignorance is far from bliss', which looks at the experiences of women in Britain. Here Susan gives her account of what happened when she decided to be tested for HIV in 1988.

'It all started like this: I was a bit disappointed at the way my boyfriend was behaving and I thought it was best to make a clean break. I decided to have an AIDS test . . . I went to a doctor who asked me why I wanted it. He asked if I'd ever had a bisexual boyfriend, taken drugs or been a prostitute – and I answered no. He then said I looked fine and he didn't think I needed to take the test.' Susan is 32 and despite her doctor's assumptions, has been HIV positive for four years. (Critchley, 1992)

EXERCISE

Answer these questions on the Critchley extract above.

1. What assumptions did the doctor make?
2. What might be some implications of such assumptions?

EXERCISE RESPONSE

Susan's doctor assumed that she was not at risk because she was not a prostitute or drug user and was not aware that any of her boyfriends had had homosexual relations. He did not enquire whether Susan always used condoms when having sex. He did not take into account that many women do not know about their male partners' other relationships, whether heterosexual or homosexual. The doctor assumed there could be nothing wrong with her because she looked healthy; he assumed that people who are HIV positive are bound to look ill.

The doctor, undoubtedly influenced by medical and media discussion at the time, thought there were certain patterns of high risk behaviour (intravenous drug-taking, promiscuity and homosexuality) through which the virus was exclusively transmitted. Such assumptions might mean that women who were involved in what were considered 'normal' heterosexual relations were not tested or educated in relation to AIDS. Ignorance about AIDS (perpetuated by such doctor/patient exchanges) could put real lives in further danger. Three writers who recently examined the history of AIDS found that: 'as women became infected . . . they found that the information available often did not apply to them, that most services were geared towards men, and that doctors and other professionals were often unprepared for the particular issues that women would raise' (Bury, Morrison and McLachlan, 1992: 1).

The neglect of various health matters of central importance to women and the early neglect of AIDS and its impact on women in the West are not the only effects of a male-dominated medical profession that concern women. In terms of gynaecology and obstetrics, it is arguable that male doctors have been too invasive in their treatment of women. The move from almost universal home births in the nineteenth century to almost universal hospital births in the late twentieth century in Western countries has occurred without adequate understanding of whether or not the increasing medicalization of childbirth is in the interests of women and the babies they bear. Rona Campbell and Alison Macfarlane (1987) have carefully examined all the historical and contemporary evidence in the debate about the best place for birth to occur and conclude, among other things, that there is no evidence to support the claim that the safest policy is for all women to give birth in hospital. Another relevant issue is that parts of women's reproductive systems are sometimes removed unnecessarily and in almost cavalier fashion (Roberts, 1990; Bellos, 1994; Dyer, 1994a, b).

Women encounter problems because of their race as well as their sex. Not only do black workers in the NHS have trouble because of racist assumptions, but health provision for ethnic minorities is also influenced by racism. Despite relatively recent race relations initiatives in the NHS, the provision of services in areas with large populations of ethnic minorities can still be hampered by racism (Torkington, 1983; McNaught, 1987, 1988). Allan McNaught has studied many reports of racial discrimination within the NHS and has concluded that people from ethnic minority groups receive poor treatment as a result of their racial or ethnic origin in all of the following areas: patient reception and handling; clinical consultation; patient consent to medical treatment; nursing care; and health surveillance and diagnosis (McNaught, 1988: 58–9).

The experiences of a black woman suffering from sickle-cell anaemia (a disease specific to certain ethnic groups) illustrates the effects racism can have on an individual. This woman has clearly suffered what McNaught classifies as 'offhand treatment' in nursing care:

> I said to a Senior Staff Nurse, 'They're never going to believe me'. After the blood transfusions, injections, and everything else, I was still in a load of pain. They just couldn't understand it! In the end they started giving Pethidine to me through the vein, because they realized the injection wasn't getting to me any more! So they contradict themselves . . .
>
> I met a man in hospital, we were on the same ward for a couple of days. He appears to have had no trouble. My brother goes to a different hospital admittedly, but their attitude is completely different, they take him a lot more seriously. They know that when he's in pain, when he asks for an injection, asks for help, he needs it! More often than not it's, 'Do you need . . .', 'Are you in pain . . .'. Whereas I had to demand, and maybe two hours later I'd get it. By then I was in double the pain – so that's what they call being 'hysterical'!? Being left in pain! (Smartt, 1983: 20)

This quote suggests the importance of distinguishing experiences of racial minorities by gender, but systematic studies on whether black women receive greater discrimination than black men remain to be carried out.

The women's health movement

The women's health movement began with the premise that women's health is political and that it is necessary to challenge those who set themselves up as 'experts' and sit in judgement over us. It is possible for women without medical training to learn enough to challenge professionals. This knowledge can be shared in small discussion groups. Knowledge sharing is important because it gives individual women power over their own lives. This has helped women to take preventive measures often not addressed by the medical profession. The white middle-class women who founded the movement aimed to spread knowledge to enable women to choose whether or not to become mothers: the 'right to choose' was a key slogan of the movement. They argued that such a choice would enable women who were not suited to motherhood to lead happier lives: all women would have the freedom to discover their special talents and strengths. So the women fought legal restrictions on abortion, imperfections in contraceptives, poor sex education, and poor health care services that prevented women from having the key control over their own bodies.

The book *Our Bodies, Ourselves* (Boston Women's Health Book Collective, 1989), which has become a feminist classic, provides an excellent example of the women's health movement at work. The writers say:

> For us, body education is core education. Our bodies are the physical bases from which we move out into the world; ignorance, uncertainty – even, at worst, shame – about our physical selves create in us an alienation from ourselves that keeps us from being the whole people that we should be. (Boston Women's Health Book Collective, 1989: 11)

At its beginning, those in the women's health movement were generally white, middle-class and able-bodied. Since then, many other voices have become audible: black women, older women, lesbian women and differently abled women. The proliferation of campaigns at grassroots level by women with different needs is mirrored in the health handbooks that are now available for women (Shapiro, 1987; Hepburn and Gutierrez, 1988; White, 1990). These illustrate that white middle-class women's campaigns to ensure women's right to choose not to become a mother address only one among many health matters concerning women. As women, we can share common ground in talking about our bodies, health and medicine, yet we do inhabit different bodies; our experiences and needs depend on the nature of this body and how it is perceived by others.

Issues in the Politics of Women's Health

In the past, women's health issues were confined to matters concerning reproduction. Now feminists consider all health issues by gender. This part of the chapter has two sections. First, we look at birth control, abortion and reproductive technology under the heading 'Reproductive rights'. Second, mental health, an issue concerning both women and men, is examined from women's perspective.

Reproductive rights

Fertility control is usually a positive thing for women if it is controlled by women themselves, and if it serves to increase the choice women have over whether and when to have children. However, there have been many cases of the abuse of birth control and abortion, and many feminists today are suspicious of the new reproductive technologies when they are controlled primarily by a male-dominated medical profession. We stress the fundamental interconnection of birth control, abortion and reproductive technology through the themes of control and choice.

Birth control

Women have had to fight for the right to contraception. At the turn of the century the law stood in their way. In 1877 birth control campaigners Annie Besant and Charles Bradlaugh were tried in England for publishing a pamphlet on sex and contraception; the court said it was obscene (Banks and Banks, 1964). In 1916, Margaret Sanger was arrested for opening the first American birth-control clinic. Over five hundred mothers attended the clinic in the nine days before it was raided and closed as a 'public nuisance' (Corea, 1985: 132). The needs and demands of women were ignored by the men in office.

The following extract is taken from a collection of letters written by working-class women in the early twentieth century, describing the great hardships that resulted from a life of continual child-bearing and child-rearing.

> [My husband's] earnings was £1 a week; every penny was given to me, and after paying house rent, firing, and light, and clubs, that left me 11s. to keep the house going on; and as my little ones began to come, they wanted providing for and saving up to pay a nurse, and instead of getting nourishment for myself which we need at those times, I was obliged to go without. So I had no strength to stand against it, and instead of being able to rest in bed afterwards, I was glad to get up and get about again before I was able, because I could not afford to pay a woman to look after me ... About two months before my [sixth] confinement the two youngest fell ill with measles, so I was obliged to nurse them, and the strain on my nerves brought on brain-fever. All that the doctor could do for me was to place ice-bags on my head. Oh, the misery I endured! My poor old mother did what she could for me, and she was seventy years old, and I could not afford to pay a woman to see after my home and little ones; but the Lord spared me to get over my trouble, but I was ill for weeks and was obliged to work before I was able ... my life was a complete misery. (Davies, 1978: 18–19)

This woman bore eleven children alive and had two miscarriages: birth-control would indeed have improved her life.

Birth control should be and has been liberating for women in many ways. Women have achieved greater sexual freedom and greater control over their lives: in Britain today, women can choose when to have a baby. Birth control can, however, be used against women's interests. Policies about birth control can be used as a means of social control. If the development of new methods of contraception is left in the hands of a male-dominated medical professional, women's health may be adversely affected. If forced on women, birth control deprives women of choice about their reproductive lives.

Too often governments or Western organizations have tried to introduce heavy-handed birth-control policies in developing countries, failing to take account of the views and culture of the indigenous population. This passage describes the situation facing some women in Central America:

> Rather than being able to make informed choices about what birth control might be appropriate to them, women have been the objects of population control programmes promoted by planning agencies (usually foreign). One year that might mean the Pill, another the coil, another year, injections of Depo-Provera. Most controversial of all is enforced sterilization. Clinics have been allocated quotas for sterilization which they must meet in order to ensure continued funding. (El Salvador and Guatemala Human Rights Committee, 1993)

Abortion

Debates about abortion have ranged over many different issues, including ethics (see box 8.1 on the 'Abortion law debate' on pages 172–3). In this section we will focus on the power of the law and its implications for women. Laws against abortion have been the target of feminist campaigns since the 1970s because they are a clear expression of male control over women's bodies. Laws against abortion do not stop abortions from happening: they simply criminalize the act, push abortion underground and endanger women's lives. Women are forced into abortions in some States (one form of control) and in others are criminalized for having abortions (another form of control). Both methods take away women's choices.

You can examine these issues of control and choice in relation to abortion in the novel *The L-shaped Room*, published in 1961. Author Lynne Reid Banks describes the situation of single woman Jane Graham who finds herself pregnant and unmarried in London. Although she is 26 and in a good career (an assistant public relations officer), she still has to hide her pregnancy from friends and family and to find accommodation away from her parents (the L-shaped room). Abortion was in most cases illegal until 1967 but Jane was openly offered it by a private Wimpole Street doctor, whom she visited for a pregnancy test. He said the law could be evaded if he signed a certificate to say she was 'psychologically unfit'. He told her the operation would cost 100 guineas.

I stood up and the room rocked for a moment. I felt a bubble of nausea come up into my throat. I closed my eyes, and swallowed, and felt better. I picked up my coat which was over the back of the chair.

'Where are you going?' the doctor asked sharply.

I held on to the back of the chair and looked at him. There was so much to say that I couldn't find words for any of it.

'Well now, look here,' he said in an altered voice. 'I can quite see it might be difficult for you to get hold of a lump-sum like that, especially if you can't turn to the man for help. I'm always so afraid of what you silly little girls will rush off and do to yourselves . . . You must realize I have certain basic costs to meet, but in the circumstances I can waive my own fee, and my colleague would do the same, I'm sure. Let's say sixty guineas all-in. There, what could be fairer than that?'

My mind was suddenly as cold and clear as ice-water. I said, 'One thing could be.'

'What's that?'

'You could make some effort to find out whether I'm really pregnant before you charge me sixty guineas for an operation that might not be necessary.'

His face didn't change but his hands paused about the business of polishing his lenses.

'You might even stop to ask me if I want to get rid of my baby, if there is a baby.' I clutched the back of the chair with both hands. I could feel a fever of choking beginning in my wrists and knees. 'But I suppose when all those guineas are at stake, nothing else seems important.' (Banks, 1961: 35)

Jane refuses an abortion at first, then telephones the doctor's practice, leaving a message that she has changed her mind. Her conversation with the receptionist is overheard by an older fellow tenant, Mavis, 'an elderly and upright spinster', who tells her that the doctor is a known crook. Jane is shocked when Mavis indicates there may be a cheaper alternative:

I was staring at her as if she were turning into a witch in front of my eyes. I felt faintly hypnotized.

'What are you suggesting?'

'Oh, nothing wrong dear,' she said, giving me a clear-eyed look of total innocence. 'Don't think that. But you know, there are ways, without any sort of tinkering about. Now, look here.' She picked up her heavy knitting-bag and took out a half-bottle of gin and a small tin of Nescafé – only it wasn't Nescafé, because it rattled. I had a good idea what was in that. It was the gin that surprised me. It was a good brand. Did Mavis drink? Where did she get the money? Again as if she read my thoughts, she said: 'After I heard you talking on the phone, I nipped out and bought this – you can pay me back, if you like. Mother's ruin. Now you know why they call it that – one reason anyway. Of course, you have to drink lots of it – "lots and lots, no tiny tots," as they say.' She tittered genteelly . . . The whole situation was so grotesque, so funny and so preposterous. 'Nothing wrong, dear!' Oh no, nothing at all wrong. It was all just like being given a new recipe or a knitting pattern. (Banks, 1961: 163–4)

EXERCISE

Answer these questions on the extracts from *The L-shaped Room* by Lynne Reid Banks.

1. What was the doctor's attitude to Jane and her predicament?
2. What was Mavis's view?
3. What were Jane's choices?
4. In what ways do you think Jane's experiences would have been different if abortion had been legal?

EXERCISE RESPONSE

Although Jane is an educated woman, the doctor calls her a 'silly little girl' in a way that is sexist and patronizing. As a male professional he is aware of the power he has and he uses it to try and exact money from Jane. Mavis thinks she is helping but, like the doctor, she has a very fixed idea about what Jane should do. Neither stops to ask Jane if she wants the baby or to discuss the possibilities with her.

Throughout history women have used and shared the knowledge of methods of abortion and contraception, ranging from herbalism and old wives' tales to acts of violence on their own bodies. It is this traditional female world that is referred to here. Mavis is described as a 'witch' whose spells and remedies seem sinister to Jane. But to Mavis, passing on such knowledge is like passing on a 'recipe or a knitting pattern'. Unwanted pregnancy is a common problem for which women have developed their own strategies and solutions.

Jane's choices are extremely limited and she has no proper information on any of them. The doctor offers her the choice of a hygienic abortion in exchange for a large sum of money and a permanent medical record of mental illness. On the other hand, Jane could look for a back-street abortion which might be cheaper, avoids the black mark on her medical record, but is much more dangerous. Mavis offers her an inexpensive remedy which has no guarantee of causing abortion and which might simply damage the foetus instead. Jane decides she wants to have the baby despite the heavy social stigma attached to unmarried mothers. Because of her single status she is forced to hide her pregnancy and is treated like a 'little girl' by the doctor to whom she turns for advice.

If abortion had been legal, easier to arrange and available on the NHS, then perhaps Jane would not have had her baby. You might see this as 'wrong' and an argument for making abortion illegal again. On the other hand, legalizing abortion can serve to give a woman better choices which are more informed and less pressurized. As we have seen from Jane's experiences, making abortion illegal doesn't stop it happening: it simply pushes it underground, puts women in danger and makes us susceptible to the manipulations of others. Because abortion was illegal, Jane was unable to discuss it properly with anyone, and was left in ignorance and confusion about her pregnancy. If abortion had been legal she could have made an informed decision to have her baby, feeling that she was in control.

When *The L-shaped Room* was written, abortion was a criminal offence in England and Wales, punishable by anything from three years' to life imprisonment. In 1967 this changed. The 1967 Abortion Act says a legal abortion (performed by a doctor) can take place if two doctors agree 'in good faith' that either:

(a)   the continuation of pregnancy would involve risk to the life of the pregnant woman or an injury to the physical or mental health of the pregnant woman or any existing children, greater than if the pregnancy were terminated, *or*

(b)   there is a substantial risk that if the child were born it would suffer from such physical or mental abnormalities as to be seriously handicapped.

This does not mean that a woman has a 'right' to abortion in England. It is up to two doctors to decide whether she fits into one of these categories; there are still a few doctors who refuse to agree to abortion under any circumstances. Attempts are being made, all the time, to erode women's access to legal abortion in England and Wales. In 1967 abortion was allowed to take place up to twenty-eight weeks after conception. Bills to amend the Act were defeated in Parliament in 1975, 1977, 1979, 1986 and 1988. The time limit on abortion was finally reduced to twenty-four weeks by the Human Fertilisation and Embryology Act 1991, although later abortions remain permissible if continuing the pregnancy will result in permanent injury to the woman's health.

The problem of access to abortion is very disturbing if we look at it in global terms. It has been estimated that about 200,000 women die in the world every year through unsafe, illegal abortions. Most of these deaths occur in developing countries (McLaurin et al., 1993). Where contraception is illegal or insufficiently available, women are forced into a cycle of continual pregnancy which, compounded by poverty and hard work, leads to acute sickness and despair. Illegal abortion, however dangerous, is the only alternative for many women.

In China a strict state family planning policy aims to restrict the size of families to one child only, in order to control the increase in the total population. In the cities women are forced to have an abortion if they become pregnant again. In the countryside, grassroots officials and their task forces 'seek out pregnant women and perform forced abortions'; this is often followed by compulsory sterilization (Bose, 1992).

Because women are seen as second-class citizens, the birth of a male child is valued more highly than that of a female child. It is now possible to find out the sex of your child before birth and in some places this has led to parents deciding to abort female foetuses. It is clear that in India and China selection in favour of male foetuses, differential neglect of girl children and female infanticide have been carried out to such an extent that the sex ratios of the populations of these countries are now out of balance. This is so dramatic in China that of the 205 million single people over 15 years of age there are nearly 300 men for every 200 women. In India the ratio is about 266 single men for every 200 single women (Shenon, 1994). The position is made worse in China by the strict population policy of the government. These are examples of abortion being used against females: mothers who want more children are forced into abortions; and future female children are denied life because of their sex.

BOX 8.1	## The Abortion Law Debate

Throughout the world, legislation on abortion (termination of pregnancy) attempts to define:

(a) Whether and in what circumstances abortion is permitted.
(b) By whom it may be carried out.
(c) What the time limit should be, that is, the number of weeks after conception during which abortion can take place.

Debates on these points tend to centre around two positions, which are often regarded as diametrically opposed:

(a) The 'pro-choice' position which emphasizes the rights of a woman to control her own fertility
(b) the 'pro-life' position which emphasizes the rights of the foetus.

Woman's Body, Woman's Right

Lobby groups, such as the National Abortion Campaign (NAC) in Britain, were set up to fight for the total repeal of abortion legislation. The aim of the pro-choice lobby is to give every woman the right to make her own decision to continue or to terminate pregnancy and the right of free access to information on the subject. Abortion should be a woman's own moral dilemma, not one which the State has prejudged for her. The pro-choice lobby also stresses that, in States where termination is banned or restricted, illegal 'back-street' abortions still take place in circumstances which are hazardous to women's health.

The Rights of the Foetus

Pro-life organizations – such as LIFE and the Society for the Protection of the Unborn Child (SPUC) in Britain – aim to reduce, and ultimately remove, access to legal abortion. They argue that the foetus is a living being in itself, and that to abort a foetus is murder. Abortion, for them, is an issue in which the State must intervene because the silent foetus cannot speak for or defend itself.

The Time Limit

Views differ as to when a foetus can be regarded as a being with individuality separate from the mother. Here are just three points of view:

1. Roman Catholic doctrine teaches that a life begins and is sacred from the moment of conception. All abortion is therefore morally and spiritually wrong.
2. Some people argue that, since a foetus has a nervous system and is sensitive to pain after six to eight weeks, then this should be the time limit for legal abortion.
3. Others argue that a foetus should be seen as part of the mother's body until it reaches the stage of development when it could theoretically survive outside the mother's body. It is difficult to establish what this actually means. In a few cases babies have lived, with extensive medical support and sustenance, when born after just twenty weeks of pregnancy.

Reproductive technology

At the same time as women in developing countries are sometimes being forced to limit reproduction, women in the West are being offered the luxury of medical intervention to 'cure' problems of infertility, to give them the 'right of motherhood'.

Here are just some of the hormonal therapies and laboratory techniques that have been developed to treat infertility:

- Artificial Insemination by Donor (AID). Sperm from a male donor is introduced into the woman's vagina, near the cervix, using a syringe.
- In-vitro Fertilization (IVF). The woman is given hormones to make her 'superovulate' or produce more than the normal one egg per month. An operation is carried out to remove the eggs, which are fertilized in the laboratry and then planted in her womb.
- Surrogacy. One woman agrees to carry a child for another. In the USA this is enforced by a legal contract between the two parties, usually involving payment of money. The surrogate mother may or may not be the genetic mother of the child. In some 'rent-a-womb' situations, a fertilized egg from another woman is planted in a surrogate mother's body.

For feminists the debate centres on whether reproductive technologies (either all or some of them) are oppressive or liberating to women. Do medical developments in the fields of gynaecology and embryology free women by giving the infertile the chance to give birth? Or do these techniques, designed primarily by the male medical establishment, simply turn women into 'baby machines' or 'wombs on legs'? What are the pressures exerted in society which make a woman feel 'incomplete' if she cannot give birth?

These are difficult questions to answer because the control of reproductive technology is not always in the same hands. AID can be carried out by any woman in her own home with relative ease. Lesbian health groups in Britain and the United States carry out their own AID and pass information on self-help to other women. No one can prevent a woman finding a male friend to donate sperm and administering AID to herself. However, when IVF and similar treatments are administered by traditional medical institutions single women and lesbians tend to be excluded in favour of married middle-class heterosexual white women. Ann Oakley (1984) has quoted a report of the Royal College of Obstetricians and Gynaecologists' Ethics Committee on in-vitro ferilization and embryo replacement and transfer:

> In considering whether or not doctors are obliged to treat everyone who wants the new technique [IVF], the Committee voices 'grave reservations' about use in circumstances that are not those of a 'stable heterosexual "marriage" '. (Oakley, 1984: 283)

Many feminists are sceptical about the claims made by the medical establishment:

> In the case of in-vitro fertilization – hailed as a 'miracle cure' for infertility – feminist research has clearly shown that IVF is a failed technology. It does not work: out of 100 women who enter an IVF programme only 5 to 10 have a chance of leaving with a baby . . . biased reporting of success also obscures the fact that IVF

presents serious risks to the health of the woman. The 'hormonal cocktails' administered to superovulate them, that is to stimulate the ovaries so that they will
produce more than one ripe egg per month, bring with them the risk of burst
ovaries. (Arditti, Klein and Minden, 1989: xii)

As well as needing to consider the known and unknown health risks to mother
and child associated with the new reproductive technologies, we need to think
about the attitudes to women inherent in the whole enterprise of developing
reproductive technology. For example, Gena Corea has voiced her concern that
women will be reduced to reproductive objects within the capitalist system
(Corea, 1988).

Certainly, today in the United States people pay women to be surrogate
mothers, and pay for fertile eggs. It could be argued that women have a right to
sell their reproductive capacity and parts as much as they have a right to sell their
'labour' in other spheres of economic activity. Might it be best to accept that the
technology is with us to stay (even though we might wish it had never been
developed), that it is firmly embedded within capitalist relations, and that what
must be done is to improve the pay and conditions of women who choose to work
in this trade?

Infertile women who do successfully conceive and bear children through IVF
programmes are generally ecstatic. It cannot be denied that some individual
women receive immense individual benefit from these technologies. Feminist
arguments which criticize the developments suggest, however, that these individual benefits are outweighed by the suffering experienced by women who do not
conceive, by the dangers of unknown consequences of the programmes, and by the
damage done to all women by the continuing ideological emphasis the programmes give to biological motherhood as the be-all and end-all of women's lives.
What do you think?

Mental health

Women and the mental health services

Women are more likely than men to come in contact with the mental health
services in the West. In 1986 in Britain, there were 482 females per 100,000 and
364 males per 100,000 of the population admitted to hospital for psychiatric care.
Women in general are also more likely to report psychological distress, especially
depression, than men (Ussher, 1991). However, such statistics are very difficult to
interpret. It is unclear whether or not they indicate that women in fact are more
mad than men or whether women are more likely to be classified as mad. There
is an influential stream of thought in the West dating back centuries which
considers women are naturally more unstable than men. Others argue that in our
society women do indeed have more mental health problems than men, but that

this is because of gender inequalities and tensions, not because of any natural difference.

Given that a significant number of women do receive medical treatment for mental health problems, let's look briefly at some information about the ways women are treated. It has been argued by many critics of the practices of the mental health services that their function is to silence the protest of the mad. R. D. Laing (1967) has called madness 'a perfectly rational adjustment to an insane world' (quoted in Ussher, 1991: 147). Feminists have added a gender dimension to such critiques. They have suggested that most traditional treatment of women for mental health problems is designed to stifle any complaints women may have about the circumstances of their lives, and to ensure that women adjust to the role that is expected of them (Ussher, 1991).

Women are more likely to be prescribed anti-depressive drugs than men (Wheeler, 1994). Among those diagnosed as depressed, women are between two and three times as likely as men to receive electric shock treatment (ECT) (Showalter, 1987). It comes with a price. ECT can cause long-term memory loss, disorientation, confusion and woolly thinking. It has been argued that women are more likely to be given such treatment because' "they are judged to have less need of their brains" ' (quoted in Ussher, 1991: 174).

At its worst, the power imbalance in relationships between mental health practitioners and women has led to physical abuse of the patients. In mental hospitals, where women are the majority of patients, sexual abuse can sometimes occur when male staff have control over women patients. Even if direct rape is not involved, the treatment of female psychiatric patients by male nurses can be sexually intimidating. As one patient described an event she witnessed in her ward:

> I've seen a woman who'd just found out that she'd lost access to her son, so she was upset and started throwing things around. And out of nowhere were six male nurses, you know, big men. I couldn't believe it. They stripped her. Why they stripped her I don't know. I was absolutely still with fear. They injected her and were laughing because she passed out with fear before they got the syringe out of her bottom. (Harding and Stiles, n.d.: 6)

Women who are not white, middle class and heterosexual can face additional problems. Lesbian women (and women who choose celibacy) can be faced with therapists who seek to 'cure' them by re-orienting their sexuality. The diagnosis of a woman's central problem as being the lack of male sexual contact can be extremely insulting and reduces a complex situation in a simplistic way. Sexual preference is not the only 'problem'. Working-class women living in urban areas are three times more likely than professional women to suffer from depression (Whitehead, 1992) and if they seek help, are more likely to be dismissed with a prescription for psychotropic drugs rather than being provided with the support services they need (Ussher, 1991).

Immigrant groups share with women a greater likelihood of admission to psychiatric hospitals in Britain. A 1989 study concluded that black people (both men and women) are diagnosed as schizophrenic on their first admission to a psychiatric hospital between four and ten times more frequently than whites (Wheeler, 1994). Erica Wheeler (1994) has highlighted the lack of mental health services for black and ethnic minority women in one health district in Britain. Black writers argue that it is the racism and ethnocentrism of the psychiatric services that explain these differences.

Femininity and mental illness

If we look historically, we can see how ideas about appropriate femininity contributed to definitions of women's mental health, and to the creation of different 'cures' for alleged mental illness in women.

An example from the nineteenth century is provided by the experience of Charlotte Perkins Gilman – an outstanding American feminist – with the 'rest cure' invented by Silas Weir Mitchell. When his patients showed the symptoms of 'neurasthenia' (a nineteenth-century classification of one kind of mental illness in women) – loss of weight, anxiety, and depression – he ordered them into his clinic. This description of the 'cure' by Elaine Showalter begins with Mitchell's own words. The women received:

> 'a combination of entire rest and of excessive feeding, made possible by passive exercise obtained through steady use of massage and electricity.' For six weeks the patient was isolated from her family and friends, confined to bed, forbidden to sit up, sew, read, write, or to do any intellectual work, visited daily by the physician, and fed and massaged by the nurse. She was expected to gain as much as fifty pounds on a diet that began with milk and gradually built up to several substantial meals a day. (Showalter, 1987: 138–9)

Charlotte Perkins Gilman was a brilliant writer and lecturer who suffered, in her words, from 'a severe and continuous nervous breakdown tending to melancholia – and beyond' for many years after her marriage and the birth of her first child (Gilman, 1913: 19). She was prescribed the 'rest cure' then sent home with the advice 'to "live as domestic a life as far as possible," to "have but two hours' intellectul life a day," and "never to touch pen, brush, or pencil again" as long as [she] lived' (Gilman, 1913: 20). Sticking to these instructions made her even worse. With the help of a friend she decided to disobey the doctor:

> I cast the noted specialist's advice to the winds and went to work again – work, the normal life of every human being; work, in which is joy and growth and service,

without which one is a pauper and a parasite – ultimately recovering some measure of power. (Gilman, 1913: 20)

She was then able to write a short story called *The Yellow Wallpaper*. This is in the form of a journal, describing vividly a woman's descent into the abyss of mental illness, made worse by her doctor husband's order to rest and do nothing except take fresh air, gentle exercise and eat as much as possible. She is under strict orders not to write, but confides to her journal secretly. In the story, the couple are staying in a country house for three months in order to aid the woman's recovery. They occupy the nursery at the top of the house, chosen by him because it is large, airy and has plenty of light. Gilman is here making the point that the rest cure turned the patient into a child instead of encouraging her to full adult responsibility. The nursery walls are covered in yellow wallpaper which, as the three months progress, becomes an increasing obsession for the central character. At the beginning the writer of the journal discusses other matters, the house, the garden, the view, what her husband is doing and saying, but the narrowness of her world quickly becomes evident. Description of the wallpaper becomes more and more dominant, until the central female character becomes part of the very story she has woven about the paper:

Hurrah! This is the last day, but it is enough. John is to stay in town over night, and won't be out until this evening . . .

As soon as it was moonlight and that poor thing began to crawl and shake the pattern, I got up and ran to help her.

I pulled and she shook. I shook and she pulled, and before morning we had peeled off yards of that paper . . .

I declared I would finish it today! . . .

I don't like to look out of the windows even – there are so many of those creeping women, and they creep so fast.

I wonder if they all come out of that wallpaper as I did?

But I am securely fastened now by my well-hidden rope – you don't get me out in the road there!

I suppose I shall have to get back behind the pattern when it comes night, and that is hard!

It is so pleasant to be out in this great room and creep around as I please!

I don't want to go outside. I won't, even if Jennie asks me to.

For outside you have to creep on the ground, and everything is green instead of yellow.

But here I can creep smoothly on the floor, and my shoulder just fits in that long smooch around the wall, so I cannot lose my way.

Why, there's John at the door! . . .

'What's the matter?' he cried. 'For God's sake, what are you doing!'

I kept on creeping just the same, but I looked at him over my shoulder.

'I've got out at last,' said I, 'in spite of you and Jane. And I've pulled off most of the paper, so you can't put me back!'

Now why should that man have fainted? But he did, and right across my path by the wall, so that I had to creep over him every time! (Gilman, 1892: 17–19)

A physician in Kansas wrote to Gilman after the publication of this story to tell her that it was the best description of incipient insanity he had ever read, and enquired politely whether Gilman 'had been there' (Gilman, 1913: 19). Gilman had grippingly depicted the slow deterioriation of the mind of a creative, intelligent and imaginative woman condemned to do nothing: she wove a world for herself out of the meagre fabric with which she was provided. At the same time the story is a moving metaphor for the imprisonment of all women: 'Sometimes I think there are a great many women behind ... But nobody could climb through that pattern – it strangles so; I think that is why it has so many heads' (Gilman, 1892: 15). Yet later, there appears some hope. The women escaped during the daytime: there were many of them, but they were still 'creeping', yet they managed to do this 'fast'. The end is brilliant: her complete descent into madness – identifying herself with the wallpaper and the fantasy she had created about it – also stands for her liberation: the only route of escape from the torture of the rest cure was to be found in the sanctuary of insanity.

The Yellow Wallpaper is an artistic representation of a key idea we are presenting in this section, that certain aspects of women's condition in society contribute to the level of unhappiness among women. The 'rest cure' was simply an exaggerated version of the life all middle-class women were supposed to lead. The nameless 'I' in *The Yellow Wallpaper* could stand for every woman locked into the meaninglessness of middle-class Victorian female existence, the gentle but firm John for every husband and every father determined to keep their women in this position.

While some circumstances of women's lives have changed since Victorian times, *The Yellow Wallpaper* continues to have relevance today. Those working to achieve understanding of women's mental illness suggest that the social construction of femininity contains so many irresolvable contradictions and constrictions that the possibility of women achieving healthy mental stability within this framework is severely compromised.

Conclusion

Both Nawal El Sa'adawi in Egypt and Annie Besant in Victorian Britain were denied knoweldge about menstruation and sexuality. The effects this had on both women illustrate two key points we have made in this chapter. First, to achieve and maintain good health, knowledge about our bodies and health is essential. And second, the society women live in influences the way we feel about our bodies.

Understanding of health and illness as socially produced highlights the importance of looking at where power lies in medicine. The domination of mainstream medicine by white men has sometimes led to key women's health matters being under-researched and underfunded. Sometimes the implications of major diseases for women are played down. In terms of gynaecology and obstetrics, mainstream medicine has been too invasive. Sometimes women and those from ethnic minorities are discriminated against by mainstream medicine.

Criticisms such as these led women in the women's liberation movement in the 1970s to seek a feminist analysis of women's health. Feminists have tried to spread knowledge about women's health matters so that individual women are empowered. Many issues have been addressed. In this chapter we have discussed reproductive rights and mental health.

Early second-wave feminism stressed the importance of a woman's 'right to choose'. Women in the late-nineteenth and the first part of the twentieth centuries had to fight to make contraception available for women. More recently, women have campaigned for and gained in many countries the de-criminalization of abortion. These changes have certainly improved many women's life choices. However, black women's voices within feminism drew attention to the abuses of fertility control. Discussion in this chapter of some women's experiences in China and Central America follows that perspective: when fertility control is forced on women it is often against women's own interests. Recent debates about the new reproductive technologies raise related issues. Some infertile women claim they have a 'right to choose motherhood' at any cost. However, some feminists have suggested that there are many dangers inherent for women as a whole in IVF programmes as they are currently carried out.

Our discussion of mental health further highlighted the ways in which the social construction of femininity affects women's health. The constraints and contradictions within notions of appropriate femininity, both historical and modern, make the achievement of healthy womanhood extremely difficult.

However, we want to end with a picture that is not entirely bleak. Feminist understanding of the politics of women's health has led to the creation of many alternative treatments and therapies for both physical and mental illness. The health handbooks discussed in this chapter are a good place to start finding out more about what is available.

REFERENCES

Arditti, Rita, Duelli Klein, Renate and Minden, Shelley (eds) 1989: *Test Tube Women: What Future for Motherhood?* London: Pandora Press.

Banks, Lynne Reid 1961: *The L-shaped Room.* London: Chatto & Windus.

Banks, J. A. and Banks, Olive 1964: *Feminism and Family Planning in Victorian England.* Liverpool: Liverpool University Press.

Bellos, Alex 1994: Women set up fund to prosecute zealous surgeons. *Guardian*, 24 September, 3.

Besant, Annie 1893: *An Autobiography*. London: T. Fisher Unwin.

Bose, Ajay 1992: Who believes in a woman's right to choose: India. *Guardian*, 11 August, 15.

Boston Women's Health Book Collective 1989: *The New Our Bodies Our Selves*. British edition edited by Angela Phillips and Jill Rakusen. Harmondsworth: Penguin.

Bullough, Vern and Voght, Martha 1973: Women, menstruation and nineteenth-century medicine. *Bulletin of the History of Medicine*, 47, 66–82.

Bury, Judy, Morrison, Val and McLachlan, Sheena (eds) 1992: *Working With Women and AIDS: Medical, Social and Counselling Issues*. London: Routledge.

Campbell, Rona and Macfarlane, Alison 1987: *Where to be Born: The Debate and the Evidence*. Oxford: National Perinatal Epidemiology Unit.

Corea, Gena 1985: *The Hidden Malpractice: How American Medicine Mistreats Women*. New York: Harper Colophon.

Corea, Gena 1988: *The Mother Machine*. London: The Women's Press.

Critchley, Laurie 1992: Women and AIDS: why ignorance is far from bliss. *Guardian*, 21 May, 36.

Daly, Mary 1979: *Gyn/Ecology*. London: The Women's Press.

Davies, Margaret Llewelyn (ed.) 1978: *Maternity: Letters from Working-women*, collected by the Women's Co-operative Guild. London: Virago reprint. [First published 1915.]

Dyer, Clare 1994a: Removal of womb leads to charge. *Guardian*, 24 September, 3.

Dyer, Clare 1994b: Teacher sues leading gynaecologist for negligence and assault over removal of her ovaries. *Guardian*, 16 August, 4.

El Salvador and Guatemala Human Rights Committee 1993: Information sheet 'Health' in *Gathering Strength: Women in Central America* information pack. London: El Salvador and Guatemala Human Rights Committee.

Gilman, Charlotte Perkins 1892: The Yellow Wallpaper. *New England Magazine*, January. Reprinted in Ann J. Lane (ed.), *The Charlotte Perkins Gilman Reader: The Yellow Wallpaper and Other Fiction*, London: The Women's Press, 1981.

Gilman, Charlotte Perkins 1913: Why I wrote 'The Yellow Wallpaper'. *The Forerunner*, October. Reprinted in (ed.) Ann J. Lane, *The Charlotte Perkins Gilman Reader: The Yellow Wallpaper and Other Fiction*, London: The Women's Press, 1981.

Harding, Jenny and Stiles, Jenny n.d.: *Women's Health and Mental Illness*. London: London Women and Mental Health Group (broadsheet).

Hepburn, Cuca with Gutierrez, Bonnie 1988: *Alive and Well: A Lesbian Health Guide*. New York: The Crossing Press.

Laing, R. D. 1967: *The Politics of Experience*. Harmondsworth: Penguin.

Laws, Sophie 1990: *Issues of Blood: The Politics of Menstruation*. London: Macmillan.

Laws, Sophie with Hey, Valerie and Eagan, Andrea 1985: *Seeing Red: The Politics of Premenstrual Tension*. London: Hutchinson.

McLaurin, Katie E., Senanayake, Pramilla, Toubia, Nahid and Ladipo, O. A. 1993: Post-abortion family planning: reversing a legacy of neglect. *Lancet*, 30 October, Vol. 342.

McNaught, Allan 1987: *Health Action and Ethnic Minorities*. London: Bedford Square Press, for the National Community Health Resource.

McNaught, Allan 1988: *Race and Health Policy*. London: Croom Helm.

Martin, Emily 1987: *The Woman in the Body: A Cultural Analysis of Reproduction*. Milton Keynes: Open University Press.

Mihill, Chris 1993: *WHO* warns women of AIDS spread. *Guardian*, 8 September, 3.

Oakley, Ann 1984: *The Captured Womb: A History of Medical Care of Pregnant Women*. Oxford: Basil Blackwell.

Roberts, Helen (ed.) 1990: *Women's Health Counts*. London: Routledge.

Sa'adawi, Nawal El 1980: *The Hidden Face of Eve: Women in the Arab World* (trans. and ed. Dr Sherif Hetata). London: Zed Press.

Shapiro, Jean 1987: *Ourselves, Growing Older*. London: Fontana.

Shenon, Philip 1994: Lonely Chinese face uphill search for Ms Right. *Guardian*, 17 August, 18.

Showalter, Elaine 1987: *The Female Malady: Women, Madness and English Culture, 1830–1980*. London: Virago.

Showalter, Elaine and Showalter, English 1972: Victorian women and menstruation. In Martha Vicinus (ed.), *Suffer and Be Still: Women in the Victorian Age*, Bloomington: Indiana University Press.

Smartt, Dorothea 1983: Sickle cell anaemia: women speak out. *Spare Rib*, 126, January, 19–22.

Smith-Rosenberg, Carroll 1974: Puberty to menopause: the cycle of femininity in nineteenth-century America. In Mary Hartman and Lois W. Banner (eds), *Clio's Consciousness Raised*, New York: Harper and Row. Reprinted in Smith-Rosenberg (1985) *Disorderly Conduct: Visions of Gender in Victorian America*, Oxford: Oxford University Press.

Torkington, Ntombenhle Protasia Khotie 1983: *The Racial Politics of Health: A Liverpool Profile*. Liverpool: Merseyside Area Profile Group, Department of Sociology, University of Liverpool.

Ussher, Jane 1991: *Women's Madness: Misogyny or Mental Illness?* Hemel Hempstead: Harvester Wheatsheaf.

Wheeler, Erica 1994: Doing black mental health research: observations and experiences. In Haleh Afshar and Mary Maynard (eds), *The Dynamics of 'Race' and Gender: Some Feminist Interventions*. London: Taylor & Francis.

White, Evelyn C. (ed.) 1990: *The Black Women's Health Book: Speaking for Ourselves*. Seattle: The Seal Press.

Whitehead, Margaret 1992: *The Health Divide*. Harmondsworth: Penguin (published together with *The Black Report*, the whole volume titled *Inequalities in Health*).

CHAPTER
9 Friendship

Jennifer Coates

Plate 9 © Negotiating Friendship. Sally and Richard Greenhill.

In this chapter I shall look at the concept of friendship and, in particular, I shall try to tease out exactly what friendship means for women. It's one of those concepts we don't think about much, an aspect of our lives that we just take for granted. In order to start thinking about the concept, we shall look at evidence from a wide range of different societies, and will examine the claim that female friendship differs from male friendship. When you reach the end of this chapter, you will probably feel differently about the idea of friendship, and it may cease to be such a taken-for-granted part of your life. You will have learned about friendship in different cultures and at different points in history, and will have been introduced to various theoretical frameworks which attempt to make sense of the facts in different ways.

We all have friends. And I imagine we all think friends are important: life would be significantly worse without them. But what makes a good friend? And how exactly do we define friendship? The following extract is taken from the diary of a fourteen-year-old girl, and is part of an account of a weekend spent at the home of her best friend, Gina. Read it, then think of the friends you had in your early teens and answer the questions that follow the extract.

Extracts from a teenage diary:

February 1 1957

. . . In Bilge & Music sat with Gina. French dragged. Longed for end of day. Lost homework notebook. Gina cross – she thought we'd miss bus. Boy on 31 just like John Owen – he was the only decent one. Gina & I giggled & tried to make jokes with Chamberlains. Walked home. Gina explained our row. It was all my fault really. Chops for tea Brussel sprouts Ugh. Mrs Jones said I could stay till Monday. Floogey . . . Gina & I read diaries to each other. Whitened gym shoes. Talked about Sybil and Adrienne. Gina smashing and friendly. Am writing this in Gina's bed.

February 3 1957

. . . Went to Pott Shrigley in car. Climbed hill & walked along canal. 3 decent boys. Gina & I chattered and were silly. Tied our shoelaces together. Saw lovers. Had decent tea – poached egg on toast. Washed hair. Gina shy. Invented word: Ishish = putting on act. Mr & Mrs Jones tried to guess. Listened to Redgauntlet. Gina in trouble cos she came in to my room to do diary. Did skiffle group. I made scale of jam jars. It was super.

EXERCISE

Now think of an episode from your own girlhood when you spent time with a friend or friends. What did you do? Make a list of the things you used to do with your friend as a teenager. Did you have a 'best friend'? What was special about this relationship? Can you put your finger on what made being with your best friend (or a close friend) enjoyable? Spend a little time thinking about this.

EXERCISE RESPONSE

Compare your list of activities, and your summary of what was special about your relationship with your best friend, with the account given by Helena Wulff in her report of a long-term study of the lives of twenty adolescent girls in South London (Wulff, 1988). She spent time with them at the Youth Club, on the street corner, at school and in their homes. She describes the typical activities of the girls as: talking, listening to music, hanging around the street corner, going swimming, ice-skating, bowling, going shopping (or just window-shopping), going to the cinema, discos, parties. You will probably want to add things to this list – for example, I spent a great deal of time just going for walks with friends, round the block or in the local park. These activities are not exotic; they are part of the everyday fabric of teenage life: what counts is doing things together.

Wulff describes best friendship as follows:

> But some friendships were more important than others; the 'best friend' was more than an ordinary friend. The essential meaning of best friendship for the girls was to have someone to whom they could tell secrets and be sure nobody else would find out about them. Secrets mainly concerned clandestine events and those boys whom the girls admired covertly. But a best friend was also someone to have fun with, to the point of 'being stupid' with, as the girls said. The affective feature of friendship . . . is that a friend comprehends you and elucidates you to yourself; a person can see himself [*sic*] reflected in a friend. (Wulff, 1988: 74)

There are three key points here; check whether these match your sense of what is central to friendship:

(a) you can trust your best friend with secrets (the diary writer says: 'Gina & I read diaries to each other' – diaries are not normally shown to anyone)

(b) you can 'be stupid' with your best friend (the diary writer calls it 'silly': 'Gina & I chattered and were silly. Tied our shoelaces together.' Tying your shoelaces together – so that you have to walk as in a three-legged race – is a good example of 'being stupid')

(c) you get to know yourself better and thus strengthen your sense of your own identity through seeing yourself relected in your friend (Gina and her friend mirror each other's confused feelings about boys, minor struggles with authority figures, conformity to school norms, interests in language and writing etc.).

Our examples so far have all related to girls rather than women. Is friendship important throughout women's lives? And are the three points listed above, together with the enjoyment of doing things together, still relevant for older women, or are there other characteristics of friendship that we need to consider?

The following extract describes the friendship of two older women, and is taken from a study of London elderly Social Services clients carried out by Pat O'Connor (1992).

Older friends:

Helen Brown is a 79-year-old housewife ... Apart from a touch of arthritis, Helen's health is still quite good ... The day-to-day 'bread and butter' of affection and intimacy in her life is provided by Vera, her
5   71-year-old card-playing friend of thirty years' standing. Helen describes her as 'a lovely person, a lively, happy, healthy person'. She says of her: 'She's all I've got'. Vera lives just ten minutes away from Helen. Helen says that she would feel 'terribly
10 lost' if she moved: 'My life would be terribly lonely, it would be a blank' ... 'We are proper pals. We can trust each other. She knows that she can come around any time she likes' ... They are together at the luncheon club on Tuesday and Friday afternoons, at
15 Bingo on Tuesday evening, at a local whist drive on Wednesday evening ('we've done that for thirty years'), and in their own homes on Monday, Friday and Saturday afternoons ... 'We can tell each other anything. We can trust each other. If I want anything she'll give it, if
20 she wanted anything, I'd give it to her.' 'There's nothing that I'd do or be ashamed of that I can't talk to Vera about' ... The relationship with Vera is identity enhancing in the sense that Vera sees her as 'the sort I am'. However, it also contributes to
25 Helen's sense of her own self-worth indirectly because Helen sees Vera as someone who has done well in

life . . . 'as a woman to a woman I admire her. She's all
the things I would like to have been and I haven't got
the guts'. (O'Connor, 1992: 133)

EXERCISE

Read through this account of friendship between two older women again, checking for
the four criterial features identified earlier: shared activities, trust, 'being stupid',
enhanced sense of identity. After you've done this, compare what you've found with the
summary below.

EXERCISE RESPONSE

Shared activities — the account mentions the lunch club, bingo, whist and talking ('we
can tell each other anything').

Trust — it is clear that this is an important component of Helen and Vera's friendship:
Helen says: 'we can trust each other' (lines 11–12); 'we can tell each other anything. We
can trust each other.' (lines 18–19).

'Being stupid' — we can infer from Helen's statement — 'There's nothing that I'd do
or be ashamed of that I can't talk to Vera about' — that the friends are able to self-
disclose about their most foolish moments; there is nothing in the passage to tell us
whether 'being stupid' in the sense of having fun together to the extent of making
idiots of themselves is a feature of their friendship.

Sense of identity — this was obviously an important ingredient in the friendship, to
judge from what the passage tells us about Helen: 'The relationship with Vera is
identity enhancing in the sense that Vera sees her as 'the sort I am'.

Up to now, I have assumed that female friendship is a reality — that you, the
reader, have experienced significant friendships in your life — both as a girl and as
a woman. This is certainly true for me, the writer (the diary extracts come from
my old diary). But some theorists dismiss the idea of serious friendship between
women. In order to consider the different theoretical positions taken on the subject, let's look at an extract from an article by Dorothy Jerrome (1984) which
summarizes three of these. Read the passage, and then do the exercise which
follows.

Three views of women and friends:

There are three views about women's capacity to make
and keep close friends ... According to one, which
corresponds with a popular stereotype, women are
naturally incapable of forming bonds with each other.
5   They are competitive and distrustful. Unlike men, who
bond naturally with a sense of inborn camaraderie,
women have emotionally superficial and precarious
relationships with their own sex. The cartoon
caricature of women's friendships – the suburban
10   clique engaged in recipe-exchanges and coffee drinking
– is a reality. It is rooted in the biological
characteristics which make women the 'natural'
home-makers and child-rearers, the nuclear family the
basic unit of human social groups, and same-sex
15   friendships secondary to the heterosexual pair-bond.

According to another view of women's friendships, this
situation exists because it is convenient in a
male-dominated society. If women do not form and
sustain close friendships it is because they have been
20   socialized to be dependent on men at the expense of
their relationships with other women. Recent social and
demographic changes such as rising divorce rates and
women's employment have exposed the situation and
indicated the need to restructure intimate
25   relationships. In particular, women's solidarity and
independence from men need to be fostered.

A third approach, which combines historical,
developmental and functional perspectives, stresses the
strength and pervasiveness of female friendship.
30   Contrary to popular opinion, women of all ages have
always made intimate relationships with other women and
derived many benefits from them. This fact has been
overlooked in much sociological and historical
literature, and women themselves have been encouraged
35   to devalue their friendships. This has been the case in
America particularly in the twentieth century. The task
facing the Women's Movement, in this view, is not to
teach women how to be friends but to restore legitimacy
to women's friendships ... so that both women and men can
40   take them seriously. (Jerrome, 1984: 710–11)

EXERCISE

Let's examine the three positions presented in this extract. What are the key words or phrases in each of the three paragraphs?

EXERCISE RESPONSE

The position summarized in the first paragraph is that women are incapable of close friendship with other women because of innate biological factors. Key words are: natural/naturally (lines 4, 6, 12); inborn (line 6); biological (line 11).

The position summarized in the second paragraph is that women are socialized into not valuing relationships with women and prioritizing (heterosexual) relationships with men. Key words/phrases are: male-dominated society (line 18); socialized (line 20).

The position summarized in the third paragraph is that friendships between women are, and always have been, strong, but that both historical and contemporary accounts have neglected this aspect of women's lives. Key words/phrases are: strength and pervasiveness (line 29); always (line 31); restore legitimacy (line 38).

You may have picked out other important words or phrases; the ones I have mentioned are not the only ones. As you'll have noticed, the position put forward in both the first and the second paragraphs assumes that women don't have strong friendships, but position two is in agreement with position three over the importance of female solidarity. So we can see that position two is an intermediate position, between one and three.

So how do we evaluate these different positions? The evidence we have looked at so far suggests that female friendship does exist, and is important for women. Here's the view of Erica Tate, chief protagonist of Alison Lurie's (1974) novel *The War Between The Tates*. Erica is a typical 1960s middle-class American woman: she has a college degree and is now married to Brian (an academic); they have two children and live in a large house on the edge of a university town. She is aware of a growing dissatisfaction with her life; a crucial factor in her increasing self-awareness is her friendship with the more radical Danielle. In this passage, Erica ponders the meaning of friendship:

> Men are often jealous and suspicious of friendship between women, though they value it among themselves. According to Danielle's feminist friends, this is because

it contradicts their idea of women as lacking the political virtues, as desiring neither liberty, equality nor fraternity. ('You notice you never hear anyone talk about sorority.') We are held to be capable of devotion to our husbands and children, but catty and competitive with all other women, without true affection for them.

Whereas the truth is, as anyone can see, that women are far better friends to each other than men are. We are not naturally selfish and aggressive, and we do not have to be. Brian is directly in competition with his 'friends' in the Political Science Department here, and indirectly with those elsewhere. ... Only rarely, as with Leonard Zimmern, can he have a friendship untainted by either rivalry or calculation – and then it must lack professional intimacy, for Leonard is in another field. Women, however, are all in the same field, yet not in competition. Brian must hoard his ideas for publication; but if she [Erica] passes on a new recipe she earns her friends' gratitude and loses nothing. (Lurie, 1974: 161).

In the first paragraph of this extract, Erica examines a position very like position one above, where women are viewed as innately incapable of friendship with each other, because of their predisposition to nurturing husbands and children. She discards this in favour of what we have called position three: i.e. she asserts the reality of female friendship in women's lives. (Note that she makes the strong claim that it is men who are 'naturally' incapable of friendship – we will return to this point later.)

Let's turn from fiction to fact, in order to build up a picture of what women's friendships are like. In the next section of this chapter we'll look at evidence from different periods of history and from a variety of cultures. In particular, we'll try to establish whether there are characteristics of female friendship which hold good across time and space.

We'll look first at two examples of women's friendships in the past, one from England, the other from America.

Women's Friendship in Seventeenth Century England

The following verses are from a poem written by Katherine Philips (1631–1664), which appears in 'Poems by the most deservedly Admired Mrs. Katherine Philips, The Matchless Orinda' (1667). Katherine Philips was admired by her contemporaries for her poetry in which she expressed her friendship for 'Lucasia' (Anne Owen). She was viewed as a model of the perfect romantic friend; men at the time saw such relationships as ennobling. Thomas Heywood wrote that love between women 'tends to the grace and honor of the Sex' (for a fuller account see Faderman, 1985: 68–71).

To my Excellent Lucasia, on our Friendship

I did not live until this time
  Crown'd my felicity,
When I could say without a crime,
  I am not thine, but thee . . .

For as a Watch by Art is wound
  To motion, such was mine:
But never had Orinda found
  A Soul till she found thine . . .

No Bridegrooms nor Crown-conquerors mirth
  To mine compar'd can be:
They have but pieces of this Earth,
  I've all the World in thee.

The poem expresses strong feelings, feelings we associate more usually with love poetry between women and men. In the first verse, 'Orinda' says that until she became friends with Lucasia she was not really alive ('I did not live until this time . . .'); and the claim 'I am not thine but thee' is a very strong statement of the merging of two selves often claimed in a close relationship. In the second verse given here, the writer compares her former self to a watch, implying that she was just an efficiently working machine until she met her 'soul' in Lucasia. In the final verse Orinda compares herself to bridegrooms and conquerors, archetypally successful men; she claims that what they have gained is only a bit of the world, while she by comparison, in gaining Lucasia, has gained the entire world. Let's turn now to a period two hundred years later, in America.

Women's Friendships in Nineteenth Century America

In the USA in the late eighteenth and early nineteenth centuries, gender roles were far more rigid, and women and men inhabited virtually separate worlds, with men's lives going on largely *outside* the home, and women's lives being centred *inside* the home. The historical evidence suggests that women had very strong ties with other women, both with female relations (of the same and of different generations) and with female friends. Intimate relationships between women were in no way taboo, and women's letters and diaries of the period show that women felt able to express strong affection for each other openly. The following extracts from the letters of two nineteenth-century women are taken from the work of Carrol Smith-Rosenberg (1975), who analysed the letters and diaries of women and men in 35 families between the 1760s and 1880s in America.

Sarah Butler Wister met Jeannie Field Musgrove in the summer of 1849 when Jeannie was sixteen and Sarah fourteen. They then spent two years together in boarding school and developed an enduring friendship. The quality of this friendship can be sensed from the following brief extracts from their correspondence. After Sarah married, Jeannie used to go to stay regularly. In a letter inviting Jeannie to stay (written in 1864) Sarah writes: 'I shall be entirely alone [this coming week]. I can give you no idea how desperately I shall want you . . .'. After one of these visits, Jeannie writes to Sarah: 'Dear darling Sarah How I love you & how happy I have been You are the joy of my life . . . I cannot tell you how much happiness you gave me, nor how constantly it is all in my thoughts . . . My darling how I long for the time when I shall see you . . .'. In another letter, Jeannie writes to Sarah: 'I want you to tell me in your next letter, to assure me, that I am your dearest . . . I do not doubt you, & I am not jealous but I long to hear you say it once more & it seems already a long time since your voice fell on my ear. So just fill a quarter page with caresses & expressions of endearment. Your silly Angelina.' Angelina was the name adopted by Jeannie in much of their correspondence; Sarah used a masculine nom de plume.

What strikes us most when we, reading at the end of the twentieth century, examine these two examples of women's friendship in the past is the intimacy revealed. Today, such strong expressions of friendship would be regarded with suspicion by members of our more homophobic culture. There are much stronger taboos today relating to behaviour in same-sex relationships: it is not normally acceptable to express strong affection either verbally or physically.

Now we'll look at the evidence from different cultures. The first example comes from nineteenth-century China (so provides us with historical as well as cross-cultural evidence); the second comes from Crete.

Chinese Marriage Registers

In the Guangdong (anglicized as Canton) regions of China, a particular type of female friendship known as Sworn Sisterhood (or Blood Sisterhood) emerged in the early nineteenth century with the particular social and economic conditions involved in the development of the silk industry. Women's key role in that development (primarily as spinners and weavers) meant that they could be economically self-sufficient. It is estimated that perhaps 10 per cent of Cantonese women remained unmarried in pre-Communist China. These women have been named 'marriage resisters' (Raymond, 1986). According to Janice Raymond, there were two types of marriage resisters – the *pu lo-chia* and the *tzu-shu nu*.

> Both types often formed societies of six to ten members who designated themselves by titles such as 'never-to-wed' or 'all-pure'. They were generally made up of pairs of

sworn sisters. *Pu lo-chia* is the Chinese term for women who were forced to marry but who did not consummate the marriage or cohabit with their husbands. It literally translates as 'not going to the family', meaning the family of the husband, as all Chinese women became members of their husband's family . . . The second type of resister was the *tzu-shu nu*, literally translated as 'never to marry'. This type became known as 'self-combers', women who comb or arrange their own hair. It was traditional at a Chinese women's marriage that her long single plait of hair was bound up into a bun. The *tzu-shu nu* put up her own hair. This 'self-combing' demonstrated to society that the non-marrying woman's life was to be lived 'as if married', that is, she could not be engaged to any man and her lifestyle was as sacred and honorable as that of a married woman. That 'never-to-marry' women took their unions with each other seriously is well exemplified in the ceremonies that marked the occasion of their coming together. A hairdressing ceremony initially signalled the woman's intention to leave home, and it was treated like a marriage ritual. As one *tzu-shu-nu* in Singapore explained, 'It is really like a marriage ceremony and the couple swear everlasting friendship and mutual help'. (Raymond, 1986: 131–2)

The following account describes the experience of Lady Hosie (Dorothea Soothill, a nineteenth-century traveller in China), who developed a strong friendship with two Chinese women. This extract starts at the point when one of the Chinese women proposes to Lady Hosie that they should become Blood Sisters:

'Shu Hua and I have been Blood Sisters for many years, as you know,' Blossom explained. 'Shu Hua spoke to me two nights ago in bed and asked me if I would consent to make you a Blood Sister with us, and my spirit was full of joy at this. First you shared our troubles, and then there was the long waiting in the Law Court, and finally we shared joy and peace together at Ch'ien Lung's Pool: so Shu Hua said that you are certainly our sister already in soul, and it is fitting you should become one by the correct rites.' [This refers to a ceremony involving readings, prayers, blessings and incense.] I could feel her soul calling to my soul, and I knew she was asking herself if any foreign women, not to mention myself in particular, had sufficient sobriety in her character to endure the implications of the Oath of Friendship. (Hosie, 1948: 157–8)

According to Hosie, the ceremony ended with the prayer 'that there might be nothing but truth between us'.

The next example comes from a society contemporary with ours, but very different in its culture.

Women's Friendships on Crete

Robinette Kennedy spent a year on the island of Crete, studying women's friendships in a small village at the western end of the island (Kennedy, 1986). In this small village, everyday tasks are strictly divided according to gender. Women and men spend little time with each other and there is a great deal of animosity between the sexes. Men have more independence than women, and spend most of their time outside the home. Women, by contrast, spend most of their time in the home and feel cut off from the outside world. The women Kennedy talked to use the word *androcratia* (= rule by males) to describe their position. As one woman said: 'Men rule. There are many things we cannot do because we are women. For instance, we want to go to Chania [the local town]. We have to go and ask our husbands, "Will you permit me?" . . . And if he says "No", then we can't go.' The women expressed a longing for freedom, but were resigned to the status quo. One of them said: 'If I had the 250 drachmae for the boat passage to go to Athens . . ., which I don't, then where can I go? What can I do there? Nothing. Which shall I be: a maid or a whore? So I am better off here. I have my house, there is plenty of horta [= wild greens] in the hills, fruit on the trees, so I am better off here.'

According to Kennedy, one way that women cope with the harshness of their lives is through female friendship. 'Women's friendships are both a powerful coping mechanism and a unique expression of special energies that are not adapted to the dominant culture' (Kennedy, 1986: 127).

> Women . . . consider the practicalities involved in carrying on a future friendship, for example, the proximity of a potential friend's house and whether it is in the same neighbourhood. It is not considered correct social behaviour to be outside one's neighbourhood for a purpose not recognized by mainstream culture, and visiting a woman friend is not supported by the dominant culture. This proscription means that visiting often must occur in relative secrecy, either in someone's kitchen while men are in the fields or at places like the village springs while women are performing laundry tasks. Moreover, unlike men, who have the social institution of the kafeneion, women have no place or time specifically designated for social intercourse and relaxation. Even while gathered under shade trees in the late afternoon to rest before beginning their evening chores, most women and young girls are sewing handwork to be included in somone's dowry or to be sold in Chania.
>
> . . . Once a friendship is begun, the relationship is seen as adding a positive dimension to a woman's life, making it happier and more interesting. The course of friendship . . . is regarded as a similarly positive experience. The reason, say the women, is because of their deliberate cultivation of the relationship – keeping secrets, trusting, understanding, and being good to each other. Many women explained to me that in their everyday lives they experience incongruity between how they feel and how they must behave in order to conform to social norms. The quality of their lives improves, however, when they have a friend, and they value the unique feelings they experience when they are with their friend, for example, the feeling of being understood, and of being able to speak openly and tell their secrets and problems to someone else. Being able to express themselves openly with a friend enables them to experience emotional and behavioural congruency, an experience they claim is rare in their everyday lives.

Women spoke of the transformative quality of friendship – being with a friend changes a mundane talk such as baking into one of pleasure and intimacy ... In addition, their identity is affirmed and they may feel understood, believed in, comforted. (Kennedy, 1986: 129–30)

EXERCISE

Now you have read these four examples of women's friendships in different cultures and/or at different points in history, do you think the evidence supports position one ('women are biologically incapable of close friendship'), or position two ('women don't have close female friends because they've been socialized into dependence on men'), or position three ('women's friendships have always been significant, but they have been ignored by historians and other researchers')?

EXERCISE RESPONSE

The evidence of all these passages, from different historical periods and from a variety of cultures, is that women do have female friends, and that these friendships are a significant part of women's lives.

Now that we've established our position on women's friendship, let's look again at the concept of friendship.

Friendship: A Gendered Concept?

So far I have used the term friendship as if it were synonymous with female friendship. But clearly the term friendship is also used to refer to certain male relationships. Are male friendships similar to female friendships? Or are there significant differences between women and men in terms of the kinds of relationships they have with members of their own sex?

EXERCISE

Read Erica Tate's account of women's and men's friendships again (pages 190-1), concentrating on the second paragraph. Make two columns, one headed 'Women' and the other 'Men', and note down the key words and phrases used in this paragraph to describe women and men and their relationships.

EXERCISE RESPONSE

Compare your lists with these:

Women	*Men*
not selfish	in competition
not aggressive	rivalry
all in the same field	calculation
not in competition	
pass on recipe	hoard ideas

These words and phrases sum up Erica's view, which is that women have good friendships while men have difficulty in getting close to each other. (Note that her view of the poverty of men's friendships directly challenges the claim that men 'bond naturally' which was put forward in position one.) She claims that women's relationships are characterized by co-operativeness, while men's are characterized by competition. This claim depends on another claim: that men are rivals at work, while women 'are all in the same field' yet not rivals. Is such an extreme position fair?

Let's look briefly at the evidence. We have little evidence so far about the nature of men's relationships with each other, though one important difference emerges from the cultures we have discussed: men tend to inhabit the public sphere, the world outside the home (this is true both for nineteenth-century America and twentieth-century Crete) while women are largely confined to the domestic sphere (though this was not true of the Cantonese silk workers who became Sworn Sisters). As a result, in most cultures, an important aspect of women's friendships is that they are carried on inside the home; men's friendships, on the other hand, are carried on in the public world outside the home. You will recognize the following description (taken from a contemporary American novel) of the typical setting for women to 'do friendship'.

> My friends and I always sit in each other's kitchens when we visit so we'll be near the coffeepot, the liquor bottles, the food and the telephone. When we really settle

down to talk we always go into the kitchen. It's in there that we excavate our old memoirs and explicate their meanings. It's there that we examine ancient confidences, as if they were poems, and reassemble memorable incidents from our pasts. Sometimes we talk substantively about our work, but most often we play with gentle visions of ourselves, trying out different images just as we do when we try on each others' new clothes. More and more often now we can anticipate each others' conclusions about most subjects. That's nice. (Raskin, 1988: 120)

Contemporary accounts of male and female patterns of friendship (Pleck, 1975; Johnson and Aries, 1983a, b; Miller, 1983; Seidler, 1989; O'Connor, 1992) suggest the following contrasts:

Women's friendships *are characterized by:*	*Men's friendships* *are characterized by:*
intimacy – 'face-to-face'	sociability – 'side-by-side'
mutual self-disclosure	self-disclosure rare
focus on *talk*	focus on *activity*
context = home	context = pub/sports club/etc.

Let's look at these contrasts in more detail. The distinction between intimacy and sociability comes from the work of Joseph Pleck (1975). He argues that, in the case of the American male, friendships are sociable rather than intimate. 'Male sociability is closely connected with male sex-role training and performance and is not characteristically a medium for self-exploration, personal growth or the development of intimacy' (Pleck, 1975: 233). Stuart Miller says in the preface to his book on men's friendships: 'Most men ... will admit they are disappointed in their friendships with other men ... [these] are generally characterized by thinness, insincerity, and even chronic wariness' (Miller, 1983: xi). The findings of these American researchers are echoed by Victor Seidler, a social theorist working in Britain. Seidler argues that 'masculinity is an essentially negative identity learnt through defining itself against emotionality and connectedness (Seidler, 1989: 7), and goes on: 'We [i.e. men] learn to identify our sense of self so strongly with our individual achievements and successes in the public world of work that we do not realize the damage this may do to our capacities for open and loving relationships with others' (p. 18).

Fern Johnson and Elizabeth Aries carried out a study to investigate the meaning of friendship for American adults. They gave a questionnaire on same-sex friendship to 176 college students, as well as interviewing twenty women and twenty men in a New England city. Their findings support those of other researchers. About men, they say: 'To the degree that activity, behavioral exchange, and light conversation replace [*sic*] a deeper sharing between male friends, their abilities to articulate personal concerns and to engage close friends in the solving of personal problems is probably diminished' (Johnson and Aries, 1983b: 235). One of the most interesting findings of their study was that talk is 'the substance of women's friendship' (Johnson and Aries, 1983a: 354). This is supported by Valerie Hey's (1988) research on adolescent girls' friendships in West London schools: 'They did their friendship through the practices of day-to-day talk' (p. 392).

If you ask girls or women what they do with their friends, they will say 'We talk', whereas men will mention activities: playing a sport, or going to the pub, or going to watch a football match. This doesn't mean that men don't talk, of course, but talk seems to have a less significant role in men's friendships. Not only does talk seem to be a key component of women's friendship, the talk is of a particular type: intimate and self-disclosing. The following are some quotations from Johnson and Aries' female informants:

> 'I can discuss things with her – whatever – that I don't with other people . . . things that involve something personal.'

> 'If I've got a problem and I want someone to talk to, I'd go to her.'

> 'I feel when I'm with her . . . I can say whatever I want to.'

> 'You can't talk to your husband the way you can to your best girlfriend. I wish I could.'

One of my women informants, in a similar survey, said: 'the friendships that I've made have always been around, you know, sort of straight talking, vulnerable talking, and it's exchanged vulnerable talking.' Whereas one of my male informants said: 'I think it's sad that men can't express what they feel.'

We've looked at some of the differences between women friends and men friends: now we need to try and place these differences in an explanatory framework. In other words, why do women and men 'do friendship' differently?

We'll look at two explanations. The first is psychological in origin, the second sociological. They are presented in boxes 9.1 and 9.2. Read the boxes and then do the exercise which follows.

Explanatory Theory 1: Connection and Separateness

BOX 9.1

One explanation for gender differences derives from the work of Nancy Chodorow, in particular her book *The Reproduction of Mothering* (1978). Chodorow argues that gender identity is formed within the psychodynamics of the family, and in particular that gender differentiation can be explained in terms of the child's initial relationship with its mother. All over the world, it is women who have primary responsibility for early childcare. So girls are cared for by – and experience their first intense feelings of love and hate for – a caretaker of the same sex. Boys, on the other hand, are cared for by, and experience their first intense feelings for, a caretaker of the opposite sex. So a boy's development is marked by discontinuity: he has to define himself against his mother, as not feminine, while girls develop in connection with the mother. As Chodorow says: 'The basic feminine sense of self is connected to the world, the basic masculine sense of self is separate' (Chodorow, 1978: 169). Connected and separate are key terms in Chodorow's work. (You can refer back to box 2.1 on 'Theories of identity formation', pages 18–20, and the discussion in chapter 3, pages 46–7, for further elaboration of Chodorow's work.)

In terms of same-sex friendship, Chodorow's theory allows us to predict that women's friendships will typically be more intimate: women are uncomfortable with separateness, and tend to define themselves in relation to others. Women's need for connection with others is fulfilled in part by friendship with other women. Men, on the other hand, are threatened by intimacy: they are uncomfortable with connectedness and define themselves as distinct from others. Friendships with other men are therefore characterized by more impermeable boundaries and less closeness.

BOX 9.2

Explanatory Theory 2: Social Structure – Patriarchy

This theory draws attention to the wider context of patriarchy and to male dominance in society. In a patriarchal society where men are dominant and women subordinate, same-sex friendships, it is argued, like other social relations, will perpetuate existing social structures. One researcher on female friendship suggests that 'the maintenance of an intimate style of relating amongst females and a non-intimate one amongst males reflects and ultimately reinforces power relationships between the sexes' (O'Connor, 1992: 33). In other words, men's friendships are as they are because men need to defend their position of dominance and cannot afford to expose themselves to their (potential) rivals. Women, on the other hand, have nothing to lose from expressing their vulnerability. Like oppressed groups the world over, they develop solidarity with each other as a way of ameliorating their daily lives. But their friendships do not challenge the status quo: on the contrary, their friendships with each other make them more content with their lives.

Some researchers even argue that female friendship is a necessary adjunct to marriage. Based on her work on the friendships of a group of middle-class, elderly women in Sussex, England, Dorothy Jerrome (1984) argues:

> Friendship is vital as a counterpoint to marriage. The meetings provide light relief, time-off from the performance of marital roles, an escape from one aspect of conventional femininity – the need to be acceptable to men. However, it should not be thought that the women's friendships compete with their commitments to husbands and families. The exclusiveness and solidarity of the group is in no sense threatening. On the contrary it promotes existing gender roles by providing moral support and advice for their performance. Conventional values are confirmed and a conservative ideology of marriage is upheld. (Jerrome, 1984: 710)

EXERCISE

Attempt to assess the value of these two explanatory theories. How far does each of them account for the evidence we have looked at in this chapter? Ask yourself the following questions:

1. What is the strength of Chodorow's theory in relation to gender differences in friendship? What are its weaknesses?
2. What is the strength of the theory of patriarchy in relation to gender differences in friendship? What are its weaknesses?

EXERCISE RESPONSE

The strength of Chodorow's theory is that it gives us constructs – connection and separateness – to explain gender differences in friendship patterns. Its weakness is that it remains at the level of the individual and ignores issues of dominance and oppression. The second approach, by contrast, focuses on dominance and oppression, and explains gender differences in same-sex friendship by reference to social structures. The main weakness of this approach is that, while it acknowledges the strength of women's friendships, it sees them as a conservative rather than as a potentially subversive force.

In the final section of this chapter, I'll examine the case for viewing female friendship – and friendship in general – as a liberating force.

Women's Friendships – A Radical Perspective

Far from being a relationship that helps to perpetuate the status quo, some argue that friendships between women are potentially liberating. The evidence we've looked at is mixed: on Crete and in nineteenth-century America, women's friendships helped them to tolerate their lives in male-dominated societies. So, in a sense, they served to maintain the smooth running of those societies. But the Blood Sisters in nineteenth-century China were clearly resisting rather than helping to perpetuate normal social practices. And Erica's friendship with Danielle, in Lurie's novel *The War Between the Tates*, is the starting point in her struggle to break out of the conventional mould.

Like Lurie, many twentieth-century women writers argue that female friendship can be a form of resistance. The friendship that develops between Celie and Shug, in Alice Walker's (1983) novel *The Color Purple*, enables Celie to talk about the terrible things that have happened in her life: through expressing her grief over these things, she is able to move on, to escape the grip of the past, and to move out of the power of men.

> Don't cry, Celie, Shug say. Don't cry. She start kissing the water as it come down side my face. . . . My mama die, I tell Shug. My sister Nettie run away. Mr. _____ come git me to take care his rotten children. He never ast me nothing bout myself. He clam on top of me and fuck and fuck, even when my head bandaged. Nobody ever love me, I say. She say, I love you, Miss Celie. And then she haul off and kiss me on the mouth.
>
> Um, she say, like she surprise. I kiss her back, say, um, too. Us kiss and us kiss till us can't hardly kiss no more . . . (Walker, 1983: 97)

Celie and Shug's friendship is expressed physically as well as in other ways. As we have seen, there is evidence from other cultures and other times that the line between female friendship and lesbianism is a very fine one. This may be an uncomfortable idea for you – you may find yourself resisting it. But it is probably true to say that we find our closest friends attractive not just in terms of their personalities and their lifestyles, but physically.

Adrienne Rich writes about the importance of coming to terms with – and redefining – the notion of lesbianism. She writes: 'It is the lesbian in every woman who is compelled by female energy, who gravitates toward strong women, who seeks a literature that will express that energy and strength. It is the lesbian in us who drives us to feel imaginatively, render in language, grasp the full connection between woman and woman' (Rich, 1980: 200–1).

Others have coined new words such as gyn/affection. This word was first used by Janice Raymond, who defines it as follows: 'female friendship . . . a loving relationship between two or more women . . . a freely chosen bond which, when chosen, involves certain reciprocal assurances based on honour, loyalty and affection' (Raymond, 1986: 9). For all these feminist writers, female friendship is something to be celebrated, and is seen as a powerful subversive force. Certainly the evidence of the Hite Report (1987) is compelling: 87 per cent of married women and 95 per cent of single women reported that they had their deepest emotional relationship with another woman. Current statistics on marital breakdown throughout the Western world suggest that traditional structures of marriage and the nuclear family are in trouble.

Some commentators see friendship as the relationship of the future. Friendship is unlike other close relationships we have in our lives: there are no formal contracts, no socially accepted rituals, no rites of passage associated with friendship. It is also unusual in that the relationship is based on equality. Even when there are differences of age or social class or ethnic background, friendship can only be sustained – will only deserve the name – if participants treat each other as equals. In other words, friendship is a symmetrical relationship. Most of our kinship relations are asymmetrical (parent–child, aunt–niece, even sister–sister since one is older and therefore has different status in the family). And it could be argued that, as long as societies construct women and men as unequal, then marriage is also an asymmetrical relationship.

Both these aspects of friendship – its fluidity as a cultural form, and the fact that it is a relationship of equals – make it a significant model for relationships in the twenty-first century. 'Friendship arguably represents the relational genre of the future' (Simmel, 1971, quoted in O'Connor, 1992: 8).

Conclusion

In this chapter, I have tried to establish what friendship is, looking at evidence from a wide range of different societies. We have examined different views of female friendship, and have looked at the evidence that female friendship differs from male friendship. We have weighed up the strengths and weaknesses of different theoretical frameworks, and have considered the possibility that female friendship is a potentially liberating force.

Each one of you will have brought to your reading different experiences of friendship, and will therefore probably come to slightly different conclusions. Once we start to think about friendship – and it is only very recently that it has been considered an appropriate topic for serious study – we begin to realize what a complex subject it is. This chapter has only covered a little of the relevant ground. I hope it has at least made you begin to think – at both the personal and the general level – about the role of friendship in our lives.

Postscript

You may have noticed that this chapter has omitted any discussion of what might be called the 'dark' side of female friendship, which has been written about so brilliantly in Margaret Atwood's (1989) novel *Cat's Eye*. I have omitted this issue because, in my view, friendship is a misnomer for this kind of interactional behaviour. What do you think? Has your experience of friendship been good (life-enhancing), or bad (manipulative/destructive)? These are questions you might like to think more about.

REFERENCES

Atwood, Margaret 1989: *Cat's Eye*. London: Bloomsbury.
Chodorow, Nancy 1978: *The Reproduction of Mothering*. Berkeley, CA: University of California Press.
Faderman, Lillian 1985: *Surpassing the Love of Men*. London: The Women's Press.
Hey, Valerie 1988: The company she keeps: the social and interpersonal construction of girls' same-sex friendships. Ph.D. thesis, University of Kent.
Hite, Shere 1987: *The Hite Report: Women in Love*. Harmondsworth: Penguin Books.
Hosie, Lady (Dorothea Soothill) 1948: *The Pool of Ch'ien Lung*. London: Hodder & Stoughton.
Jerrome, Dorothy 1984: Good company: the sociological implications of friendship. *Sociological Review*, 32, 4, 696–715.
Johnson, Fern and Aries, Elizabeth 1983a: The talk of women friends. *Women's Studies International Forum*, 6, 4, 353–61.
Johnson, Fern and Aries, Elizabeth 1983b: Conversational patterns among same-sex pairs of late-adolescent close friends. *Journal of Genetic Psychology*, 142, 225–38.
Kennedy, Robinette 1986: Women's friendships on Crete: a psychological perspective. In Jill Dubisch (ed.), *Gender and Power in Rural Greece*, Princeton: Princeton University Press.
Lurie, Alison 1974: *The War Between the Tates*. London: Heinemann.
Miller, Stuart 1983: *Men and Friendship*. San Leandro, CA: Gateway Books.
O'Connor, Pat 1992: *Friendships Between Women: A Critical Review*. Hemel Hempstead: Harvester Wheatsheaf.
Philips, Katherine 1667: Poems by the most deservedly Admired Mrs. Katherine Philips, The Matchless Orinda ('To my excellent Lucasia, on our Friendship' reprinted in H. J. C. Grierson (ed.), *Metaphysical Lyrics and Poems of the Seventeenth Century*, Oxford: The Clarendon Press).
Pleck, Joseph 1975: Man to man: is brotherhood possible? In N. Glazer-Malbin (ed.), *Old Family, New Family*, New York: Van Nostrand.
Raskin, Barbara 1988: *Hot Flashes*. New York: Bantam.
Raymond, Janice 1986: *A Passion for Friends*. London: The Women's Press.

Rich, Adrienne 1980: 'It is the lesbian in us . . .'. In Adrienne Rich, *On Lies, Secrets and Silence: Selected Prose 1966–1978*, London: Virago.

Seidler, Victor 1989: *Rediscovering Masculinity*. London: Routledge.

Simmel, George 1971: *On Individuality and Social Forces* (ed. and introduction by D. N. Levine). Chicago: Chicago University Press.

Smith-Rosenberg, Carrol 1975: The female world of love and ritual: relations between women in nineteenth-century America. *Signs: Journal of Women in Culture and Society*, 1, 1, 1–29.

Walker, Alice 1983: *The Color Purple*. London: The Women's Press.

Wulff, Helena 1988: *Twenty Girls: Growing Up, Ethnicity and Excitement in a South London Microculture*. Stockholm Studies in Social Anthropology 21, Stockholm: Department of Social Anthropology, University of Stockholm.

CHAPTER
10 Women in the Arts and Media

Joanna Thornborrow

Plate 10   Remedios Varo, *Exploration of the Sources of the Orinoco River*, oil on masonite.
© Exploration Fuentes Rio Orinoco.

There are very many different aspects we could consider with regard to the role of women in the arts and the media. For example, we could examine the role of women as producers of art and literature, or of women as 'consumers' of art and of media texts: as readers of books, as buyers, watchers, and users of television and radio, of videos. We could also look at how women are actually represented in paintings, in literature, in films, on the television screen and in advertisements. Obviously we can't deal with all of these aspects in one chapter, but I shall address at least some of them as an introduction to the topic, albeit necessarily a rather selective one. I hope you will feel able to use this initial discussion as a springboard to help you to carry out your own investigations into further related areas of reading and study.

We're going to go backwards chronologically in this chapter, starting with a look at some aspects of the position of women as readers and consumers of contemporary media texts, something that we are all familiar with, and then taking a step backwards in time to examine the role of women as writers and artists in previous centuries. So the chapter will be divided into two main parts, the first taking a contemporary perspective where we will talk about how women are represented within the media and also how they use media texts, the second a more historical perspective, in order to examine the role of women as producers of art and literature. After reading this chapter you will have become more familiar with the concept of discourse, and become aware of some of the ways that women are represented in and addressed by contemporary media discourse. You will also have gained an insight into the historical role of women in the arts world and begun to think about their position and work within literary and artistic movements.

Reading Women: Teenage Magazines

First of all let's have a look at some examples from a media genre that we have probably all come into contact with as young women: the teenage magazine. The publication that these examples are taken from, *Shout Magazine*, is aimed at a market of young teenage girls, and contains articles about pop bands and singers, pictures of and gossip about the 'stars' of the pop music scene, as well as fashion features, competitions, beauty advice, problem pages and letters from readers. The list of sentences at (1) below are taken from a feature article on a singer, Jason Orange, in the band Take That, entitled 'Are you his type?'. The second text (2) is a typical problem page letter, based on one found in the same magazine from a young teenage reader, with its accompanying reply. (For copyright reasons it is not possible to reproduce the article or letter and response in their entirety.) Read these extracts and then do the exercise following.

(1)

1.a 'If you're an Aries, Scorpio or Pisces you could be the love of Jason's life.'

1.b 'Jason won't tell any fibs so if he says he loves you, he means it!'

1.c 'As a typical Cancerian, Jason likes the traditional life, so the more wholesome recipes you know, the better! Start raiding Mum's kitchen now!'

1.d 'A sure way to make him notice you is to send him lots of cards.'

1.e 'Mrs Orange [his mother] is the special lady in his life. Hit it off with her and you'll be laughing.'

1.f 'He can be very moody so don't make a fool of him behind his back.'

(2)

2.a My obsession

Please can you help me with my problem – it's Take That. I can't help sitting in my room at home all the time watching videos of them or listening to their music. Then all I can do is cry because I know that it is impossible for me to get to know them. This makes me so angry and depressed that I take it out on my family, and when I think about people who have met them it gets even worse. I find myself having conversations with my posters of Jason. I don't want to talk to my friends any more and can't concentrate on my school work. I am taking my GCSEs this summer and I'm sure I'm going to fail every one.

My sister likes them too but she just thinks I'm crazy to be so obsessed by them. I have got tickets to their concert next month but I'm scared this will make my infatuation even worse. What can I do?

2.b Reply

Fancying someone like Jason Orange is a normal feeling at your age and something that many other girls experience. It shouldn't be making you feel so miserable and upset though, and your infatuation is obviously doing just that. Remember that you can't really get to know the boys from Take That, and that although you like and enjoy their music, what you are fantasizing about is only an image of them. Do you think that it's worth the risk to the relationships you have with your family and friends, as well as to your future school work, if this obsession takes over your life? It may sound impossible right now, but try to control your feelings and accept that you are only in love with a dream figure. There are plenty of real boys out there to get to know, and that will be lots more fun than sitting in your room with your fantasies. The real world is out there waiting for you, don't run away from it – start to enjoy it.

EXERCISE

From the extracts in (1), and the response to the letter in (2), make a list of what the reader is advised to do in each text, e.g.:

(1) 'Are you his type?'
    be nice to his mother
(2) 'My Obsession'
    don't run away from the real world

What strikes you as contradictory about the messages that the reader is being given by these texts? How useful do you think the advice given to the reader about her 'problem' is?

EXERCISE RESPONSE

In the original article as it appeared in the magazine, the title was: 'Could you be his ideal girl?'. It is inviting the reader to consider the possibility of being Jason Orange's girlfriend, giving us advice about how we should behave and what we should do to 'win him'. The letter, on the other hand, expresses the distress of a young reader due to her obsession with an unobtainable pop star. The advice she is given in the reply, to live in the real world and work hard to get over this 'crush', is in direct contradiction to the kind of things she is invited to consider as the reader of the feature article. These two extracts, appearing within pages of each other in the same issue of the magazine, illustrate some of the highly contradictory messages that adolescent girls have to deal with as readers of this particular genre of media text. If you can remember reading this type of magazine as a teenager, can you think about how you felt about them at the time?

The teenage magazine is not the only place where women are given conflicting messages about who they are and what sort of behaviour is expected of them, however. When we read. whatever we read, the text addresses us as a particular kind of reader, gives us a specific social role, and positions us in a specific relationship with 'the world' as it is represented by the text. We call these representations **discourses**. The discourse of extract (1) above sets up the reader as a potential partner for Jason, telling her the 'intimate' details of his personal life, how he feels about his mother, and what sort of person he is. The discourse of the problem page letter and its reply, however, positions the reader as an 'ordinary girl', warning her of the impossibility of really knowing the singer, and of the dangers of letting a fantasy get out of hand, and I think almost blaming the reader for this. So within the space of a few pages the reader has been positioned by two conflicting discourses, on the one hand being invited to consider the impossible, then being firmly told this is not a sensible thing to do.

You might think now about what sort of things you read at that age, and what you can remember your male contemporaries reading. If you have teenage children, what sort of things do they read? If you can, collect some examples of these texts, and try to decide how the different discourses position their readers as people in the world, just as we have done for the two extracts above. How do the discourses which address young women differ from those which address young men?

There are other kinds of contradictory pressures created by the messages women receive from the pages of magazines, the advertising media, and television. For example, the kind of discourses addressed to women often present ideal images of what we should look like, and then make us worried because we do not shape up to that ideal. Ros Coward (1984), writing about the effect of advertising and magazine images on readers, claims that women are constantly being told to see their own bodies as fragmented into different areas which can be 'worked on'. If these areas don't correspond to the 'right' shape, or the 'right' size, represented by the models in the pictures of glossy magazines, then we will not gain men's attention, and on that attention (so the story goes) depends our future happiness:

> Advertising in this society builds precisely on the creation of an anxiety to the effect that, unless we measure up, we will not be loved. We are set to work on an ever-increasing number of areas of the body, labouring to perfect and eroticize an ever-increasing number of erotogenic zones. Every minute region of the body is now exposed to this scrutiny by the ideal. Mouth, hair, eyes, eyelashes, nails, fingers, hands, skin, teeth, lips, cheeks, shoulders, arms, legs, feet – all these and many more have become areas requiring work. Each area requires potions, moisturizers, conditioners, night creams, creams to cover up blemishes. Moisturize, display, clean off, rejuvenate – we could well be at it all day, preparing the face to meet the faces that we meet. (Coward, 1984: 80)

Coward explains how women, from a very early age, are presented with fragmented images of their body, broken up into its separate parts, and then encouraged to embark upon a constant remaking of themselves (with the help, of course, of all the products mentioned above). This remaking does not always stop at the physical aspects of being a woman either, as along with cosmetic restructuring goes the remaking of personality and femininity. In the passage below, Suzanne Moore (1993) explains how women are constantly being constructed according to socially and politically determined norms, taking the example of two prominent women in American culture: First Lady, Hillary Clinton and television personality Roseanne Arnold. Commenting on one woman politician's advice to ambitious women to 'lose two stone and buy a suit', she says:

> While male politicians may have got themselves a decent suit, they are not required to make over their personalities as well. For as Roseanne has her spare parts physically removed, Hillary Clinton is having her personality cosmetically altered, to judge by the endless profiles in the American media. Hillary the cover-girl, Hillary the saint, Hillary the loving wife and mother. Forget Hillary, one of the hottest lawyers around; see her in the kitchen scrambling eggs for sick little Chelsea. All this is about as convincing as Margaret Thatcher's 'I'd rather bake cakes than drive a tank' act.
>
> Paradoxically, though, all this mannered domesticity is an attempt to show us the 'real' Hillary. This tinkering with her image, this toning down and dressing up, is no doubt the result of long thought-out strategies. A photogenic First Lady is still more important than a clever one.
>
> It is the malleability of female identity that is on show, however, with both Hillary and Roseanne. While men just are, women are continually becoming. To admit to cosmetic surgery or to being aware of one's image is always, for men, a feminizing move. These days, there is little comfort to be found in the idea of the natural. Indeed, successful women parade their transformations in public as if they were the most natural thing in the world. No one is born a 'real' woman, but hey, we get the picture. With the right light, enough liposuction and a feigned interest in the right way to scramble an egg, any of us can do a damn good impersonation of one. (Moore, 1993)

So the key themes present in these two accounts are that women are constantly being urged to rework their physical and personal image. As well as the fragmentation of their bodies, women also have to deal with the fragmentation of their social roles into separate constituent parts which are often presented as incompatible. As Moore points out above, there is an implied conflict between Hillary Clinton being a 'loving wife and mother' and her professional status as a lawyer. As a result, women are supposed to be continually engaged in a process of trying to become something or someone else, in order to suit the prevailing notions of what the 'real woman' should be like, and the prime channel for the expression of what these notions are is through the media.

Watching Women: Representation of Women in Advertisements

So far, then, we've looked at how media texts addressed to women set up these tensions between the reality of what we are and the ideal of what we are told we should be. There is another area we need to look at – that of how the media use representations of women to sell products ranging from ice-cream to cars. In the next part of this chapter we will talk about the kind of images of women that are used in advertising, and the discourses which accompany these images.

First of all, look at Figure 10.1, which is a recent advertisement for a Rover Metro car seen in the *Guardian* (11 June 1993).

EXERCISE

Try to answer the following questions on the advertisement:

1. How does the text of this advertisement create a link between the woman in the photograph and the car?
2. What kind of relationship between men and women does this advert use to sell the car?
3. What does the ethnic origin of the woman signal?

EXERCISE RESPONSE

Right, so the link between the woman and the car is created by the use of particular shared features: women, like cars, are 'noticed' and 'looked over' (i.e. they are the focus of the male gaze); they can 'attract the wrong kind of attention' (i.e. sexual interest); and they can also be 'stolen' by rivals (there is a central-locking and anti-theft alarm); they can be bought (there is a price on the woman's body). So this advert hinges on an asymmetrical, heterosexual relationship of property and ownership, through the implication that men can 'possess' this car in the same way that they can possess a woman. The fact that the woman in question is 'exotic' (to match the colour options for this car) reinforces the discourse of ownership by mobilizing a range of cultural assumptions related to racial and sexual stereotypes, particularly the domination of the white male and the sexuality of the Polynesian woman. Just imagine how the discourse of the advert would be changed if the tattoo had been inscribed on a different kind of woman, for example a white, spiky-haired punk with rows of earrings and a pierced nose.

Can you think of any car advertisements which are specifically addressed to women? If so, are there any differences between them in the way women are represented? Some adverts do address women rather than men, but not necessarily for the same type of products. Car manufacturers in particular draw on repre-

TATTOO GOOD TO BE TRUE?

Polynesian Turquoise, Pearlescent Nightfire Red, and Pearlescent Caribbean Blue.

Blink!

At £5,995, Metro Rios will certainly be noticed. But in case they attract the wrong kind of attention, the Rio Grande includes remote central locking and anti-theft alarm for just £6,795.

Inside there's a special Rio trim for the party season. And outside there's a rear wash wipe, for the monsoon season.

Look them over at your Rover dealer. But keep your shades handy.

METRO rio

Figure 10.1   Rover Metro car advertisement

Source: The Guardian, 11June 1994. Reproduced with permission from Rover Cars and LINTAS *i* (formerly KMM).

sentations of heterosexual relationships (not always as offensive as this one) to sell their products. There is an interesting comparison to be made here with a 1990s television advertisement for a Renault Clio car (Papa? Nicole?), which is constructed around a father/daughter relationship. In this advert, although the potential driver of the car is a woman, it is suggested that it is the father who buys the car for the daughter, rather than the daughter who buys it for herself. The discourse of car advertisements in general makes an interesting study into media representations of women, as they are often constructed around stereotypical background assumptions concerning the relationship between men, women, money and control. This is an area you may wish to consider in more detail.

Now that we have looked at some examples and thought about the way women are portrayed in different types of advertisements, we can discuss some theoretical positions relating to women and how they are represented in the media. In an article in the magazine *Cosmopolitan* in 1989, Judith Williamson argued that advertising techniques change to take account of the potential market, and that the hard-bitten, self-centred images of the 1980s would give way to more human, caring images in the 1990s:

> But advertising is like a barometer – it can't make the weather, but it can tell us when the weather's on the turn. I predict that the nineties will be brighter, freer, more caring and more daring than the last which I, for one, was very glad to leave behind. (Williamson, 1989)

So Williamson claims that women were portrayed as hard and self-centred in a decade that was characterized by values of individualism and self-promotion, and that those images will change as one set of values is replaced by another, different set. This idea that advertisements reflect changes that are happening in society contrasts with Ros Coward's (1984) theory that all media discourse – including advertisements, of course – works to construct social positions for us as viewers, listeners, readers, since we are constantly being addressed by texts as if we actually occupied those positions.

We can summarize these two theoretical positions as follows:

1. The media adapt to and reflect social changes.
2. The media are actively involved in the process of constructing idealized roles that women are always being urged to take up.

BOX
10.1

Theoretical Positions: Representation

We can summarize the main issues of representation of women in the texts we have been looking at so far in the following way:

First, women are frequently represented in media texts and discourses as either fragmented or incomplete in some way. We are faced with broken down images of ourselves: physical images of the body as parts to be 'worked on' as Ros Coward (1984) describes, or as somehow incomplete – being in a process of continually 'becoming', as Suzanne Moore (1993) discusses in her article on Hillary Clinton and Roseanne Barr. Our social roles are also fragmented and often represented as incompatible: for example being a scientist and being a mother are seen as mutually exclusive, whereas being a scientist and being a father are unproblematic.

Second, media discourses also set up social positions for women to occupy that are often based on stereotypical images of who we are and what we do. Because media texts are widely accessible, and play a large part in our social lives, they play an important part in constructing and reproducing these positions. Whether or not we see ourselves personally as occupying the roles that texts construct for us (the reader of a 'problem page', a 'Take That Fan'), it can be difficult to speak and be heard from different positions which challenge these stereotypes.

Third, many representations of women in media discourse, be it advertising, television, or the press, are **asymmetrical**. That is to say that there is an imbalance between the way men are represented and the way women are represented in these texts. Imagine the Metro car advertisement which used a picture of a man instead of the woman, and how this would affect the 'message' of the text.

EXERCISE

You could think about these issues in greater depth, taking as your starting point the two claims above. In the light of the arguments presented here, and by collecting evidence of your own, try to assess the two theoretical positions.

Watching Women: Women as Media Consumers

To conclude this part of the chapter, I want very briefly to discuss how women use the media. Women are consumers of media texts, in the sense that we read newspapers, watch television, rent video-tapes, go to the cinema. In a recent study into how women use television and video, i.e. what kind of videos women watch on television and when they watch them, Ann Grey (1992) found that women tended to choose 'one-off', or what she terms 'unique' films when renting videos for their own viewing, rather than select a film by genre. In other words, the women she interviewed for her study tended not to choose videos according to their classification as thrillers, Kung Fu movies, westerns, etc., but according to their knowledge of particular, 'individual' titles. However, Grey also found that this personal choice was not imposed on other members of the family, and that when choosing films for family viewing, women tended to select the type of films that would appeal to the rest of the family rather than according to their own personal preference.

Another significant finding of Grey's study is that women working at home tend to regard time taken watching television or videos as 'stolen time', and that they often felt guilty about their viewing rather than considering it as valid relaxation or leisure time. As a result, many of the women said that they often watched television or videos at the same time as doing other household tasks. (See discussion in chapter 6 on women's uses of time/space at home.) Grey makes a further observation, based on the claim that certain areas of a family's living space are 'colour-coded' for gender into blue and pink areas (for example, the garage is a 'blue area', the kitchen is a 'pink area'), while other rooms are neutral. She says that 'with the increased technologization of the sitting-room, particularly in relation to leisure and entertainment, this potentially neutral area of relaxation is also becoming 'colour-coded', (Grey, 1992: 248). If this coding is extended further to audio-visual technology, Grey suggests that there are colour-coded operating modes for the television and video recorder too, ranging from lilac for the record/ rewind/play controls, blue for the timer, and an even deeper shade of indigo for the remote control!

So Grey is saying that according to the results of her study, the space for relaxation and leisure in the home is becoming progressively more and more 'blue', i.e. the sitting-room is becoming a masculine domain, and that women frequently do not have a place where they can get away from domestic work and take control of their own leisure time. Furthermore, she argues that watching television and videos is not seen as a legitimate leisure activity, and that women's viewing often takes place at the same time as other household tasks.

Think for a minute about your own viewing patterns. When do you watch television, how do you choose what you watch, and if you have a family, do your choices correspond to theirs? If you possess a video recorder, who sets the timer?

And if you are watching television with other family members, who holds on to the remote control? Then consider whether your own experience would support Grey's conclusions.

This notion that whichever members of a household occupy particular areas of the living space, and thus to a great extent control what goes on within that space, is one that has been evoked at the beginning of the century in relation to women writers, and in the next part of this chapter we are going to look at how different kinds of space have affected the literary and artistic production of women as writers and painters.

Writing Women and Creative Space

Virginia Woolf, writing in 1929, felt that women's access to both space and time of their own was crucial for them to develop their literary and artistic potential:

> In future, granted time, books, and a little space in the house for herself, literature will become for women, as for men, an art to be studied. Women's gift will be trained and strengthened. The novel will cease to be the dumping ground for the personal emotions. It will become, more than at present, a work of art like any other, and its resources and its limitations will be explored. From this it is a short step to the practice of the sophisticated arts, hitherto so little practised by women – to the writing of essays and criticism, of history and biography [. . .]
>
> So, if we may prophesy, women in time to come will write fewer novels, but better novels; and not novels only, but poetry and criticism and history. But in this, to be sure, one is looking ahead to that golden, that perhaps fabulous, age when women will have what has so long been denied them – leisure, money and a room to themselves. (Woolf, 1929, quoted in Cameron 1990: 39–40).

The material conditions mentioned here by Woolf are one kind of space necessary to literary and artistic production. But there is also the psychological space, a kind of freeing of the mind which is necessary in order to concentrate on a different kind of work, removed from domestic concerns. Stella Bowen, a British artist who was married to the novelist Ford Madox Ford for eight years, had this to say in her autobiography about the effect of married life on her work as a painter:

> My painting has been hopelessly interfered with by the whole shape of my life, for I was learning the technique of quite a different role: that of consort to another and more important artist, so that although Ford was always urging me to paint, I simply had not got any creative vitality to spare after I had played my part towards him and Julie and struggled through the day's chores . . .

Ford never understood why I found it so difficult to paint when I was with him. He thought I lacked the will to do it. That was true but he did not realize that if I had the will to do it at all costs, my life would have been oriented quite differently. I should not have been available to nurse him through the strain of his daily work; to walk and talk with him whenever he wanted, and to stand between him and circumstances. Pursuing an art is not just a matter of finding the time – it is a matter of having a free spirit to bring it on . . . I was in love, happy and absorbed, but there was no room for me to nurse an independent ego . . .

A man writer or painter always managed to get some woman to look after him and make his life easy and since female devotion, in England anyhow, is a glut on the market, this is not difficult. A professional woman, however, seldom gets this cushioning, unless she can pay money for it. (Bowen, 1984: 82)

EXERCISE

Read both these passages again, and make a note of what you think are the key words in each one. In what ways does Bowen's account of the difficulties faced by women artists differ from Woolf's?

EXERCISE RESPONSE

Bowen describes a rather different problem from the issues of space, time and money that Virginia Woolf talks about. Bowen put her own work second to that of what she describes as 'a more important artist', a pattern which repeats itself frequently in the lives of many promising women artists of the early twentieth century. Many of them had access to training at art schools, but subsequently abandoned their career to further that of their more 'gifted' partners (cf. Greer, 1979: 54). Some of the reasons for this are evoked by Bowen in the passage above: the conflict between her role as a wife and mother, and her creative vitality, which needed space to develop her independent spirit and ego.

The Spanish painter Remedios Varo, a member of the early surrealist movement, was able to combine both a professional career as a painter and marriage towards the end of her life (though it is probably significant that she had no children and that her last husband was very wealthy). Her association with the surrealist movement started in Paris in the 1930s, where she was part of a group of artists and poets led by André Breton. She married another member of the group, the poet Benjamin Peret, emigrated with him to Mexico, and for many years earned a living painting advertisements for a drug company until her work became publicly recognized after an exhibition in 1955.

An important influence on Varo's work was her close friendship with another artist and writer living in Mexico, Leonora Carrington. The two women used to paint each other's dreams, and write together too. One of the problems she had faced as a painter within the surrealist movement was the contradiction between Breton's poetic ideal of woman as the 'femme enfant' (de Beauvoir, 1949: 375) – a 'child-woman' who never reaches maturity – and the achievement of her later work as a mature woman. Disillusioned by the surrealists and their dogma, in her later work Varo moved away from the ideology enshrined in Breton's (1924) *Manifeste du Surréalisme*, and developed her own, independent style of painting (see the illustration at the front of this chapter, 'Exploration of the sources of the Orinoco River'). This struggle to achieve self-definition, and to break free from the predominantly male power to define views of ideal womanhood, is one which is explored in depth by de Beauvoir in *The Second Sex*.

Being successful as a painter does not only depend on personal gift, however. Recognition also depends on external influences, on the people who decide what counts as art, on the people who have the money to buy paintings. We can take the example of another painter, Frida Kahlo (1910–54), who was married to the Mexican muralist Diego Rivera. Compared to Rivera, Kahlo's work had not been given much attention, particularly in Mexico, until some of her paintings were bought in the mid 1980s by the singer Madonna – a woman with enough money and consequently enough power to influence what is valued as 'good art'.

Old Masters – Old Mistresses?

How many women painters can you name? Although there have been women making a living from their art for many centuries, their number is not reflected in the canon of 'great masters' that we associate with the Western artistic tradition. The art world has been predominantly controlled by men; in France, for example, in the eighteenth century, only four women were allowed to be members of the Académie Royale de la Peinture at any one time. As Germaine Greer (1979: 6) points out, this number is completely arbitrary, and does not reflect at all accurately the actual number of women artists during that period.

Women often assisted with large-scale paintings by men without getting much credit for it. Women obtained training as artists, often working within the family tradition, but remained in subordinate positions in relation to the male artists in whose studios they worked. As a result, historically the work of women painters has often either not been recorded at all, or it has been attributed to men. There is also the issue of what kind of work women artists are mostly remembered for.

Greer, in her account of northern European commentaries on art in the early seventeenth century, notes that:

> None of them mentioned Mechteld toe Boecop, a much more considerable artist than some of those who were included, for she painted religious pictures in large format for 30 years, while other women are better known for a few sheets of scissorwork and portrait drawing. (Greer, 1979: 4)

So women artists have tended to be associated with the small scale and the intimate, rather than with the major paintings to which they frequently contributed while working for a better-known male contemporary. One artist whose name and work are the exception to this absence of women from historical accounts and commentaries is Artemisia Gentileschi (1593–1653). Gentileschi came from a family of painters and learned her skills working in her father's studio in Rome. She travelled around Europe earning a living from her painting, and was the first woman to be admitted to the Florence Academy. Although some of her work has since been wrongly attributed to her father, several of her paintings have survived and been recognized as her own work. However, her fame as a painter was matched by her notoriety at the time, and one of her most famous paintings (*Judith Beheading Holofernes*) has been interpreted as revenge for the humiliation of a seven-month rape trial during which her reputation was held up to very public scrutiny. Although her subject matter was one of the popular biblical themes of the time, the fact that such a brutal scene could have been painted by a woman has continued to shock.

So we need to consider the question of what and how women paint, and think about whether what they paint is in some way intrinsically a woman's view of the world, in the same way as writers such as Virginia Woolf and Dorothy Richardson, another modernist writing at the same time as Woolf, have claimed that sentences by women are inherently different from those of male writers because they are trying to use language to express 'a less linear conception of time and space' (Cameron, 1990: 10). Again, the difference between women's and men's literary writing is one that you might like to consider further at some stage, and a useful overview of feminist literary theory can be found in Moi's (1985) *Sexual/Textual Politics*.

EXERCISE

Here are two accounts of women's painting, one fictional, one biographical. The first is an extract from a play (written by Howard Barker) where these conflicting world views are expressed in a discussion of how a battle was portrayed by a woman painter. The second is taken from the biography of Remedios Varo, and describes the particular characteristics of her painting.

1.a
Galactia is the artist (loosely based on Gentileschi), Suffici the admiral who led the battle of Lepunto (October 7, 1571)

Suffici: She cannot be allowed to do this thing which is – in effect a calculated offence to me and to the sailors who so heroically laid down their – what is this, what are all those bodies doing – it is all bodies, everywhere with gaping – I do not pretend to be an artist but it was not like that!
(Scene 13, p. 290)

1.b
Ostensibile: Signora, we do not understand your painting.
Galactia: It is a painting of a battle at sea.
Ostensibile: It is a slaughter at sea.
Galactia: A battle is a slaughter.
Ostensibile: No. It is the furtherance of political ends by violent means.
Galactia: I showed the violence.
Ostensibile: But not the ends. So it is untruthful. The ends were the freedom of the seas, the affirmation of the Christian faith, the upholding of a principle. Why did you not paint those?
Galactia: How do you paint the upholding of a principle?
(Scene 14, p. 292)
(Howard Barker, 1990, 'Scenes from an execution')

2.
The public seemed to welcome Varo's delicacy of touch and exquisite concern for detail, enlivened by her rich sense of irony. The muralists did huge, serious paintings blazoned on public walls; Varo's canvases were intimate, often humorous, depicting personal narrative and scaled to private response. It is this private quality that is so striking in her paintings. They are quite small, very quiet, and invite the kind of personal contemplation evoked by an illuminated prayer book [. . .]. The work is not bright or flashy or broad in any way. It is intimate, both technically and thematically, and it elicits an intimate response. (Kaplan, 1988: 133–4)

First, write down what you think are the *main* characteristics of the paintings being discussed in the two texts above. Now, think about whether these characteristics could be seen as stereotypically 'feminine'.

EXERCISE RESPONSE

In the first passage, the painter's representation of the battle focuses on its violence. This view is doubly unacceptable to the male figures in the play, firstly because it shows the horror rather than the glory of the battle, and secondly, because the ability to portray such violence does not correspond to stereotypes of 'the feminine' (as we saw in the discussion of Gentileschi's work above). Varo's painting, on the other hand, is described as personal, delicate, private, intimate, small and quiet – all qualities which, as we will see, are specifically associated with women and their artistic production.

In her account of the work and condition of women artists, Greer notes that when women do paint, this is often considered as something exceptional, abnormal almost. She explains the absence of women from the records of art history in the following way:

> The unreliability of the classic references when it comes to women's work is the consequence of the commentators' condescending attitude. Any work by a woman, however trifling, is as astonishing as the pearl in the head of the toad. It is not part of the natural order, and need not be related to the natural order. Their work was admired in the old sense which carries an undertone of amazement, as if they had painted with the brush held between their toes. In a special corner reserved for freaks they were collected and disposed of, topped and tailed with compliment. By the time the next commentators came around, no one could remember why they had ever been included, they appear and disappear, leaving the serious student baffled to know whether there ever were any considerable works, let alone where they have since disappeared to. (Greer, 1979: 4)

If women's contribution to art was perceived in previous centuries as a freakish exception to the 'natural order' of male artistic creativity, it is perhaps no accident that women's contribution to literature should find its beginnings in the novel: a genre that was considered to be their 'natural' domain, and a genre that was largely 'uncolonized' by men, originating as it did with the semi-private form of letter writing, in the epistolary novel (Donovan, 1980). The novel did not require the formal rhetorical skills of what were considered to be the highest literary forms, and in the eighteenth century, sentimental fiction was particularly associated with women, and as Donovan (1980: 41) points out, again this association 'relied on stereotypes of what is the feminine'. As the novel developed in the nineteenth century, these 'natural' feminine characteristics remained central to critical accounts of women's writing. Elaine Showalter (1978) describes the Victorian attitude to women writers in the following passage.

Victorian critics agreed that if women were going to write at all they should write novels. Yet this assessment, too, denigrated and resisted feminine achievement. Theories of female aptitude for the novel tended to be patronizing, if not downright insulting. The least difficult, least demanding response to the superior woman novelist was to see the novel as an instrument that transformed feminine weaknesses into narrative strengths. Women were obsessed by sentiment and romance; well, these were the staples of fiction. Women had a natural taste for the trivial; they were sharp eyed observers of the social scene; they enjoyed getting involved in other peoples' affairs. All these alleged female traits, it was supposed, would find a happy outlet in the novel. 'Women' wrote E. S. Dallas, 'have a talent for personal discourse and familiar narrative, which, when properly controlled, is a great gift, although too frequently it degenerates into a social nuisance.' Such an approach was particularly attractive because it implied that women's writing was as artless and effortless as birdsong, and therefore not in competition with the more rational male eloquence. (Showalter, 1978: 82)

At this stage you might like to refer back to the passage by Virginia Woolf on page 217 before considering the three theories outlined below which account for why women came to start writing novels rather than other literary forms such as poetry or drama:

1. because the novel is the literary form closest to experience – women are innately good at writing fiction, it comes naturally to them, and fits their life experience and pattern
2. because of their lack of education – women wrote novels because this was all they could write – they didn't have the formal education necessary to write anything else
3. because the novel was a new form, not limited by classical models and rules, women as cultural outsiders, i.e. not part of the classically educated male elite, adopted it (see box 10.2).

Access to education, and the availability of time and space to write, is only half the story for women though. In order for their work to be recognized, women writers needed publishers, and the publishing business was until recently a male-dominated world, with its own preconceived judgements about what women could and should write: for example, sentimental novels rather than 'serious' fiction. For this reason, in the nineteenth century, some women novelists, such as Mary Anne Evans and Charlotte Brontë, published their fiction under male pseudonyms (George Eliot and Currer Bell) rather than use their own names.

The rise of women's publishing houses in the early 1970s, such as The Women's Press and Virago, has provided a forum for women writers, and has done much to redress the predominantly male bias of the publishing world. Virago was created in 1973, and made a declaration on the opening page of every book that it was a 'feminist publishing company', refusing for many years to publish fiction by male authors. However, this refusal is currently the subject of discussion, and the inclusion of non-fiction titles by men on Virago's lists is seen by some as a gradual move towards lifting the ban on publishing male writers. In a report on Virago's twentieth anniversary celebrations, Catherine Bennet comments that:

> Now the opening pages in Virago's books are as blank as anyone else's. This is understandable. The world is not what it was in 1973. Then women in publishing were few and mostly subordinate: it was difficult to publish books like Fenwomen; hard to get them noticed on literary pages; books by living black American women writers and dead white English women aristocrats were not to be had for love or money. Today women reign over Random House, the enormous publishing conglomerate; women editors thrive elsewhere, bidding great sums for feminist books and frightening men with their formidable group, Women in Publishing. (Bennet, 1993)

Finally, I would like to point out another stereotype at work here, which is the use of the term 'frightening' as a label for women who hold positions of power and financial control. Substantial progress may have been made by women in the traditionally male domains of art, literature and the media, in terms of recognition of women's creativity, as well as providing the means to market that creativity. But, just as Gentileschi's paintings had the power to scare and shock, not through the violence of their subject matter, but through the fact that a woman was capable of representing such violence, today women who hold positions of power are still represented as threatening to the 'natural order'; as 'frightening' and 'formidable', some kind of exception to the rule of what is seen to be stereotypically 'feminine' behaviour.

It has been a real problem choosing which aspects relating to the place of women in the arts and the media to look at in detail in this chapter, and the choice has inevitably been influenced by the focus of my own experience and interests. I hope, however, that this selective introduction to the role of women in the Arts and the Media has given you an idea of how and where to start thinking about some of these issues in more depth than I have been able to cover here.

BOX 10.2

Theoretical Positions: Artistic and Literary Creativity

In her study *The Obstacle Race*, Germaine Greer (1979) makes two important claims about the history of women painters.

First, that the absence of women from art history does not mean that there were really very few women painters, great or otherwise, but that art historians and commentators did not record their work. The history of art has therefore been predominantly the history of male artists.

Second, that as a result of this absence, the woman artist has lacked female 'role models', and the art that she studies and is inspired by is primarily 'the artistic expression of men'. Greer comments that 'given the present orientation of art history she is not likely to have seen much women's work and less likely to have responded to it. She certainly would not, unless she grew up in a very strange environment, be able to say that she responded primarily to women's work. If she does she is probably not referring to painting, but to textiles or some other "minor" art in which women have not been inspired, led, influenced, taught and appreciated by men.' (Greer, 1979: 325).

We can see a parallel here in Donovan's (1980) observation that women may have started to write novels because it was the only thing they could write, not having access to the necessary classical education where the rules of 'high' literary forms such as poetry were only made available to a male elite. So the novel as a literary genre is rather like textile and design within the art world – these are 'minor' artistic forms lacking the rigour and aesthetic value of what is regarded as 'major' or 'high' art.

Donovan, however, also puts forward a contrasting theory as to why women adopted the novel as a genre. Not because they were 'naturally' good at this kind of writing as the Victorian critics claimed, but precisely because this was a new form, and that as cultural 'outsiders', i.e. not part of the educated male elite, women did not have to adhere to the rules of classical models of literature, but were free to explore new forms of writing. It was therefore a liberating genre for women writers.

ACKNOWLEDGEMENT

I would like to thank my sister Bridget Thornborrow for her help and advice in writing the section of this chapter dealing with women painters.

REFERENCES

Barker, Howard 1990: Scenes from an execution. *Collected Plays Vol. I*. London: Calder.
Bennet, Catherine 1993: The House that Carmen built. *Guardian*, 14 June.
Bowen, Stella 1984: *Drawn from T. Life*. London: Virago.
Bretan, A. 1924: *Le Manifeste du Surréalisme*. Paris: Gallimard.
Cameron, Deborah (ed.) 1990: *The Feminist Critique of Language*. London: Routledge.
Coward, Ros 1984: *Female Desire, Women's Sexuality Today*. London: Paladin.
de Beauvoir, Simone 1949: *Le deuxième Sexe*. Paris: Editions Gallimard.
Donovan, Josephine 1980: The silence is broken. In S. McConnel-Ginet, R. Barker and N. Furman (eds), *Women and Language In Literature and Society*, New York: Praeger.

Greer, Germaine 1979: *The Obstacle Race*. London: Secker & Warburg.

Grey, Ann 1992: *Video Playtime, the Gendering of a Leisure Technology*. London: Routledge.

Kaplan, Janet 1988: *Unexpected Journeys – the Art and Life of Remedios Varo*. London: Virago Press.

Moi, Toril 1985: *Sexual/Textual Politics*. London: Methuen.

Moore, Suzanne 1993: RIP the 'real' Roseanne. *Guardian*, 28 May.

Showalter, Elaine 1978: *A Literature of Their Own*. London: Virago Press.

Williamson, Judith 1978: *Decoding Advertisements, Ideology and Meaning in Advertising*. London: Marion Boyers.

Williamson, J. 1989: adsNAUSEAM. *Cosmopolitan*, December.

Woolf, Virginia 1929: Women and fiction. In Deborah Cameron (ed.), (1990) *The Feminist Critique of Language*, London: Routledge.

CHAPTER
11 Women, Crime and Violence

Lorraine Radford

She lives with a successful businessman, loving father and respected member of the community.

Last week he hospitalised her.

Z
ZERO TOLERANCE

EMOTIONAL, PHYSICAL, SEXUAL
MALE ABUSE OF POWER IS A CRIME

ZERO TOLERANCE CHARITABLE TRUST WORKING FOR ZERO TOLERANCE OF VIOLENCE AGAINST WOMEN

Plate 11   Zero Tolerance Domestic Violence poster. Designed and photographed: Raffles.
© Frankie Raffles Childcare Fund.

A brief review of the headlines in your daily tabloid will be enough to convince you that much of what is written in the popular press about crime compounds gender stereotypes about what women and men should do, how women and men, girls and boys are essentially, naturally different. The media and traditional criminologists have shared the view that, on the whole, women's 'roles' demand from them more constrained behaviour. If women do break the law, especially if they commit crimes of violence, it makes front page news, a good story. As the nursery rhyme suggests, when women are bad you cannot fail to notice it:

> There was a little girl
> Who had a little curl
> Right in the middle of her forehead
> When she was good
> She was very very good
> But when she was bad
> She was horrid

After working through the material in this chapter, you should be able to tackle the following key questions about women, crime and violence: (1) What is 'crime' and how does it affect the lives of men and women? (2) How has the deviance, crime and conformity of women been explained (theorized)? (3) What options are there for dealing with crime? This is a very broad area of study and debate in Women's Studies. To limit the range of our discussion to the key themes and ideas I will, throughout the chapter, refer mainly to crimes of violence against the person.

The Bad and Not so Bad

Let us begin by looking at the basic definitions of crime and deviance.

Crime is simply behaviour which the state labels as and responds to as 'illegal'. In his textbook on Sociology, Anthony Giddens (1993) defines *laws* as: 'norms defined by governments as principles which citizens must follow, formal sanctions being used by those in authority against people who do not conform' (p. 119). Crime will therefore vary over time and in relation to the principles deemed to be important by a given state. At times, the state's laws may be out of step with social norms of behaviour, so some of those who break the law, such as young homosexual men having consenting sex, may not necessarily be viewed as deviant. Crime ranges from the extremes of interpersonal and state violence (murder, genocide) to the petty infractions of everyday life (stealing a pint of milk from a doorstep). While the condemnation of certain crimes – murder and genocide – is virtually global, other acts will move in and out of criminal categories. There is less consistency across nation states in the labelling of political acts and petty offending as illegalities.

Deviance may be defined as non-conformity to a given norm or set of norms accepted by a significant number of people in society (Giddens, 1993: 116). The concept is very wide and, like crime, will vary in relation to historical and cultural contexts.

The definitions obviously overlap considerably but it is possible to conform and break the law, and to be considered law-abiding but deviant.

EXERCISE

Read through the following list of behaviour and actions. What would you rank as a crime, as deviance, as neither?

1. Stealing stationery from work.
2. Driving at 40 mph in a 30 mph speed limit area.
3. Obstructing the traffic on a public highway.
4. Stealing a bottle of nail polish from a store.
5. Drawing a beard and moustache on an image of the Queen.
6. Date rape (raping your date companion).
7. Dressing up as a: grunge; hippy; skinhead; Neo-Nazi; transvestite; baby.
8. Not going to the Mosque/Synagogue/Church on a Friday/Saturday/Sunday.
9. Smoking marijuana.
10. Abortion.
11. Begging for money on the underground.
12. Committing adultery.

EXERCISE RESPONSE

Did you, like me, find it easier to distinguish between the criminal and non-criminal than between the deviant and non-deviant? Seven of the listed acts are easily classified as crimes (1–4, 6, 9, 11). Two of them (adultery and abortion) have been crimes and accordingly punished at some time in the UK and in other nation states. You might sympathize with some of the crimes, perhaps begging on the underground? Clearly, class, poverty and moral beliefs have a part to play in our perceptions of crime and deviance.

Law and order has been a major political issue in recent years, especially around election time when concerns about 'rising crime rates' gush out from campaigning platforms. However, official (i.e. government) statistics on crime do not give us a true picture of criminal behaviour in society. They show us only the tip of the iceberg of crimes which are committed. Many more stay in the 'dark shadow' of crimes which are not detected, reported or prosecuted. For instance, employment-related crimes committed by professionals (white collar or corporate crimes) are notoriously difficult to detect and to prosecute, thus rarely figure in official statistics. Crime surveys and self-report studies, which ask people about the crimes they have committed or experienced as victims, provide additional information on these more 'hidden crimes', although their accuracy depends upon the truthfulness of the people interviewed. Official statistics and crimes surveys show that most lawbreaking is done by young people, particularly young men aged between sixteen and twenty-one years old. Women make up a very small proportion of the offenders dealt with by the police, courts and prisons. On the whole, women's crimes are less serious and less frequent than are men's, women are less likely to become persistent offenders (**recidivists**) and to be sentenced to imprisonment. Of the 541,100 persons found guilty or cautioned for indictable offenses in 1992, 81 per cent were males and 19 per cent were females (Criminal Statistics, 1992). Of the offenders found guilty by the courts in 1992, women committed:

- 8.7 per cent of crimes of violence against the person
- 2 per cent of sexual offenses
- 3 per cent of burglaries and robberies
- 3.5 per cent of thefts, handling stolen goods and forgeries. (Criminal Statistics, 1992)

Self-report studies of crime suggest that official statistics exaggerate the differential offending rates of men and women. These indicate that the discrepancy between males and females is more like two males to every one female admitting responsibility for crimes, although *the sex ratio increases with offence seriousness* (Hedderman and Hough, 1994). Only among drug offenses do we find some degree of 'equality'. Here the proportions of men and women sentenced to imprisonment for drug offenses are roughly equal at around 14 per cent of those charged (Hedderman and Hough, 1994).

It is reasonably easy to conclude, given these figures, that there is a male dominance in reported *crime* but this does not mean necessarily that women are less criminal nor less deviant than are men. The trial of nurse Beverley Allitt in 1992 for the mass murder of children in her care stands as evidence that women can match men at the extremity of criminal violence. Why they do not do it more often is an interesting question.

There has been extensive discussion about why women figure less in official reports of crime (see Farrington and Morris, 1983). Otto Pollack, a criminologist writing in the USA in the 1950s, pioneered an argument known as the 'masking' thesis. This was based upon the belief that there exists an undercurrent of 'hidden' female crime, especially female violence (Pollak, 1950).

The masking argument rested upon the following assumptions about women's crimes:

1. Women are just as capable of, and just as likely to commit crimes as are men, they are not essentially more moral beings.
2. Because women's sphere of influence is limited to the home and the family, not the public space, women lack the opportunity to commit crimes. Where the opportunity exists they take it. Thus they shoplift, abuse children, poison relatives when cooking and, as servants, they steal from their masters.
3. Women are more devious than are men and therefore they are better at covering up their crimes and evading detection. They are often accomplices to, or the main instigators of, men's crimes but they are rarely punished.
4. Women offenders are not treated equally within the criminal justice system. They are more likely to be cautioned or acquitted from charges than are men.

How plausible do you find these assumptions that women's crimes are under-reported, not detected or dealt with more leniently when brought to the attention of the criminal justice system?

Clearly, there are many crimes which are 'hidden', whether committed by men or women. Attempts to prove that women's crimes are more likely to remain concealed, particularly the idea that women are treated more leniently or 'chivalrously' in the criminal justice system have not been very successful. First, because counter evidence exists and, secondly, because it has been suggested that women's crimes are treated *differently*, rather than leniently. Counter evidence can be found to show that women's crimes are not 'covered up' and in fact, poor women, black women, prostitutes and battered women who kill are especially harshly dealt with by the criminal justice system (Edwards, 1984; Player, 1989; Jones, 1991).

> A woman who commits a crime is in essence breaking two rules – one the rule of law and the other a rule constructed by society as to how she is expected to behave. (Nadel, 1993: 135)

Women are cautioned more often by the police than are men but this is because the crimes for which they are cautioned are less serious. Ideas about appropriate behaviour for girls and women can be very demanding and research suggests that girls have been treated very harshly by the courts and social services for 'status offenses' (doing things a girl should not do) such as running away from home or sexual promiscuity (Cain, 1989). Looking at the biographies of women in prison, Pat Carlen (1988) concluded that contact with the social services early in a girl's life, or being taken into care, was a significant feature in the development of criminal careers. In adulthood a woman's worth is often judged on the basis of her sexuality and mothering status.

A woman appearing before a criminal court is almost twice as likely as a man to be dealt with by psychiatric rather than penal means (Allen, 1987). Women report more psychiatric symptoms than do men, are more frequently diagnosed as mentally ill and more frequently subjected to psychiatric treatment. Recent studies of convicted women show unusually high levels of psychopathology (Carlen, 1983; Dobash, Dobash and Gutteridge, 1986; Casale, 1989). Courts may even order psychiatric treatment for women in the absence of a medical diagnosis. Yet in a review of homicide cases tried at the Central Criminal Court ('Old Bailey'), Hilary Allen (1987) found that the judiciary are more likely to see men as totally mad than women. Male offenders do not get psychiatric treatment as frequently because they are seen as being too dangerous to be anywhere but in prison. Women are more likely to be given psychiatric treatment when convicted of a crime because they seem *less disturbed, disordered and dangerous* than do men.

Safety and Fear of Crime

In the previous section we looked at the under-representation of women as offenders in criminal statistics. Women do however figure highly in official statistics on victimization where they almost equal men as *victims* of crime. In this section I will review the position of women in official statistics as victims of crime and I will develop our discussion of 'hidden' crimes by looking at the fear and experience of crime in 'public' and 'private' spaces.

EXERCISE

Make a list of the safety precautions you routinely take (if any): when at home; when going out at night. Do not spend too long over this. Limit yourself to ten points for each category.

EXERCISE RESPONSE

The Home Office (1988) publication *Practical Ways to Crack Crime* recommends women take a number of steps to protect themselves from crime, including the following:

> Draw your curtains after dark to discourage any Peeping Tom. If you think there is a prowler outside, don't go out to check – dial 999 . . . Use only your surname and initials in the telephone directory and on the doorplate if you live in a flat, that way a stranger cannot tell whether a man or woman lives there . . . When you are at home, keep your external doors locked . . . Avoid short cuts through dimly lit alleys or across waste ground . . . Walk facing the traffic so a car cannot pull up behind you unnoticed . . . Walk on the street side of the pavement so an attacker lurking in an alley has further to come to reach you . . . Don't hitch hike or accept lifts from strangers . . . If you regularly go jogging or cycling try to vary your route and time so you can't be waylaid by an attacker . . . If you regularly walk home after dark, consider buying a screech alarm . . . Always park your car in a well-lit preferably busy area – and take a moment or two to look around before you get out . . . When you come back to your car have your key ready and check there is no one in the car. (Home Office, 1988)

EXERCISE

How useful do you think the Home Office's advice would be to protect you from crime? Has the Home Office told you anything you did not know or did not have on your own list already? Read through the extract again and answer the following questions. What assumptions do you think are made about:

1. the types of crimes threatening the public
2. the type of person who commits these crimes
3. who is at risk of crime
4. a victim's responsibility to protect herself and not to invite crime.

Do you think that the value of the Home Office advice would vary with the age or race or physical or mental vulnerability of a reader?

Try to imagine advice on self protection for men. Do you think it would be just as relevant to suggest, for instance, that men do not accept lifts?

EXERCISE RESPONSE

Safety advice for women flows liberally from the Home Office, the AA and RAC, from cell phone and safety alarm manufacturers. Like the extract, most of this advice is aimed at women's fears of 'stranger-danger', the unknown man, lurking like a predator outside the haven of the home. Women are rarely told how to protect themselves from *known* men – husbands, lovers, fathers. There is also a conspicuous lack of advice for *men* on how to protect themselves. It is assumed that men *know* how to protect themselves (though, as I will show, they are not very good at it). Government sponsored crime surveys show that fear of crime is greater for women than it is for men and greater among women living in city and urban areas (Mirlees-Black and Aye Naung, 1994). Fear of crime affects men differently, there being no female cultural equivalent of the 'Ripper' waiting to prey upon males. When victimized, men are more likely to experience anger than fear (Stanko and Habdell, 1993).

The feminist criminologist Betsy Stanko talked to men and women about their personal safety and found that, when men express fears, they are more likely to be concerned about their property, and also about the personal safety of others:

> When men do worry about crime, it is about their property rather than their persons ... Men learn to negotiate physical danger, largely in the company of other men. Safety comes from strength, backed up by physical ability and enhanced by the advantages of economic, racial or sexual status. A 'real man' is a strong, heterosexual male protector, capable of taking care of himself and, if necessary, guarding his and others' safety aggressively. (Stanko, 1990: 109–10)

Yet, the reality is that it is *young men* who are most at risk from 'stranger-danger'. They are especially at risk of violent assault and robbery. For males, over 51 per cent of circumstances of recorded incidents of violence against the person occurred in the 'public context' of a street or pub brawl, or an attack on public servants. Men are more than twice as likely than are women to be killed by strangers (Home Office, 1992).

For women, it is the home or 'private sphere' that presents the greater danger. Known men more often abuse women than do 'strangers'. Women are more likely than men to be victims of sexual assault, domestic violence and theft from the person. Crime surveys show that 50 per cent of the offenses of violence against female victims involve domestic violence, as compared with 6 per cent for males. Women are at greater risk of homicidal violence or rape from known men, particularly from men within the home. In 1990, 43 per cent of female homicide victims were killed by their male partners in contrast to 9 per cent of male homicide victims. In two-thirds of the reported rape cases the suspect was known to the victim (Criminal Statistics, 1991). This figure is likely to underestimate the risk of rape and violence from known men as women are less likely to report crimes by men they know. A 1991 self-report survey of 1007 married women found: one in seven women reported having been raped by their husbands, half had been raped six times or more and 91 per cent of the women never reported the rape or discussed it with an official agency (Painter, 1991).

The media perpetuates the myth that sex crimes are committed by beasts or fiends, rather than by 'ordinary' men:

BABY FACED SEX BEAST SET TO KILL (*Star*)

SCHOOLGIRL RAPED BY YOUNG 'FOX' (*Sun*)

M4 COPYCAT FIEND GRABS GIRL (*Sun*)

HOW COULD THEY LET THIS ANIMAL LIVE?
JUROR SLAMS KIRSTY KILLER (*Star*)
(Extracts from Soothill and Walby, 1991)

Press representations of sex crimes create a distinction between 'real' rapes and assaults and 'normal', justifiable behaviour. 'Real' rapists and murderers are referred to as 'beasts' , 'fiends', 'monsters' or even heroically as 'Fox', 'Panther', 'Ripper', 'Strangler' (see also Cameron and Fraser, 1987). Law and press reports on domestic violence and assaults by known men upon women are put together so that the victim appears to be to blame:

Humiliated Husband Goes Free after Killing Wife During Row
A man who killed his elderly wife during a row over his burnt dinner received a suspended sentence yesterday. Mr Frederick Burton, a retired company director, aged 76, was described as a long-suffering husband who was attacked and humiliated by his 79 year old wife . . .The judge accepted there had been considerable provocation. (The *Guardian*, 7 June 1989)

Sympathy for Killing 'Bully Wife'
A man who killed his bullying, alcoholic common law wife, was given a two-year suspended jail sentence yesterday after the judge, Mr Justice Popplewell said: 'This lady would have tried the patience of a saint.'
Joseph McGrail, 45, . . . was regularly subjected to abuse from Marion Kennedy, 40, who began drinking in 1981 and was addicted to sleeping pills . . . On February 27 he attacked her after returning from work to find her drunk. She died from internal bleeding. (The *Guardian*, 1 August 1991)

The media invariably point out judges 'findings' that men tried for killing wives or lovers were truly 'good men'. Their trial for murder or manslaughter is portrayed as an injustice:

> Roy Greech ... was given two years' probation for killing his wife because she was having an affair. Mr Greech stabbed her 23 times and left the knife in her throat before calling the police. The judge told him: 'You have not only been a man of good character but you are a good man also.' (The *Guardian*, 11 April 1994)

In contrast, women tried for murder or manslaughter are never cast as 'good' women, although sympathies may occasionally extend to them as 'helpless victims'.

The idea that the lust-crazed psychopath carries much of the responsibility for crimes of violence against women has been criticized by feminist criminologists on two chief grounds. The first is that, as the preceding discussion has shown, women experience a considerable number of 'hidden crimes' in the 'safety' of the home or in intimate relationships with men. Violence is an essential component of the relations between men and women and it is used by men in a power relationship to control and humiliate the victim. Secondly, it has been argued that there are links between the actions of the lust-crazed psychopath and those of the 'normal' man.

There are two key points to note here. The first is the idea, put forward by Liz Kelly (1988), that there is a sexual violence continuum. The continuum links a panoply of abusive acts (rape, sexual harassment, domestic battery, homicide etc.) with the everyday abuses and safety precautions in women's lives. Male control and domination of women's bodies expresses itself as aggressive male sexuality (and its converse, passive, masochistic female sexuality). Dominance is eroticized, interwoven with sexuality (MacKinnon, 1982, 1983; Hester, 1992). Thus, it is argued that acts such as violent rape, forced and consensual sex share common rituals of conquest and submission which make it difficult to distinguish the 'normal' from the 'aberrant' (Kelly, 1988). Men are therefore able to argue that victims of rape said 'No' but meant 'Yes', scratched, bit and kicked but none the less 'wanted it' because these things happen in 'normal sex'. In the climax of the film *Gone With The Wind*, Rhett Butler rapes/seduces Scarlet O'Hara while she passionately screams resistance. Today, in the 'bodice rippers' from Mills and Boon and in reports from the courts, Scarlet O'Hara clones scream resistance while yearning to be overwhelmed:

> He closed in on her, his warm mouth brushing her ear. 'The impenetrable Alexia has a heart after all', he whispered in her ear, keeping up the teasing pressure on her breast [. . .] 'No', she rasped, terrified of the need he has aroused so alarmingly from deep inside her. (Fox, 1992: 1)

As the gentlemen on the jury will understand, when a woman says 'No' she does not always mean it. Men can't turn their emotions on and off like some women can. (Judge Raymond Dean, Central Criminal Court, April 1990)

It is not just a question of saying 'No'. It is a question of how she says it, how she shows it and makes it clear. If she does not want it, she only has to keep her legs shut and he would not get it without force. (Judge David Wild, Cambridge Criminal Court, 1982)

The second key point to note is that male violence is said to work in a self-perpetuating way, where fear of crime in the 'public' reinforces women's risks of crimes in the 'private'. Hanmer and Saunders (1983) carried out a community study of women's victimization in West Yorkshire as a response to the short-comings of the first British Crime Survey. On the basis of their results Hanmer and Saunders theorized male violence as working in a closed, circular system where the fear and experience of violence is self-perpetuating. There are six steps to the cycle:

1. Fear of public abuse is fed by the media, informal rumour, personal experience of women, their friends and acquaintances. Women are expected to behave in appropriate ways in public places and are often held responsible if an attack occurs.
2. Fear of public spaces leads women to change their behaviour either by avoiding dangerous places (alleyways, cities at night, empty trains) or by not going out alone.
3. These restrictions reinforce women's dependency upon men as protectors in the home and escorts in public places.
4. This puts women at greater risk of abuse from known men. Known men who abuse learn that there are few sanctions against them as women's culturally defined responsibility for violence increases with the closeness of the relationship.
5. The criminal justice system and welfare agencies reinforce division between public and private crime by refusing to intervene in 'domestics' (the term police use to refer to violence to women from known men) or in situations of sexual violence between men and women in intimate relationships. The problem of abuse to women is turned around so that the primary emphasis becomes her behaviour, how she invited or provoked the attack. The battered wife is blamed for causing her own abuse by not walking out from the abuser. The victim of rape is blamed for inviting it by hitch-hiking, dressing 'provocatively' or having sex with a man in the past.
6. If the criminal justice system and the police are seen as unhelpful, this reinforces the fear of public crime.

EXERCISE

Remember the masking argument? Look back to page 232 if you need to refresh your memory. Do you think that Hanmer's and Saunders' suggestion that men's 'private' crimes are covered up detracts from the claim that women's crimes are 'masked'? How and why do you think crimes are hidden and who benefits? How could this self-perpetuating cycle of violence be broken? Write down five ideas.

EXERCISE RESPONSE

The first point to note in response to this exercise is that 'hidden' crimes are just as relevant to men as to women, so proving equity between the sexes in the under-current of violence is still more elusive. In the opportunity for crime argument, women would presumably have equality of opportunity to abuse spouses yet they far outnumber men as spousal homicide victims. (They do however make use of their power and opportunity to abuse children.) 'Leniency', in terms of lack of enforcement of the criminal law, can also be seen to work for men's crimes of violence to women. All too often the violence is excused and the offender's behaviour is not recognized as criminal. Furthermore, if you accept Hanmer's and Saunders' argument, the *opposite* to masking takes place for men's 'public' violence; it is given a high profile, thus fuels women's fears so that their movements are restricted. We will return to the question of how to break the 'cycle' of violence later on in the chapter when we look at the criminal justice system and options for dealing with crime. Hold on to your notes.

Women in Criminology

The feminist approach to criminology has, until recently, existed mainly as a critique that women have been 'left out' or, worse still, had inappropriate, patriarchal explanations for crime grafted on to their experiences (Naffine, 1987; Heidensohn, 1993). There is now a substantial literature on the topic but you can get at the essence of the feminist critique of criminology by working through the next exercise.

EXERCISE

Read through the following extracts. For each extract make a list of the offender's characteristics and the circumstances which seem to be associated with the crimes.

A. Louise C.:
    At three she was a thief and laid hands on her mother's money, on articles in shops, on everything . . . that came in her way. At five she was arrested and conveyed to the police office, after a determined resistance . . . She shrieked, tore off her stockings, threw her dolls into the gutter, lifted up her skirts in the street. . . . Lombroso, by looking at her murky photograph, could identify 'the exact type of the born criminal. Her physiognomy is Mongolian, her jaws and cheekbones are immense; the frontal sinuses strong, the nose flat with a prognathous under-jaw, asymmetry of face, and above all, precocity and virility of expression. She looks like a grown woman – nay a man.' (Jones, 1991: xiii)

B. Linda Hewitt:
    Ask Linda Hewitt what went through her head at the moment she took a carving knife and plunged it into the neck of the man she loves, and she replies simply: 'Don't ask me . . . ask the other woman.'
        The other woman in question answered to the name of Linda Hewitt, looked like her, was her as far as the outside world was concerned . . . Just what turns a happy, loving woman into a knife-wielding maniac can be summed up quite easily.
        'The doctors have a technical word for it' said Linda yesterday. 'They say I was suffering from post-natal depression, and at the time my condition was aggravated by pre-menstrual tension. I was in a total trance . . . The first time I realized what I'd done was when I was giving my statement to the police.' (Benn, 1993: 52)

C. Zoë, aged 28, lone parent:
    I got this house when Sylvie was seven months old. I was still paying off my electricity bill that we'd had the first winter 'cos Sylvie had had bronchitis and I'd had heating on twenty-four hours a day. I got myself into a complete and utter mess within six months of being in this house. I got rent arrears; I had gas bills. I'd managed to pay my electricity bill off and I had a coin meter installed for my gas. They set it so low that I was virtually getting nothing for my money. A lot of the time, once Sylvie had gone to bed, I was sitting with no fire. I was freezing cold. I started shoplifting. (Carlen, 1988: 115)

EXERCISE RESPONSE

The individualist emphasis upon mind or body in extracts A and B contrast with the material and social circumstances influencing the crime for Zoë in extract C. My lists for the three extracts included the following points:

Louise	Linda	Zoë
Past history	Being 'out of herself'	Duty as mother
Body	Not knowing/passive/ not responsible	Rational choice
Man-like	Pre-menstrual	Poverty
Lifting skirts	Medical experts	Lack of options
Innate/incurable	Treatable	Social cure

In Louise's extract it is the child's *physical* appearance which it is claimed leads her to commit crimes. Her crimes are taken to include not only the stealing but also 'inappropriate' behaviour for a girl, fighting or lifting one's skirts. Her crimes are incurable, being innate, Louise is a 'born' criminal. In the extract she is described as having 'masculine' features, leading her to later commit crimes which were 'unwomanly'.

In Linda's case her pre-menstrual, bodily condition is said to have affected her mind and hence responsibility for her violent crime. She is portrayed as a passive being who lacks the intent to be wicked (being 'out of herself'). Her condition is temporary, possibly fleeting, and curable with therapy. While it is her 'abnormal' hormonal condition which essentially afflicts her, for the court it is her state of mind which is the focus of concern, whether at the time of the offence she was temporarily 'mad' or just plain 'bad'. There is also an ambiguity in her statement, 'the doctors have a technical word for it . . . they say I was suffering . . .', which suggests that the doctors have had some control over what can be said about her condition and her crime.

In Zoë's case her social conditions and role as a lone mother combine to lead her into crime. Her criminality is a conscious decision, perhaps a rational choice, which she takes. She is not a passive victim of her body or mind, although, depending upon your political views, she might be seen as the victim of a society which penalizes single mothers. Indeed her crime could be said to be caused by 'society', the social constraints upon Zoë's life together with the expectation that she should, none the less, provide for her child. Zoë's criminality holds the prospect of reform; a government could either encourage her to change her status as a lone mother (marry her off to a man or take her child into care), or help her to cope with or improve her status in society (with social work intervention or access to a decent income).

This exercise leads us into two central concerns of the feminist critique of criminology: (1) a woman's body and biology as limiting, causing or justifying her crimes; (2) the limits imposed upon women's behaviour by sex 'roles', the family and socialization. These two strands form the basis of the 'foundational critique' of criminology (Brown, 1986) which saw either biology or society as ultimately to blame for women's crimes or women's conformity. I will review the main features of these two strands of critique in turn.

Body, biology and crime

Carol Smart, in her pioneer work *Women, Crime and Criminology*, published in 1976 saw criminological writings about women and crime as stuck in a pre-sociological, biological quagmire. In classical criminology, it was argued, women were seen either as 'naturally', biologically, conformist or as so unstable and under the sway of hormones it is hard to see why we are not all out committing crimes 25 per cent of the time. The nineteenth-century Italian criminologist, Cesare Lombroso, mentioned in Louise's extract above, has generally been the starting point for feminist critiques of criminology. Lombroso measured skull sizes and foreheads to detect 'criminal types' and concluded that women who committed crimes were, like Louise, physically more like men than women. One hundred years later it is not difficult to see the quantum leaps in logic required to construct links between physical characteristics such as a low forehead or square jaw and crime. While there has been research (sponsored by organizations such as NATO) into matters such as aggression and testosterone, contemporary criminology, when looking at men, has placed less emphasis upon biological explanations. For women, however, physical conditions arising in the pre-menstruum, post-natal or menopausal phases have been well used in courts as grounds for mitigation and defence of crime. Women's hormones (natural physiology) are said to affect the mind to the extent that some women commit crimes when 'out of themselves'. In killing her lover, Linda has no responsibility or agency for her crime. Her criminality is virtually excusable and treatable with hormone therapy, in her actions she is passive, victim to the sway of her hormones.

Biologically based explanations of crime individualize and divorce crime from its social, cultural and political context. Criminal activity appears to be irrational and illogical yet this might not be the case, as Zoë's extract shows, if there are no alternatives, crimes may have a rational motivation.

Women's 'roles'

For women, there is the expectation that they should not break the law. Role theory was based on the idea that women are naturally more conformist than men and are constrained in their behaviour by the family and society. Women's criminality is seen to be curtailed by their 'differential association', socialization and lack of opportunity to commit crime (Smart, 1976; Naffine, 1987). In other words, who a woman mixes with, where she goes and what she does in her daily life, limit her opportunities and motivation to commit crime. When women do break the law it is either due to some physical abnormality (sickness, hormones) or because of poor socialization: 'From infancy girls are taught that they must be nice, while boys are taught they must be rough and tough' (Sutherland and Cressey, 1966: 142). Taking away the restraints on women releases the hidden tide of women's criminality we discussed earlier when looking at the idea of 'masking'.

The woman who casts off the shackles of her 'feminine role', becomes lesbian, and turns into aggressor to terrorize men has been popularized as a male fantasy in films such as *Thelma and Louise*, press hype over female serial killers such as Aileen Wuornus (a hitch-hiking prostitute who stood trial in the USA in 1992 for killing seven men in self-defence), female gangs, or over women who, like Mrs Bobbitt (who cut off her husband's penis after his alleged marital rape), take the law into their own hands to put an end to abuse (see Birch, 1993, for interesting reviews of murder and representation). In the Ruth Rendell (1986) mystery story *An Unkindness of Ravens*, fifteen-year-old Sara Williams kills her father in order to get the maintenance money which he had refused her. Sara, a member of a separatist feminist organization, hoped to study medicine but needed parental maintenance to top up her grant. Having failed in her attempt to extort the money from her father through blackmail – threatening a (false) accusation of his sexual abuse – Sara creates 'false memory syndrome' of his abuse in her sister Veronica, and then enlists her help in a brutal, ritual killing of the father. The moral of this tale, provided in the closing chapter by the analysis of a male police inspector, is that feminism leads women away from the traditional confines of femininity towards crime. In trying to equal men – liberation seen here as becoming men, taking on male norms of behaviour, responsibilities and vices – women end up outdoing them in the aggression stakes, because they are able to manipulate law enforcer's expectations about their vulnerabilities. In an article in the *Sunday Times* (27.11.94) Ian Burrell and Lisa Brinkworth reported on the Busch Corner Girls, a female gang who rob women alone on the underground, who evade prosecution by 'dressing smartly and playing up to the magistrates', acting 'like Minnie Mouse'.

In 1975 Freda Adler took up this idea that as women became liberated and 'traditional' family and social restraints declined, crimes, especially crimes of violence would increase. Adler used official statistics to support her claim that women's crimes had been dramatically increased with the second wave of women's liberation from the 1960s onwards. Male and female behaviour was said to be converging as women's liberation undercut traditional ideas about what men and women should do. By implication, thus, crime was seen as 'masculine' and women's liberation as making women more manly. The assumption that liberation for women means becoming more like men, or indeed the equation of lesbianism with masculinity, is clearly faulty. Serial killing women are a rarity and not all women who break the law would identify themselves as feminists, law breaking being more associated with social marginalization than with liberation.

Lorraine Radford

Society to blame – feminist criminology

Unlike role theorists, feminist criminologists started their study of women and crime by talking to women about their experiences and by looking at how their behaviour had been socially constructed as deviant. They sought to place women's conformity and deviance within the political and historical context of patriarchy, looking at the constraints upon women's lives, at how women are 'over-controlled', made to and expected to conform. Feminist criminologists have also looked at how the criminal justice system creates women as offenders, innocents or victims and at how marginal women are more commonly defined as deviant. The social control perspective has drawn very much on the work of interactionist and labelling theory (Becker, 1963; Hall and Scraton, 1981). On this perspective, an act is not perceived as a crime until it is defined as such. The power of professionals, police and agents of the state as 'definers' is crucial in the process of definition. The existence of certain categories or 'scripts' of behaviour inevitably holds the possibility that some offenders will recognize their own behaviour within them or try to use them to fit or justify their actions. (Like Linda's account of her pre-menstrual tension and post-natal depression above?)

In the mid 1980s, the criminologist Frances Heidensohn (1985) supported the case for developing a feminist criminology. Feminist criminology involved:

- looking at how women's position in society affects their experiences as victims and offenders
- exploring the links between behaviour which is 'normal' and behaviour considered to be 'deviant'
- shifting the emphasis of debate from a concern with deviance to the analysis of conformity and control
- a critique of conceptions of crime in 'public' and 'private' spheres of life
- observation of the processes of the criminal justice system from a feminist standpoint.

Frances Heidensohn applied a social control perspective by looking at the constraints on women in four areas of life: the home, in the 'public' space, at work and in social policies. She used the concept of the 'over control' of women to explain the anomaly that, if poverty and crime are linked, women should be more criminal than men as they are poorer.

> Informal sanctions discourage women and girls from straying far from proper behaviour; parents will disapprove or impose sanctions, as will gossip, ill repute and male companions. Fear of crime, harassment or stigma all aid this process. A range of other commitments – to children, family, community etc. – occupy women much more fully than do men. Finally, public images and culture encourage deviance in men but suggest that deviant women are punished. (Heidensohn, 1993: 1028)

Pat Carlen (1988) similarly employed a version of control theory, based upon the assumption that people will outwardly conform while they perceive it to be worth their while to do so. For those in employment, the benefits of paid work, conforming and keeping one's job will usually outweigh the benefits of crime. If there is poverty, then this 'class deal' may be less attractive to potential offenders and the decision to commit a crime may be based upon a 'rational' choice. Carlen argued that women are expected to make both a 'class deal' and a 'gender deal':

> Working class women have traditionally been contained within *two* material and ideological sites of social control, the workplace and the family. Working class women have therefore been doubly controlled. They have been expected not only to make the 'class deal' but the 'gender deal' too ... The majority of women do not become embroiled in criminal careers, even if they do break the law on occasion ... while they remain in the family, they are seen to have made the gender deal and to be gender regulated. Conversely, girls in Care, single women living alone and other women 'without men' are often seen as being gender decontrolled ... *unregulated women*, they are also seen as being potential recidivist law-breakers and the authorities act accordingly. (Carlen, 1988: 13)

There is, unfortunately, no room for us to explore here the case for and against a feminist criminology. Questions which you might like to consider are, however:

1. Does the social control approach merely substitute society (as victimizer of poor, marginal women) to replace classical criminology's individualized responsibility for crime? To what extent have feminist analyses challenged the 'foundational critique' of criminology?
2. In looking at social control, constraints and the social construction of women's crimes, to what extent have criminologists fuelled or countered the idea that women are passive victims? An important question to consider here is whether or not you think that social control theory could explain women's violence and abuse of children (see Kelly, 1991).
3. Does Frances Heidensohn's concern with social control lead her outside of criminology into the study of women in society?

The 1990s has seen the growing influence of post-modernist theory where the social constructionist approach has become especially important (see chapter 7 on sexuality for a discussion of the social constructionist approach). Post-modernists have adopted an abolitionist stance, arguing an end to criminology as a subject altogether in favour of an approach which looks at gender, law and social policy as a whole (Smart, 1990; Cain, 1991). Maureen Cain (1991) argues for a 'transgressive approach' to criminology to break out of the traditional confines of the subject – where women are measured against male priorities. One outcome of these current trends has been an increasing interest in the 1990s with the study of masculinity and crime.

To sum up this section, we can see that feminist work in the area of criminology has developed in the past twenty years from a *critique* of male-centred theories about women's crimes, to a concern to work from a *feminist standpoint* (putting women back into the frame of discussion, studying the impact of crime upon women's lives), to the study of the social construction of *masculinity, femininity and crime*.

What to do About Law and Order

Policing and imprisonment have been the mainstay of conservative crime control policy. Any response to crime is linked to ideological beliefs about the value and aims of punishment, treatment or reform and prevention. There are no 'wrong' answers to the question 'What should we do about crime?', but there are plenty of 'right' answers. Options available in the criminal justice system could be used to achieve any combination of the following aims (and probably more):

(a)   retribution and revenge, the 'eye for an eye' approach
(b)   containment of an offender to protect the general public
(c)   reform/rehabilitation
(d)   protection for victims
(e)   public shaming or humiliation of offenders and/or victims
(f)   education for offenders, victims and the general public
(g)   prevention of further crime.

Return to your ideas from the exercise on page 239. Did your list of options include the criminal justice system? Did you have any of the following crime control options on your list?

- Arrest.
- Imprisonment.
- Injunctions.
- Abuser groups.
- Treatment.
- Victim compensation.
- Refuges.
- Awareness raising (as in, for example, Zero Tolerance Campaign, which involves public education about domestic violence through posters spread

across the city – an example of one of the posters used is shown at the beginning of this chapter).

- Reparation (coming face to face with a victim and the consequences of one's crime).
- Probation.
- Alternatives to imprisonment, such as community service.

To conclude this chapter I will leave you to consider the following questions:

1. How well would these responses fit with each of the identified crime control aims?
2. How would they affect the victims of crime?

Resources and Further Study

You may want to carry out your own original work and further study to develop the ideas raised in this chapter. There are plenty of opportunities for project work in the area of women and crime. Here are a few suggestions:

- sitting in the magistrates or Crown Court to observe the conduct of trials
- monitoring press, news, film or magazine representations/reports of crime
- setting up a learning or reading group to look at race, age, disability, lesbianism, or masculinity and crime
- monitoring and improving the safety provisions in your college or local community
- helping out at your local refuge or rape crisis centre
- getting involved in anti-violence public education
- organizing a conference or information day on women's safety.

REFERENCES

Adler, F. 1975: *Sisters in Crime*. New York: McGraw Hill.
Allen, H. 1987: *Justice Unbalanced*. Milton Keynes: Open University Press.
Becker, H. 1963: *Outsiders*. New York: Free Press.
Benn, M. 1993: Body talk. In H. Birch (ed.), *Moving Target*, London: Virago.
Birch, H. 1993: *Moving Targets Women Murder and Representation*. London: Virago.
Brown, B. 1986: Women and crime: the dark figures in criminology. *Economy and Society*, 15, 3, August, 355–402.
Cain, M. 1989: *Growing Up Good*. London: Routledge.
Cain, M. 1991: Towards transgression: new directions in feminist criminology. *International Journal of the Sociology of Law*, 18, 1, 1–18.

Cameron, D. and Fraser, E. 1987: *The Lust To Kill*. Oxford: Polity.

Carlen, P. 1983: *Women's Imprisonment: A Study in Social Control*. London: RKP.

Carlen, P. 1988: *Women, Crime and Poverty*. Milton Keynes: Open University Press.

Casale, S. 1989: *Women Inside*. London: Civil Liberties Trust.

Criminal Statistics 1992: London: HMSO.

Dobash, R., Dobash, R. and Gutteridge, S. 1986: *The Imprisonment of Women*. Oxford: Blackwell.

Edwards, S. 1984: *Women On Trial*. Manchester: Manchester University Press.

Farrington, D. and Morris, A. 1983: Sex, sentencing and re-conviction. *British Journal of Criminology*, 23, 3, 229–48.

Fox, N. 1992: *Revenge*. London: Mills & Boon.

Giddens, A. 1993: *Sociology*. Oxford: Polity.

Hall, S. and Scraton, T. 1981: Law, class and control. In M. Fitzgerald, G. McLennan and J. Pawson (eds), *Crime and Society*, London: Routledge.

Hanmer, J. and Saunders, S. 1983: *Well Founded Fear*. London: Hutchinson.

Hedderman, C. and Hough, M. 1994: *Does The Criminal Justice System Treat Men and Women Differently?* Research Findings No 10, Home Office Research and Statistics Department, London: Home Office.

Heidensohn, F. 1985: *Women and Crime*. London: Macmillan.

Heidensohn, F. 1993: Women and crime. In S. Jackson (ed.), *Women's Studies: A Reader*. London: Harvester/Wheatsheaf.

Hester, M. 1992: *Lewd Women and Wicked Witches: A History of the Dynamics of Male Domination*. London: Routledge.

Home Office 1988: *Practical Ways to Crack Crime*. 2nd edn. London: HMSO.

Home Office 1992: *Gender and The Criminal Justice System*. London: HMSO.

Jones, A. 1991: *Women Who Kill*. London: Victor Gollancz.

Kelly, L. 1988: *Surviving Sexual Violence*. Oxford: Polity.

Kelly, L. 1991: Unspeakable acts: women who abuse. *Trouble and Strife*, 21, Summer, 13–20.

MacKinnon, C. 1982: Feminism, Marxism, method and the State: an agenda for theory. *Signs*, 7, 3, 515–44.

MacKinnon, C. 1983: Feminism, Marxism, method and the State: toward feminist jurisprudence. *Signs*, 8, 2, 635–58.

MacKinnon, C. 1989: *Towards a Feminist Theory of the State*. Cambridge, MA: Harvard University Press.

Mirleees-Black, C. and Aye Naung, N. 1994: *Fear Of Crime: Findings from the 1992 BCS*. Home Office Research and Statistics Dept, Findings No 9. London: HMSO.

Nadel, J. 1993: *Sara Thornton: The Story of A Woman Who Killed*. London: Victor Gollancz.

Naffine, N. 1987: *Female Crime: The Construction of Women in Criminology*. Sydney, Australia: Allen & Unwin.

Painter, K. 1991: *Wife Rape, Marriage and The Law*. Manchester: Manchester University Press.

Player, E. 1989: Women and crime in the city. In D. Downes (ed.), *Crime in The City*. London: Macmillan.

Pollack, O. 1950: *The Criminality of Women*. Pennsylvania: University of Pennsylvania.

Rendell, R. 1986: *An Unkindness of Ravens*. London: Arrow.

Smart, C. 1976: *Women, Crime and Criminology*. London: RKP.

Smart, C. 1990: Post-modern woman meets atavistic man. In L. Gelsthorpe and A. Morris (eds), *Feminist Perspectives in Criminology*, Milton Keynes: Open University Press.

Soothill, K. and Walby, S. 1991: *Sex Crime In The News*. London: Routledge.

Stanko, E. 1990: *Everyday Violence*. London: Pandora.

Stanko, E. and Hobdell, K. 1993: Assault on men: masculinity and male victimization. *British Journal of Criminology*, 33, 3, 400–15.

Sutherland, E. and Cressey, D. 1966: *Principles of Criminology*. Philadelphia: Lippincott.

CHAPTER
12 Women's Spirituality

Beverley Clack and Jo-Anne Whitcomb

Plate 12   *Shiva*, © The Mansell Collection, London.

In this chapter we will consider the different issues surrounding the idea of spirituality and specifically what might be meant by women's spirituality. At the outset, we need to be clear about what we mean by 'spirituality'. At its most basic, spirituality refers to the varied and differing responses people make to the universal human experiences of birth, life and death. In other words, how do human beings make sense of such experiences; how do they give meaning to their lives? In what ways might it be possible to give meaning to the apparent meaninglessness of life in the face of death? Background and experience will influence the ways in which different people express their experiences. As such, this chapter will reflect the backgrounds of its authors, formed as they have been by the Christian tradition. However, the way in which spirituality has been explored in other religious traditions – or, indeed, by women who do not subscribe to any formal religion – will also be considered.

If spirituality, then, is defined as the responses human beings make to these universal human experiences, and if there is a difference between male and female experiences of life, will there be a difference between male and female forms of spirituality? In this chapter we shall attempt to discern the ways in which women give expression to their spirituality. What might a woman-centred spirituality involve?

After reading this chapter you will be able to define different understandings of what it means to be 'spiritual' and will be aware of different possibilities for a woman-centred spirituality.

The Historical Context

If we consider the way in which spirituality has traditionally been understood, it may be that there is a difference between male and female understandings of the spiritual life. Spirituality, at least within the predominantly Christian Western world, has been understood from a male perspective – with dramatic and often damaging consequences for women. Before we can approach the issue of women's spirituality, we need to be aware of the way in which the spiritual life has traditionally been described.

Myths of spirituality: Fall and Incarnation

The spiritual expression of people in Western Europe and America has been dominated by the Christian understanding of God. There has been a tendency within this tradition to identify men with God and the spiritual life, while women have been identified with the body and nature – occasionally even with the devil. According to one Proverb found in places as varied as Arabia, Denmark, Germany, Greece, India and Russia, 'Woman is man's Satan'. Why is this idea so widespread? In the West, the idea that men are somehow closer to God and the spiritual realm can be traced back to one of the basic Christian stories, the Fall.

The Fall of Humanity is told in the first book of the Bible, Genesis. In this creation story, God is described creating man from dust, and then creating a helpmate, woman, for him, from his rib. While the idea that woman was created out of man and is therefore subordinate to him originates from this image, it is not this part of the passage that concerns us here. The devil in the shape of a serpent tempts the woman, Eve, into eating the fruit of the tree of knowledge of good and evil. Eve, having eaten the fruit, gives some to Adam too. Through that action, the doom of humanity is sealed. God curses humanity, and as a consequence work and death become part of the human condition. And who is to blame for this state of affairs? According to the Church Fathers who developed Christian doctrine, Woman. If Woman in the shape of Eve is ultimately to blame for the Fall of Humanity, women will have to bear a special burden of guilt (see box 12.1, 'Tertullian, "On the Apparel of Women" '). As far as spirituality goes, woman by the very nature of her sex will find the spiritual life more difficult.

BOX 12.1	Tertullian, 'On the Apparel of Women'

Do you not know that you are each an Eve? God's judgment upon your sex endures even today, and with it endures the weight of your guilt. You are the devil's gateway: You are the unsealer of the tree: You are the first deserter of the divine law: You are she who persuaded him whom the devil was not brave enough to attack. How easily you destroyed God's image: man. On account of your reward – that is, death – even the Son of God had to die. (Written 200ce)

It is interesting to note that in Islam, a religion which is part of the same monotheistic tradition (in other words, believes that there is One God), the equivalent to Eve is not portrayed as the cause of evil and human suffering (see box 12.2, 'Qur'an II: 36–8'). Rather both the Man and the Woman are considered guilty of disobedience. They seek and receive forgiveness from Allah (the Arabic word for God), and it is the serpent who is perceived as the source of evil.

BOX
12.2

Qur'an II: 36–8

Then did Satan make them slip
From the (Garden), and get them out
Of the state (of felicity) in which
They had been. We said:
'Get ye down, all (ye people),
With enmity between yourselves.
On earth will be your dwelling place
And your means of livelihood
For a time.'
Then learnt Adam from his Lord
Words of inspiration, and his Lord
Turned towards him; for He
Is Oft-Returning, Most Merciful.
We said: 'Get ye down all from here';
And if, as is sure, there comes to you
Guidance from Me, whosoever
Follows My guidance, on them
Shall be no fear, nor shall they grieve.
(Ali (translator) 1975: 25–6)

Christianity itself is based on the Incarnation, the claim that God entered into the world as a human being – or rather, as a man, Jesus of Nazareth. The historical fact that Jesus was male is reflected in Christian language. Jesus is understood by Christians to be the Christ, the Son of God. It is perhaps not surprising that, as a result, God is spoken of in primarily male gender language ('He', 'Him'). God is described by male images ('Lord', 'Father', 'King'). This problem is not restricted to Christianity alone. In Islam the term 'Allah' is without gender and yet throughout the translations of the Qur'an Allah is referred to as 'He' and 'Lord'.

Yet the Christian story has an additional problem. In Islam, Jesus is simply a prophet. In Christianity, Jesus is the personal revelation of God. This means that it is possible to summarize the Christian story thus: God 'the Father' has a 'Son', Jesus Christ, and that Son picks a group of twelve male disciples who go on to found the Church. Not surprisingly, this predominantly male basis for the Church has led to the idea that men are somehow 'closer' to God than women. Now this might be taken to mean that men are somehow 'more spiritual' than women. Or it might be taken to mean that God has ordained men to be the leaders of his church. Until very recently, leadership within the Christian Church has been identified as a specifically male role.

Such an idea is not common to all religions. If we look at the Rg-Veda (Hindu classical scripture), we find that the act of worship is portrayed as a communal activity in which male and female share:

> The married couples, anxious to satisfy thee and presenting oblations together cele-brate (thy worship), for the sake of (obtaining) herds of cattle. (Rg Veda 1.131.3; cited in Sharma, 1987: 61)

The woman's role within the ritual process is seen as essential, for she is joint host to the gods. Leadership in this tradition is not perceived as a purely male preserve. However, such an understanding of male and female roles is revised in later scriptures such as the Upanisads, where leadership becomes almost exclusively male (for further reading see Sharma, 1987).

The idea that leadership must be male surfaced in the recent debate concerning the possibility of women being ordained as priests within the Church of England. The Anglican Church, in common with the Roman Catholic Church and in contrast to other denominations such as the Methodist and the Baptist Churches, until recently denied that a woman could be a priest. In other words, the church decreed that women could not represent Christ during certain rites of the church. The arguments of opponents to the ordination of women stem from a particular understanding of the respective natures of men and women.

EXERCISE

The following passage is from a speech made by a leading opponent to women's ordina-tion, Graham Leonard, a former Bishop of London, explaining why he is opposed to women priests. Read the extract and then answer the following questions.

> I believe that the Scriptures speak of God as Father, that Christ was incarnate as a male, that he chose men to be his apostles . . . not because of social conditioning, but because in the order of creation headship and authority is symbolically and fundamentally asso-ciated with maleness. For the same reason the highest vocation of any created being was given to a woman, Mary, as representative of mankind in our response to God because symbolically and fundamentally, the response of sacrificial giving is associated with femaleness . . . As the American Protestant layman Thomas Howard has said 'Jews and Christians worship the God who has gone to vast and prolonged pains to disclose himself to us as he not she, as King and not Queen, and for Christians as Father not Mother, and who sent his Son not his daughter in his final unveiling of himself for our eyes. These are terrible mysteries and we have no warrant to tinker with them.' (G. Leonard, speech to the General Synod of the Church of England, 8 November 1978, Church Literature Association for the Church Union, cited in D. Hampson, 1990: 66)

Now answer these questions:

1. What justification does Leonard give for excluding women from the priesthood? Does this create problems for viewing Christianity as an appropriate way of expressing one's spirituality if one is female?

2. How does Leonard describe the 'fundamental' nature of women? Drawing upon your own experiences, how might you respond to his idea of what constitutes femaleness?

EXERCISE RESPONSE

In answer to the first question, according to Leonard, men and women have definite and distinct roles which God has ordained for his creatures. So, maleness reflects qualities of leadership. This is further illustrated by the 'fact' that Christ and the twelve disciples were male. Femaleness, on the contrary, reflects qualities of submission. Women are to be submissive in the same way in which the Virgin Mary was submissive to God's will. Historically, Christianity reflects a male revelation of God which, Leonard claims, says something about the true nature of God; in other words, God is either in some sense male or closer to male qualities. An understanding of Christianity which so stresses maleness suggests that a woman would need to ask herself if Christianity could be an appropriate vehicle for female spiritual expression. If spirituality is an expression of one's sense of self and one's place in the world, Christianity with its male language and imagery might not be of much use for women.

Our response to the second question is that for Leonard, the fundamental nature of woman is one of 'sacrificial giving'. Such an understanding of what makes a woman 'good' has led many women to live lives which have not been fulfilled. They may feel guilty if they do not live up to the picture of the self-sacrificing martyr. Alternatively, they may have stifled their desires and hopes and lived for others. Will a woman brought up with this model of femaleness accept what is unacceptable – for example, abuse, degradation, disrespect – in the name of accepting the will of God?

What does it mean to be spiritual?

In many writings on spirituality, the very idea of 'the spiritual' aspires to traditional attributes of maleness. The word 'spiritual' has connotations of detachment, coolness, asceticism. If we say of someone, 'he's so spiritual', we're probably trying to describe that person in terms of those qualities – that is, he doesn't seem concerned with the things of this world, he leads a celibate existence, etc. There has been a tendency to link spirituality to a disregard for the body. So we read of the desert fathers who lived in caves or even at the top of pillars, trying to conquer the lusts of the body by denigrating the body. It is important to note that this is not necessarily a common feature of all religions. So while the Buddha lived an ascetic life for a time, he eventually rejected this way of cultivating the spiritual life.

While there have been women ascetics, women themselves have been closely identified with the body and nature. This identification can be traced back to the philosophies of Plato and Aristotle. Plato in his *Symposium* identifies love of woman with the natural urge to procreate (see *Symposium* 207b–208c). Aristotle associates woman with passive matter, and, by implication, with natural impulses (see Aristotle's *On the Generation of the Animals*). Both thinkers were to influence the way in which Christian doctrine was to develop. Through the acceptance of these ideas in the writings of one of the major Christian theologians, Thomas Aquinas (*c*.1225–1274), woman was linked to the body, nature and the world. Such ideas built upon those which claimed woman to be responsible for the Fall. Men, on the other hand, were linked with spirituality, reason and the mind.

In these times of increased environmental consciousness, women may feel that it is good to be identified in this way with nature. However, because the spiritual has been associated with overcoming the world and the flesh within the Western spiritual tradition, this idea has led to the belief that women are less 'spiritual' than men.

EXERCISE

Here are a selection of views from 'spiritual' men on the nature of woman. Read them and then think about the question at the end.

> Man, but not woman, is made in the image of God. It is plain from this that women should be subject to their husbands, and should be as slaves (Gratian, *Decretum* 1140).

> In such a being as the absolute female there are no logical and ethical phenomena, and, therefore, the ground for the assumption of a soul is absent ... There is no female genius, and there never has been one ... and there never can be one ... How could a soulless being possess genius? (Weininger, 1910: 189)

Weigh up these ideas with your own self-understanding. What assumptions are they making – for example, about the soul?

EXERCISE RESPONSE

What does it means to talk of a 'soul'? Both Gratian and Weininger suggest that woman does not possess this quality. For Gratian, woman does not possess the 'image of God'; some might term this quality 'the soul'. For Weininger, a being without a soul could not be a genius. When we talk of 'soul', what are we talking about? Are we talking of a metaphysical entity, something which could be defined separately from physical existence, or are we talking about the quality of humanity? Gratian and Weininger, in denying a soul to the female, are denying her basic humanity.

Women, then, have been identified with the body, with primeval nature, with chaos. If these things constitute the natural woman, how can she hope to live the 'spiritual' life (as understood by these worthy fathers)? How can she be a 'good' woman?

Within the Christian tradition, one of the principal models for the 'good' woman, as defined by men, has been the Virgin Mary. Mary, the mother of Christ, is a good woman as she is both a virgin, untouched by the impurity of sexual relations, and also a mother, the ultimate vocation of any woman under patriarchy. (See box 9.2 'Explanatory theory', pages 200–1.) Moreover, she is characterized by purity, passivity, obedience. Most pictures of the Virgin show her with downcast eyes, modest, unassuming, almost invisible. By modelling herself upon Mary, a Christian woman can escape the punishment merited by Eve's actions. (For more on Mary as role model, see Daly, 1986: 81–2.)

This negative attitude toward female sexuality can also be found in Islam, where a woman is exempt from obligatory prayers when she is menstruating, and for forty days after the birth of a child. Does this, along with the Christian attitude to sexuality, suggest that a woman is not capable of being spiritual during these times?

Perhaps we should press for a new understanding of what it means to be 'spiritual'. There is a sense in which many central experiences of women, for example, childbirth and menstruation, do not adhere easily with views of the spiritual life as one of quiet reflection, detachment and aloofness from the things of this world. Women in many ways are connected to the world, to nature, to the body. Might it be possible, then, to tie in the wild, natural side of women's nature with ideas about the spiritual? Men have often complained about the way in which women cannot be controlled. It would be interesting to incorporate female strength and determination into our model of what it means to be spiritual. If women are to be 'spiritual', this does not mean that they must curb their strength, individuality, and independence. Much creativity comes from these things, and, as we shall see in the next section, spirituality necessitates creativity.

EXERCISE

Michèle Roberts (1991) in her novel *The Wild Girl* tells the story of Mary Magdalene, one of the women followers of Christ. In Roberts' retelling, Mary is a fiercely independent woman whose spirituality has much to do with her sexuality and her sense of herself as a part of the world. In Roberts' story, Mary and Jesus are lovers. This relationship is seen as the source of Mary's spiritual awakening, suggesting that the sexual and the spiritual are closely connected. In this passage, Mary describes the way in which their sexual union opened up a new sense of the nature of reality for her.

> That night I lay with Jesus, held in his arms, in a grain-store belonging to a kindly farmer whose property lay along our route. Separated from the others only by the wall of the cloak he cast about us, we touched each other in the darkness. As we drew closer and closer towards each other we entered a new place, a country of heat and sweetness and light different to the ground we had explored together before. I felt us taken upwards and transformed: I no longer knew what was inside and what was outside, where he ended and I began, only that our bones and flesh and souls were suddenly woven up together in a great melting and pouring. I was six years old again, lying on the roof looking up at the stars, at the rents in the dark fabric of the sky and the light shining through it. Only this time I rose, I pierced through the barrier of shadow, and was no longer an I, but part of a great whirl of light that throbbed and rang with music – for a moment, till I was pulled back by the sound of my own voice whispering words I did not understand: this is the resurrection, and the life. (Roberts, 1991: 67)

How do you respond to this passage? Do you think that the sexual and the spiritual can be linked in the way which this passage suggests? What might any reservations you have about this connection suggest about your understanding of the spiritual?

This section has suggested that the traditional model for what constitutes 'spirituality' is geared towards male experience and excludes female experience. In the next section we shall explore the kind of spirituality women might seek in order to fully express their experience of the world.

A Woman-centred Spirituality

How might women create/discover a spirituality which more adequately reflects women's experience of the world? Indeed, it is experience which may prove to be of vital importance when considering spirituality, as opposed to expressions of this within a given religious tradition. Rosemary Ruether, one of the foremost theologians working in the field of women's spirituality, suggests that religion itself might be a male construct; in other words, that female spirituality has its basis in women's direct experience of life, birth and death in the world:

> Could it be that the male, marginalized from direct participation in the great mysteries of gestation and birth, asserted his superior physical strength to monopolize leisure and culture and that he did so by creating ritual expressions that duplicated female gestating and birthing roles so as to transfer power of these primary mysteries to the male? (Reuther, 1991: 238)

So to what sources might a woman-centred spirituality turn? If we are concerned with spirituality rather than religion, there is no reason why our choice of sources should not be varied, coming from many different religious traditions. This section will deal with three important areas – finding a past (which will look at the legacy of women within different traditions), finding an image (which will look at female images for the divine), and finding a future (which will look at possible ways of developing women's spirituality).

Finding a past

This section may prove more important for women already within a tradition who do not want to give up their foundation in a historical faith and community. However, all women may gain something from consideration of female mystics from different religious traditions. Mysticism may prove to be important for the creation of a woman-centred spirituality as it is based primarily in experience, although its experience is filtered through a tradition. While the experiences of female and male mystics may not differ, it is the way in which these experiences are expressed which is different. Reading the works of the mystics can be an enlightening experience, particularly as they often have a very modern feel about them. Here are a few examples.

Rabi'a al 'Adawiyya (717–801CE)

Born in Basra, little is known of Rabi'a's background. Some claim that her family were poor, and of the Sufi, or 'mystical', tradition within Islam. Others believe her to have been of noble birth. Orphaned at a young age, she was seized and sold as a slave. One day, despairing of her situation, she hears a voice saying, 'Be not sorrowful, for on the day of Resurrection thy rank shall be such that those who are nearest to God in Heaven shall envy thee' (cited by Fernea and Bezirgan, 1977: 41).

Her master, realizing the true mystical nature of his slave, sets her free to seek the ascetical life she desires. A wide variety of stories surround the life of this mystic, and the tradition tells us that she experienced severe illness during visions and recitations (a common occurrence for most mystics). Rabi'a is reported to have described her relationship with Allah as follows:

> My peace, O my brothers, is in solitude,
> And my beloved is with me always,
> for His love is the test for me among mortal beings,
> Whene'er His beauty I may contemplate . . .
> If I die of love, before completing satisfaction,
> Alas, for my anxiety in the world, alas for my
> distress,
> O Healer (of souls), the heart feeds upon its
> desire,
> The striving after union with Thee has healed my
> soul,
> O my joy and life abidingly,
> Thou wast the source of my life and from Thee also
> came my ecstasy.
> I have separated myself from all created beings,
> My hope is from union with Thee, for that is the
> goal of my desire.
> (From Fernea and Bezirgan, 1977: 45)

Rabi'a perceives Allah as the only thing she could possibly love, calling Allah her 'Beloved'. In common with other mystics, she feels that the 'Beauty' of Allah is beyond conception. Allah is not only her Beloved, but also the source of life; that which all human hearts feed on. In this excerpt, she talks of 'union' with Allah, which takes the idea of Allah as Beloved further: she is yearning for oneness with God. The language of sexuality fits perfectly with the language of spirituality:

> In my case there is not such existence, for I have passed out of self. I exist in God. I am His absolutely. (Quoted in Ferguson, 1976: 154)

Hildegard of Bingen (1098–1179)

It is important to recognize Hildegard as a woman of her time. While a strong individual, she still conforms to the negative views of women prevalent at the time. In a letter to Bernard of Clairvaux, she speaks of herself thus: 'Wretched as I am (and more than wretched in bearing the name of woman) . . .' (Bowie and Davis, 1990: 127f.).

Yet her ideas on spirituality are peculiarly resonant for today. For example, many of her experiences are concerned with creation.

God is viewed as the principle of life. At times, her ideas would seem to border on **pantheism** (that is, the idea that God and the world are one and the same). So in the *Book of Divine Works*, God speaks in the following way:

> I, the highest and fiery power, have kindled every living spark and I have breathed out nothing that can die . . . I have regulated the circuit of the heavens by flying around its revolving track with my upper wings – that is to say, with Wisdom. But I am also the fiery life of the divine essence – I flame above the beauty of the fields; I shine in the waters; in the sun, the moon and the stars, I burn . . . For I am the whole of life – life was not torn from stones; it did not bud from branches; nor is it rooted in the generative power of the male. Rather, every living thing is rooted in me. (Bowie and Davis, 1990: 91–2)

Feminism is often linked with ecology – the implication being that women have an affinity with the world. Hildegard's words seem particularly fruitful in this context. God is the life of this world. If this is so, if the world is God's body, how should we treat it?

Hildegard moves away from thinking about life in terms of a set of opposites – no longer is it a case of God or the world, soul or the body. We don't have to choose one or the other. Rather: 'The soul assists the flesh and the flesh, the soul. For every work is perfected through soul as well as flesh, so that the soul is revived by doing good and holy works with the flesh' (Bowie and Davies, 1990: 96). This seems much more positive than some of the flesh-hating/woman-hating works of the fathers of the church! Hildegard offers a holistic alternative particularly apt for considering what it might mean to be spiritual bearing in mind the ecological crisis facing today's world.

Margery Kempe (born c.1373)

Margery Kempe was a housewife and lay member of the church. She was illiterate, but not uneducated. It appears that she suffered from post-natal depression after the birth of her first child, and some writers have suggested that this illness would account for her visions of God. Perhaps what is interesting is the way in which Margery adopts the contemplative life as a means of attaining personal space. Mother to fourteen children, she used her religious experiences as a means of gaining some kind of autonomy over her own life.

An interesting aspect of Margery's spiritual life is the way in which she finds God in 'women's work'. Remember, she is not a 'professional' religious like Hildegard. She is seeking space in her own life to explore the spiritual. So her images of the divine are mediated through her experiences of life. God is found in day-to-day experiences, not in a specifically sanctified place or action.

BOX 12.3	**Margery Kempe: God in the Ordinary**

'When you provide food or care for yourself, your family or anyone you receive in my name, it will be as though you have given it to me or my mother.' (Hawker, 1988: 27)

'Everytime I see women being purified after childbirth it is as though I see our Lady.

'When I watch a wedding, in my heart I see our Lady joined with St Joseph and the joining of a soul with Jesus Christ our Lord.

'When I see children carried in their mother's arms it seems to me I see Christ in his childhood.' (Hawker, 1988: 41)

Teresa of Avila (1515–1582)

A woman in medieval times was faced with two choices: marriage or the religious life inside a closed order. Many women opted for the latter as it at least offered opportunities for greater self-expression. Theoretically, at least, the religious woman was equal to men. Teresa's reasons for entering the convent are somewhat unclear. What is clear is that she made that decision not for primarily spiritual reasons, but for a whole host of reasons, which seem to have included fear of causing a family scandal, and an awareness of the hard and unfulfilling life led by her mother. It was to be twenty years before she had what she considered to be a genuine religious experience. Her writings are particularly important for an exploration of women's spirituality as she wrote specifically for women.

During Teresa's lifetime, the Spanish Inquisition was in place. This doctrinal committee, sanctioned by church and state in Spain, decided what was orthodox (and therefore acceptable) and what was heterodox (and therefore unacceptable). Penalties for being found guilty of heresy ranged from excommunication to execution. Mystics base their understanding of God upon personal experience rather than upon doctrine and dogma. As such, Teresa throughout her life fell under suspicion of being a heretic. It is significant that during these times of trial, Teresa trusts her own experience of God, yet undergoes severe doubts about the experience only when learned men challenge her:

When I am in prayer, and on days when I am enjoying quiet and my thoughts are fixed on God, all the learned men and saints in the world might unite in tormenting me with all imaginable tortures, and, even if I wanted to believe them, they could not make me believe that this is the devil's work, because I cannot. When they did try to make me believe this, I was afraid, seeing who they were that spoke to me in that way, for I thought that they must be speaking the truth, and that I, being who I was, must be mistaken. (Quoted in Green, 1989: 163)

As Dierdre Green (1989) points out, it seems that women's religious experience has seldom been taken into account when forming religious doctrines. This has much to do with the way in which the 'non-rational' experiences of mystics have undoubtedly been mistrusted as linked with qualities which are seen as 'feminine' and irrational. Feminists are starting to challenge this approach by suggesting that we start with experience, and that experience itself is self-authenticating, regardless of cultural mores.

So what is Teresa's experience of God? She looks within herself to find God. It is in self-understanding, not self-negation, that we find the divine. It is understanding of ourselves that leads to a closer awareness of God.

Summary

Looking to mystics from different traditions may help provide not only a basis for the spiritual lives of women within those traditions, but it may also help the more general quest to find a basis for women's spirituality. Women's spirituality will have its grounding in women's experience of life, and the way in which that experience is expressed.

EXERCISE

1. Can you think of everyday experiences where you might find God?
2. What problems might there be in basing women's spirituality in experience?

EXERCISE RESPONSE

'Experience' is a notoriously difficult term with which to work. How are we to define this? Do we mean simply individual experience of life? If so, it will not be possible to speak of women's spirituality in any meaningful sense as I will always be speaking from my own situation. However, some feminists want to work with a rather different definition of experience. Women's experience can be understood as women's experience of oppression in a patriarchal society, as well as the positive experience of sisterhood. In this sense, there will be common ground between women, but also considerable difference. Perhaps discussions of spiritual experience could fit into that pattern.

Beverley Clack and Jo-Anne Whitcomb

Finding an image

One of the central problems we confronted early on in this chapter revolved around the predominantly male images of God in the monotheistic faiths. Is a male God the only image of the divine?

Hindu ideas of the goddess

In Hinduism we come across the idea that the multitude of gods and goddesses are attributes of the ultimate reality, or 'God'. Furthermore, we find that the gods and goddesses themselves are said to contain both male and female attributes (see the picture of Shiva at the front of this chapter). So it is possible for a Hindu woman to come to the conclusion that she as a woman, and therefore as an integral part of humanity, is in fact also an integral part of God. Can we then look to the Hindu goddesses as a way of finding an image to represent the spiritual life of women?

Within Hindu mythology goddesses are indeed portrayed as extremely powerful. Yet Wendy O'Flaherty (1981) in her book *Sexual Metaphors and Animal Symbols in Indian Mythology*, maintains that although the goddesses within Hinduism are perceived as powerful, they are also considered dangerous precisely because they are powerful. The dominant goddess is thus seen in a variety of ways, not all of them positive (see box 12.4, 'The dominant goddess'). Indeed, on a mundane level, female power is viewed with suspicion and feared as dangerous. It is felt that women need some kind of restraining force which will domesticate them. So stories of goddesses are told which show that although they are powerful, they are completely subservient to their husbands (see box 12.5, 'Manu-dharma-sastra'). These stories can be used to suppress the power of women. Hindu women are sometimes directed to the stories surrounding Sita, who is portrayed as entirely devoted and loyal to her husband Rama. Sita is reported to have said to Rama:

> For a woman, it is not her father, her son, nor her mother, friends nor her own self, but the husband, who in this world and the next is ever her sole means of salvation ... I shall willingly dwell in the forest as formerly I inhabited the palace of my father, having no anxiety in the Three Worlds and reflecting only on my duties towards my lord. Ever subject to thy will, docile, living like an ascetic, in those honey-scented woodlands I shall be happy in thy proximity, O Rama, O Illustrious Lord. (From the *Ramayana of Valmiki*, cited by Kinsley, 1986: 71)

Sita is thus portrayed as the perfect wife! This idea of forfeiting one's self for one's husband does not present an ideal role model for women. However, it may prove more useful to focus on the way in which the androgyny of the gods and goddesses suggests that deity itself is composed of both male and female.

<table>
<tr><td>

The Dominant Goddess

She appears as the killer of her demon lover, beheading him in a symbolic castration; she dances on the corpse of her consort, impaling herself upon his still animate phallus. This is the non-maternal goddess, with whom the worshipper does not dare seek erotic contact for fear of losing his powers. But the dominant woman also appears as the mother goddess, with whom the worshipper does not dare seek erotic contact for fear of incest. (O'Flaherty, 1981: 77)

</td><td>

**BOX
12.4**

</td></tr>
</table>

<table>
<tr><td>

Manu-Dharma-Sastra

Though destitute of virtue, or seeking pleasure elsewhere, or devoid of good qualities, a husband must be constantly worshipped as a god by a faithful wife. (From Kinsley, 1986: 70)

</td><td>

**BOX
12.5**

</td></tr>
</table>

New Age ideas of the Goddess

Arising from the 'New Age' movement and its attempt to find a relevant spirituality for today's world, some have felt the need to return to the worship of the Goddess who, it is suggested, was venerated during the prehistoric era. Does this movement merely reflect nostalgia for a time when it was perceived that to be female was to embody deity? While that is one way of considering this impulse, it may be fairer to say that the Goddess gives expression to the desire many women have for a symbol of the divine which more adequately reflects their experience than those formed within the major religious traditions by men. (For further reading see Tulip, 1991.)

So why might the Goddess be important? Women who would not consider themselves 'religious' may find goddess imagery useful for exploring different aspects of their femaleness. How might this be possible? First, the Goddess is often employed by women in an attempt to reclaim the female body. As we have seen, there has been a tendency to link women with the body and with nature in a negative way. Those who worship the Goddess, believe that their rituals link the cycles of the female body with the planetary cycles of the year. The Goddess is thus seen as the symbol of life and death, waxing and waning in the universe and ourselves. As such the female body is seen as the incarnation of natural cycles (see the next exercise).

Such an interpretation may also be useful for women who are using the language of the Goddess to make sense of their experience of life. Indeed, those involved with 'Goddess Spirituality' claim that the symbol of the Goddess has psychological and political consequences for women. Ntosake Shange (1991) expressed this when she said: 'I found God in myself and I loved her fiercely' (p. 290). The self is affirmed and accepted. At the same time, this image expresses the woman's sense of her own power to determine her own life. She will no longer be at the mercy of male society. She has found her inner strength and freedom, and will live by it.

EXERCISE

The Greek goddess Demeter was understood as a trinity – Virgin (Kore), Mother (Demeter), and Crone (Persephone). It does not take a great leap of the imagination to see how this three-phase goddess could be intimately connected to the three phases of the moon – waxing (coming to fullness), full, and waning (moving from fullness). At the same time, the life cycle of any woman can be reflected in these phases. As Shuttle and Redgrove (1986) point out, the ancients themselves probably first measured time by the moon's cycle. Women were probably aware of their menstrual cycles as part of a natural process made explicit by the stages of the moon. Modern people seem to have lost this affinity with creation.

The Goddess is described as maiden, mother and crone; images which cohere with the three stages of the moon, and the three stages of woman. Accepting this image means that all the stages of womanhood are deemed important, not just the 'youthful beauty' venerated by our culture. Write a poem or paint a picture which gives expression to this idea of the divine. How does it relate to your own experience of yourself?

Finding a future

So what is the way forward for a woman-centred approach to spirituality? Here are three possible approaches you might like to explore.

Retelling stories

Judith Plaskow's (1979) retelling of the story of Lilith is an excellent example of women taking stories with a misogynistic purpose, and giving them a whole new meaning. In the Jewish rabbinic tradition, Lilith was the first wife of Adam who refused to obey him; notably by refusing to lie beneath him while making love! Adam complains to God about his troublesome wife, and she leaves Eden, haunting the wilderness places and becoming the mother to all kinds of demons – notably the succubus who troubles men with lewd thoughts and wet dreams!

In Plaskow's retelling, Lilith is seen as expressing the power of women which is repressed under male-dominated society. Lilith comes back to tempt the submissive new wife, Eve, over the wall. The two women leave God and Adam fearful, wondering about what they will do when they return. (Ruether, 1984.)

Plaskow's intent in telling this story is to help women reclaim their own strengths, to feel at ease with themselves and to gain a sense of their power.

EXERCISE

Take a well-known story with a female anti-hero (e.g. Eve or Jezebel or Pandora), and give it a different woman-centred meaning. What problems/strengths might there be with this kind of approach?

Creating stories

In recent years there has emerged the image of a crucified woman – Christa. Seeing a woman in the place of the male Christ has often been controversial. But what is interesting about this image is the way in which women are trying to use their experience of life and relate it to particular established religious ideas. An image of a crucified woman seemed to this particular artist to reflect the position of women in a society which seeks to oppress and exclude them. In other words, women are making new stories to make sense of their experiences.

Beverley Clack and Jo-Anne Whitcomb

EXERCISE

What kind of stories might you tell to make sense of the way in which you perceive your life in this world? Is it easier to create or to reclaim a story to tell of the things which have value in and give meaning to your life?

Women-church

This movement in which women come together to explore female spirituality needn't be exclusively linked to one religious tradition. In Portland, Maine, there exists a Feminist Spiritual Community which consists of three circles of women: the circle of Sophia, which has its roots in the Judaeo-Christian tradition; the circle of Isis, which has its roots in Wicca (or witchcraft); and the circle of the Great Spirit, which has its source in the religion of the Native American peoples. Within these circles the women work on rituals which are then presented to the community as a whole. In the UK, the St Hilda's Community aims at providing a non-sexist setting where female spirituality may be explored within the Christian tradition (see box 12.6, 'God our Mother'). Within the Women-church movement, the intention is for women to meet together to explore and create a spirituality which fits their experiences.

BOX 12.6	God Our Mother: A Prayer From the St Hilda's Community

God our Mother
you hold our life within you;
nourish us at your breast,
and teach us to walk alone.
Help us so to receive your tenderness
and respond to your challenge
that others may draw life from us,
in your name. Amen.
(From *Women Included*, St Hilda's Community, 1991)

268

Conclusion

This chapter has attempted to outline the kinds of issues surrounding spirituality, and the ways in which some women are striving to correct some of the problems with spirituality as it has been formulated over the years by men. For those who think that these issues are really only of interest to women already involved in religion, these words of Mary Daly (1991) from early on in her philosophical career may be of interest:

> The becoming of women may not be only the doorway to deliverance from the omnipotent Father in all of his disguises, but, to many, also a doorway to something, namely to a more authentic search for transcendence, that is, for God. (Daly, 1991: 339)

REFERENCES

Ali, A. Y. (trans.) 1975: *The Holy Qu'ran*. Leicester: The Islamic Foundation.

Bowie, F. and Davies, O. (eds) 1990: *Hildegard of Bingen*. London: SPCK.

Daly, M. 1986: *Beyond God the Father*. London: Women's Press.

Daly, M. 1991: The spiritual dimension of women's liberation. In S. Gunew (ed.), *A Reader in Feminist Knowledge*, London: Routledge.

Ferguson, J. 1976: *An Illustrated Encyclopedia of Mysticism and the Mystery of Religion*. London: Thames & Hudson.

Fernea, E. W. and Bezirgan, B. Q. 1977: *Middle Eastern Women Speak*. Texas: University of Texas Press.

Green, D. 1989: *Gold in the Crucible*. Shaftesbury: Element.

Kinsley, D. 1986: *Hindu Goddesses: Visions of the Divine Feminine in the Hindu Religious Tradition*. Delhi: Motilal Banarsidass.

O'Flaherty, W. D. 1981: *Sexual Metaphors and Animal Symbols in Indian Mythology*. Oxford: Motilal Books.

Plaskow, Judith 1979: The coming of Lilith. In J. Plaskow and C. Christ (eds), *Womanspirit Rising*, New York: Harper & Row.

Roberts, Michèle 1991: *The Wild Girl*. London: Minerva.

Ruether, R. R. 1984: *Religion and Sexism*. New York: Simon Schuster.

Ruether, R. R. 1991: Renewal or new creation? In S. Gunew (ed.), *A Reader in Feminist Knowledge*, London: Routledge.

St Hilda's Community 1991: *Women Included*. London: SPCK.

Shange, Ntosake 1991: For coloured girls who have considered suicide when the rainbow is enuf. In S. Gunew (ed.), *A Reader in Feminist Knowledge*, London: Routledge.

Sharma, A. 1987: *Women in the World's Religions*. New York: State University of New York Press.

Shuttle, P. and Redgrave, P. 1986: *The Wise Wound*. London: Paladin.

Tulip, Marie 1991: Introduction. In S. Gunew (ed.), *A Reader in Feminist Knowledge*, London: Routledge.

Weininger, O. 1910: *Sex and Character*. London: Heinemann.

CHAPTER
13 Taking the Next Step

Lyndie Brimstone

Throughout this book, the contributors have asked you to draw on your experience as a way of engaging with a range of issues relating to particular aspects of women's lives. No doubt as you have read through the book there were times when you registered an immediate identification with something being said, a feeling that, whether painful or empowering, those words could have been your own. At other times you may have felt distant, bored, impatient, angry even, because your experience seems to have been overlooked or given insufficient attention. If you have been working on your own to maintain a 'dialogue' with the book, as suggested in the Introduction, you will have voiced these feelings and, in some cases, put words to things for the first time. If you have done this on paper you will now have a substantial record to look back on. If you have been working through the book with a group, you may have been surprised to find either that your experience *is* shared by others or, conversely, that no one else had even thought about what you take for granted as a daily reality. It is possible, too, that a life you had thought mundane and uneventful, whether your own or someone else's, has now taken on new meaning and interest. I am spelling out these possibilities because you need to recognize that it is precisely the kind of interaction that you have been engaging in here that forms the *basis* of academic Women's Studies.

It is with the emphasis on basis, however, that we come to the point of this concluding chapter for, while Women's Studies couldn't exist without it, each contributor has directly or indirectly made the point that 'raw experience' alone is not enough. Theory is both inescapable and necessary if we are to take the next step and, though we may not always have a particular name for it or a very clear idea of where it comes from, we in fact use theory all the time. The primary purpose of this chapter, then, is to encourage you to think about the sets of ideas you already hold, the theories you already support, and the ways in which they contribute both to your understanding of your experience and to the shaping of the experience itself. Rather than setting out to provide a mass of information for you to learn, this chapter will focus on the importance of what is in some ways a much harder task: asking questions.

EXERCISE

Take some time now to look back to the Introduction, paying particular attention to the sections headed 'What is Women's Studies?' and 'The Place of Theory'. Make brief notes under the following headings:

1. Why Women's Studies is political
2. Why experience as a valid form of knowledge needs justification

3. Theory – negative associations
4. Theory – as inescapable necessity.

EXERCISE RESPONSE

I hope that by the time you get to the end of this book you will think about collecting notes under a fifth heading: 'Feminist theory – stimulating and empowering'. If not, you should at least have sufficient confidence to know that you understand enough of the basics not to be intimidated by theory. My notes from the Introduction look like this:

1. Why Women's Studies (WS) is political:

- WS came into being because of unequal power relations
- WS informed by feminist scholarship
- Women's knowledge challenges traditional views, leads to change
- WS teaching challenges not just *what* but *how*
- WS aims to empower women individually and collectively

2. Why experience as a valid form of knowledge needs justification

- experience embedded in complex social context
- none of us just women (race, class, ability, sexuality etc.)
- need to understand individual experience in relation to shared/different experience

3. Theory – negative associations

- difficult, inaccessible
- associated with 'great' men
- unfamiliar language
- rules for members only
- not practical, doesn't do anything

4. Theory – as inescapable necessity

- can't understand experience, make sense of our lives without it
- can't see things on a bigger scale without it
- allows us to explain observations and experiences in a systematic way

- necessary for shared understandings
- provides basis for strategies for change

I expect that your notes include some of these points and you may also have added more that came to mind while you were reading. It's certainly very useful to set notes out in this way because it is easier to focus on, hold on to and develop smaller 'thought chunks'. Another advantage is that connections and contradictions stand out. Take the last notes in 3 and 4, for example, where on the one hand theory is rejected because it doesn't do anything and on the other deemed necessary in order to bring about the desired change. You might also like to think about the clear connection between Women's Studies and feminism in the first set of notes. Did you consider this connection so automatic as to be taken for granted or, like many Women's Studies students starting feminist theory courses, feel antagonistic towards it?

EXERCISE

Perhaps you would like to attempt two items from the questionnaire that I put to undergraduate students in their first session:

1. Is there, or should there be, a distinction between Women's Studies and Feminist Studies? Please give reasons for your answer.
2. Have you ever come across a definition of feminism? If so, please give details. If not, try to formulate a definition in not more than twenty words.

EXERCISE RESPONSE

In the last four years responses to the first question have barely changed and I have come to expect that between 30 and 50 per cent of students will argue, quite forcibly, for a distinction to be made between the two. The main reason given is that Women's Studies can embrace *all* women, including those who choose to live with husbands and identify as housewives, while Feminist Studies is really for the relatively small number of independent *Cosmopolitan* or *Guardian* readers who want careers. 'Women in the Arts and Media' (chapter 10) points to some of the ways in which this popular (mis)understanding of feminism has come about. Did it influence the definition you have given?

If you haven't already done so, have a look to see what your dictionary says. According to the *Concise Oxford* (1990), feminism is (1) 'the advocacy of women's rights on the ground of the equality of the sexes', and (2) a medical term to describe 'the development of female characteristics in a male person'. The latter is certainly a very interesting idea but I think you'll agree that, on the whole, the dictionary is not a great help.

One definition that I like comes from Chris Weedon (1987) who says: 'Feminism is a politics. It is a politics directed at changing existing power relations between women and men in society' (p. 1). This is a bold and clear statement emphasizing 'politics' and 'change'. Chris Weedon goes on to elaborate on these 'power relations' which, she says, 'structure all areas of life, the family, education and welfare, the worlds of work and politics, culture and leisure' and, as if this didn't cover enough to make feminism relevant to all women, she adds, 'They [power relations] determine who does what and for whom, what we are and what we might become'. Clearly, then, feminism is not for or about any one particular group of women, and there is no intrinsic reason why a feminist political agenda should be determined solely by the independent, highly educated, career-minded (global) minority of women. Indeed, in order to avoid repeating the same exclusionary patriarchal practices that have contributed to women's subordination for so long, ongoing open debates that can acknowledge and interrogate both commonalities and differences, connections and contradictions, are crucial.

The chapters 'Growing Up' (chapter 2) and 'Girls and Schooling' (chapter 4) directly acknowledge the vitality and importance of these debates by setting out a number of different approaches taken by feminists and pointing to some of the differences between them. Each approach has developed a framework to help us to see and understand women's diverse life experiences. Each has developed strategies within this framework that set out to challenge, in varying degrees, the patriarchal status quo. Each, whether it is made explicit or not, involves theory. As Chris Weedon puts it:

> If feminism is a politics, it is also a theory, or rather a range of theories. Whether acknowledged or not, every form of feminist politics, and there are many, implies a particular way of understanding patriarchy and the possibilities of change. (Weedon, 1987: 4)

It cannot be stressed often enough that there is no single, all-embracing, answer-everything feminist theory. What we all have to do is evaluate each of these approaches, frameworks, strategies for change, test them against the pulse, decide which we can best work with.

EXERCISE

If you have been compiling a glossary of terms, you will doubtless have made a number of entries drawn from the boxes included in 'Growing Up' (chapter 2) and 'Girls and Schooling' (chapter 4). With your glossary to hand, read box 2.1 'Theories of identity formation' (pages 18–20) and 'Feminists go to school' (pages 74–76) again, and see if you can pick out some notes and key words to put under the following broad headings:

1. autonomous individual
2. socialization and biological difference
3. social construction and the sexual division of labour
4. precarious subjectivity.

EXERCISE RESPONSE

This wasn't an easy task and if you've managed to collect just one or two terms or concepts under each, you've done well. One of the reasons for setting the exercise is that, as with any other skill, working with new theory and the language that comes with it requires practice. One reading is never enough. I would also hope that, going back over the boxes this time, you found the terms and concepts just a little more familiar and less off-putting than they might have appeared first time round.

Within the context of Women's Studies it would have been more usual to ask you to organize your notes for the last exercise under headings like 'liberal feminist', 'radical feminist', and so on. This approach is not without merit and it is important to recognize that some feminists do find close identification with a particular category productive for a variety of reasons. Not least of these is the sense of personal affirmation and collective solidarity evoked by 'I am a lesbian/radical/socialist feminist' type assertions. Others, and I would include myself in this group, aren't so sure. Jackie Stacey describes her uncertainty like this:

> . . . like many other feminists, I have long felt dissatisfied with this rigid categorization which, firstly, excludes so much feminist thinking which eludes such distinctions; and secondly, fixes individual writers and thinkers in a way that ignores the changes and developments in their work, disregarding the complexities or contradictions in one woman's feminism. Use of these categories frequently obscures more than it reveals and can lead to the unhelpful stereotyping of feminist ideas: for example, radical feminists are dismissed as essentialist, lesbians are all assumed to be

radical feminists, socialist feminists are assumed to be uninterested in sexuality, and liberal feminists are seen as naively reformist. (Stacey, 1993: 52)

This said, you will need to be familiar with the key ideas associated with different, named feminisms (such as Liberal Feminism, Radical Feminism and so forth) because so much has been written in these terms. What I asked you to do was to organize your notes not using rigid categories or labels but rather broad thematic headings that suggest different ways of perceiving both the self and, by extension, gender and social organization. It is under these broad headings that I will point out and ask you to consider selected aspects of the standard feminist perspectives that are used on most Women's Studies courses.

Autonomous Individual

There can be no doubt that the way you see, or are prepared to see, yourself and your own experience will influence your response to and willingness to engage with different feminist theories. If, for example, you believe that you are a sovereign individual with free will, one who can make, and has the right to make, rational choices (the first heading), you will probably find some aspects of liberal feminism quite attractive. Your energies are likely to be directed towards reforms in education, legislation, and work practices that would guarantee equality of opportunity and permit individual women to freely choose their paths towards self-fulfilment and happiness without the burden of sex discrimination and social pressure. This is no small agenda and I think that very few feminists of any persuasion would disagree with the need to remove institutional obstacles. The problem comes when we try to define these obstacles and work out an order for tackling them. For example, some regard the institution of heterosexuality as the biggest and most fundamental obstacle of all, while liberal feminists, including those in lesbian relationships, are inclined to take the nuclear family and existing social relations more or less for granted. What matters most to liberal feminists is that women *choose* whether and when to marry or have children, *choose* whether to work or stay at home and, most importantly, take responsibility for these freely made choices.

Can you see any problems with this reliance on free will and choice? I am not suggesting with this question that liberal feminism is wrong, a waste of time, or an inappropriate choice. That's for you to decide. I shall be asking you to look for problems and possibilities in every brief account given here. At the same time, what I shall try not to do, is to provide anything that might be read as a firm, unequivocal answer. There would be nothing wrong with me giving you my point of view providing, in accordance with feminist principles, I didn t try to pass it off as a universal truth (see discussion about language in chapter 1, page 11).

What is more useful at this stage, though, is for you to ask questions in order to clarify what you already think and recognize the theories that you already, at least in part, use.

A further point under 'autonomous individual'. Liberal feminism has its roots in humanism. Did you make this connection in your notes? The aim of liberal feminism is the creation of an androgynous society where biological difference is socially irrelevant, a society where all individuals have a right to self-determination and self-fulfilment in every sphere providing, of course, that this doesn't interfere with another's equally valid right. The ultimate aim of liberal feminism, then, is liberal humanism.

Socialization and Biological Difference

Your notes under this second heading will probably have included some reference to liberal feminism as well. Valerie Hey does, after all, suggest that 'socialization is a key term' in liberal feminist theory and that 'resocialization or changing attitudes of girls, parents and teachers' is seen as the answer to gender inequality (chapter 4, page 74). Biological difference, however, only enters the equation as a political insignificance. Yes, women have babies but, with the professionalization of domestic labour, changes in parenting arrangements and the removal of the stigma attaching to working mothers, this shouldn't make any difference unless the individual woman wants it to. Yes, 'femininity' and 'masculinity' are innate, natural, given sets of qualities but they have been grossly exaggerated to serve men's misguided interests. The powers of reason are available to both sexes and it is these, in the social world at least, that should prevail. Liberal feminism, then, only half fits under the heading 'socialization and biological difference'. It is, nevertheless, a half that's important to note because overlap, shared ground, relationship, is a characteristic of all feminist theories. The notes that I would expect to find firmly under this heading relate to radical feminism.

Radical feminists share with liberal feminists a belief in the power of socialization but disagree entirely on the place of biological sexual difference. If you understand your experience as not only strongly influenced by gender socialization but as crucially determined by your sex (see 'Key concepts' notes in chapter 7, page 134, if you are not clear about the sex/gender distinction), then some aspects of radical feminism will interest you. Males and females are understood as fundamentally different in radical feminist theory and resocialization certainly doesn't mean making girls more like boys through the extension of male-defined 'opportunities', or making women more like men through the granting of equal rights within the existing male-defined social order. Radical feminism demands far more extensive change than this for both sexes.

The bottom line in radical feminist theory is that one group, defined by biological sexual difference, is oppressed and violently controlled by the other. This same group, defined by biological sexual difference, is further disempowered through a socialization process that both creates and reinforces inferior status. Rather than seeking to dissolve, minimize, or 'androgynize' this biological sexual difference, radical feminism in the 1970s made a powerful case for wresting the power to define the world out of the hands of men and freeing women from the effects of 'false' socialization. With these newly uncovered selves, women would learn to appreciate and harness the innate, natural, given (superior), worth of our sex. No longer understood as signifiers of frailty or dependence, women's bodies and reproductive potential, together with all the gentle, nurturing, non-competitive, affective, in short, 'feminine' qualities that patriarchy has inappropriately (de)valued and used to men's advantage could be celebrated, regarded as strengths that women can redirect away from men and towards each other. At the same time, women could reclaim the qualities that men have denied us and appropriated for themselves. A prime example, here, is rationality.

For some radical feminists, this re-evaluation of what it means to be a woman involves a complete rejection of heterosexuality and the creation of separatist space in which women can discover and/or reinvent themselves outside of patriarchal definitions. For others who continue to enjoy sexual and/or emotional relationships with men, it marks a commitment to working primarily in women's interests in both the public and private spheres. There are many others who position themselves somewhere in between or move, at different points in their lives, between one position or another. This mobility is possible because radical feminist differences lie not in the foundations of the theory or, indeed, in the ultimate aim of overthrowing patriarchy, but in the ways that a feminist future and the strategies required to achieve it are envisaged.

EXERCISE

One way of checking out the ideas you already hold is to do the following: Make some notes about the kind of Utopian future you fantasize about. What would need to change to make it even vaguely possible?

On the subject of similarities and differences (again!), did you notice the repetition of the words 'innate, natural, given' in relation to both liberal and early radical feminist thought? Maybe, before we come on to the heading 'social construction and the sexual division of labour', we should give a name to this way of thinking. First, though, you need to go back over the few points I have made about radical feminism and make a note of any problems or possibilities you think there might be with this way of understanding and challenging women's oppression. When you know more about developments in each of the theories discussed here, you may change your mind. Meanwhile, not having a full account or complete understanding doesn't mean that there aren't some very important ideas that you can start to work with now. Have you asked yourself, for example, whether any of *your* ideas are **essentialist**? That is to say, are any of them based on the notion that some things, like sexuality, gender, mothering, or aggression are 'natural', 'innate', 'given'? Diana Fuss explains essentialism like this: 'Essentialism is most commonly understood as a belief in the real, true essence of things, the invariable and fixed properties which define the "whatness" of a given entity' (Fuss, 1989: xi).

Most people would agree that socialization has a significant part to play, but there is considerable disagreement about the raw material that socialization works on. Is there, underneath the layers of socialization, a 'real you' trying to get out? The fact that this sounds like the advertising copy for a hair colorant or exotic drink demonstrates the degree to which commercial interests recognize and play on the commonly held belief, supported by certain kinds of therapies, that we somehow, in some crucial respect, pre-exist socialization. In this sense, socialization is generally understood as a repressive practice, one which seeks to paper over or distort our 'true natures'. Popular expressions such as 'boys will be boys', 'just like a woman', and 'he's a real man' indicate, too, the widespread acceptance that at the very heart of each person there is a gendered kernel, a seed from which everything else develops, a point beyond which analysis cannot go. Some people believe this essential core to be genetic, some believe it forms in earliest infancy, some understand it within a spiritual framework. To pick up Diana Fuss's explanation again:

> Essentialism is classically defined as a belief in true essence – that which is most irreducible, unchanging, and therefore constitutive of a given person or thing [. . .] In feminist theory, essentialism articulates itself in a variety of ways and subtends a number of related assumptions. Most obviously, essentialism can be located in appeals to a pure or original femininity, a female essence, outside the boundaries of the social and thereby untainted (though perhaps repressed) by a patriarchal order. (Fuss, 1989: 2)

With this understanding, there is one particular problem with theories that rely on a combination of essentialism and the popular understanding of socialization theory outlined above that I would like you to consider. While these theories provide a useful general overview and have underpinned a number of very successful feminist campaigns and initiatives, they remain unable to account for the actual diversity of femininities and masculinities in society, or make theoretical use of instances of significant variation, resistance, or change. If, for example, we

Lyndie Brimstone

believe (a) that there is an essential femininity, a set of characteristics or general tendencies that every female, in varying degrees, has, and (b) that socialization moulds, limits and directs these innate characteristics so that they serve patriarchal interests, how do we understand women who refuse the life they have apparently been prepared for? Why these women and not others? Are we saying that the majority of women labour under false consciousness while a gifted, courageous, quirky or enlightened few know better and have some privileged insight into what it really means to be a woman? While much radical and revolutionary feminist rhetoric in the 1970s seemed to be saying just this and did indeed have the effect of shaking and galvanizing many thousands of women inarticulately dissatisfied with their lot, it is, I think, a dangerous assumption to make. Within this theoretical framework, women need only to be woken, made aware of their shared oppression, and empowered to oppose it. But what if, once roused, once urged to speak, some women start expressing views and visions that are different from those held by their wakers? To give a very real example, what if some women decide that rather than joining campaigns to ban the production and distribution of pornography feminists should have (a) equal access to it, and (b) the power to determine for themselves what form pornography should take?

Social Construction and the Sexual Division of Labour

The primary reason why this kind of socialization theory has difficulty accounting adequately for variation is because it is **functionalist**. In other words, it assumes a one-way system of control which always functions for the benefit of the powerful. What my simple example was intended to illustrate is that it is actually very difficult to predict or guarantee the effects of an action. Dolls with pink dresses don't always produce dutiful mothers and the resocialization of girls to recognize their power can just as easily produce 'girl gangs' as militant feminists, or sophisticated criminals instead of successful career women working for the social good.

EXERCISE

Think about the number of times 'constructionism' or 'social construction' is mentioned in this book and read again the paragraph in which it first occurs (chapter 1, page 4). You will find an account of the strengths of social construction theory when considering sexuality in chapter 7, page 138, and you might like to remind yourself, too, of the born or made, nature or nurture, body or social circumstance arguments that run through both the chapters on 'Mothers' (chapter 3) and 'Women, Crime and Violence' (chapter 11).

Constructionism is usually considered to be in direct opposition to essentialism and quite definitely, as the word suggests, supports 'made' rather than 'born that way' arguments. As Diana Fuss (1989) puts it: 'the essentialist holds that the natural is *repressed* by the social, the constructionist maintains that the natural is *produced* by the social' (p. 3). Aspects of constructionist theory have been taken up by feminists of all persuasions. Some argue that while biological difference is irreducible, the meanings built around that difference are constructed. Others would say that the whole idea of having a two-sex world, when biology is far more complicated than that, is part of the social construction of the natural. Opinions range, too, on issues like sexuality. Not just the construction of sexual identity categories (see chapter 7, page 143) but the place of the sexual in contemporary life. Are we naturally sexual? Would we attach so much importance to sex, or the lack of it, if we didn't see and hear references to it every single day? It is an interesting exercise to carry a notebook in your pocket for a few days and keep a record of every advertisement, joke, film, song, newspaper report, magazine article, television programme, conversation you come across that contains a reference to sex.

Frequently you will find 'social construction' and 'socialization' used almost synonymously and this, I think, is partly to do with the word itself. We associate 'construction', after all, with building houses, bridges, roads and the like and we know that most constructions require a foundation of some sort. It's not, of course, difficult to see that foundations, too, have to be put together, assembled from different parts that have undergone a variety of processes, but what about the ground that they are laid on? Isn't that the natural, 'raw material'? Without going into lengthy detail, here, I would suggest that it is again better to avoid rigid demarcation and, for the time being at least, think of constructionism as being *generally* opposed to essentialism while remaining, in some important ways, linked to it. We need to adopt a similar approach, too, when considering the relationship between socialization theory and constructionist theory:

> Anti-essentialists are engaged in interrogating the intricate and interlacing processes which work together to produce all seemingly 'natural' or 'given' objects. What is at stake for a constructionist are systems of *representations*, social and material practices, laws of *discourses*, and *ideological effects*. In short, constructionists are concerned above all with the production and organization of differences, and therefore reject the idea that any essential or natural givens precede the processes of social determination. (Fuss, 1989: 2–3, my italics)

Although, in the course of this book, you will have come across all the terms that I have highlighted, this is a densely written passage and you may need to read it carefully several times. The main point to note for the moment is that socialization *is* recognized by constructionists, but only as one of the processes in a complex interactive (rather than functionalist or cause and effect) *network*. Instead of suggesting a one-way process, 'Anti-essentialists are engaged in interrogating the *intricate* and *interlacing* processes which work together . . .'.

To return to our heading 'social construction and the sexual division of labour', the chapters on 'Jobs' (chapter 5) and 'Leisure' (chapter 6) are clearly going to be very important here, so you might like to refresh your memory and supplement your notes by turning to box 5.1 'Sexual division of labour', and box 6.1 'Social implications of capitalism' on pages 90 and pages 112.

Leaving aside the tricky question of what might constitute an unnatural sex difference for a moment, most feminists would agree that the 'sexual division of labour is socially constructed rather than based on natural sex differences'. Most feminists have also come to realize that despite changes in education and the availability of a mass of historical and cross-cultural evidence which proves that there really isn't anything that some women, somewhere, and at some time haven't been able to do, the notion of 'men's worlds' and 'women's worlds' maintains a powerful hold on the popular imagination. So long as this belief in two distinct sexes with their own discrete gender characteristics remains, women who step outside the designated feminine sphere have only one other conceptual place to go. These women are described as doing 'men's jobs', being 'as good (or bad) as the men', perhaps being criticized, by feminists in some instances, for 'behaving like men' (Margaret Thatcher [British Prime Minister 1979–91] is a good example, here).

While noting the extent to which most feminist theories might warrant at least a mention under our third heading 'social construction and the sexual division of labour', it is socialist feminism that I would expect to see firmly placed here. As well as making a substantial contribution to the development of constructionist theory, socialist feminists are closely associated with another related concept that you will have come across many times in this book: ideology. Given that it is Marxist in origin, it is entirely appropriate that we should take another look at ideology here. However, I would again remind you of the key word, *overlap*, and caution you against creating a sealed theory 'box'. This thinking has with doubt been most consistently sustained in socialist feminist theory, but the partial use of the concept of ideology will, like constructionism, be found in a lot of feminist writing that is not otherwise associated with the socialist project. Take a moment to look at the index now and select a couple of entries under 'ideology' to refresh your memory.

Rejecting all biological or essentialist explanations, and finding the explanatory power of socialization theories to be inadequate, socialist feminists have focused on ideology as the principle means by which the interests of one group are maintained and guaranteed through the creation and simultaneous subordination of another group.

Since this is the second time that I have talked about groups or categories being 'created' you might like to give some thought to it. In order to check whether this sits comfortably with ideas you already hold, make a note of your responses to the following questions:

1. Does it seem perfectly logical to you that those who share a biological similarity, skin colour, sexual identity or occupational band constitute a natural group?
2. How many groups do you fit into?
3. Is it a neat fit or do you find bits of yourself being compromised, left out, over-emphasized? Do all the identity groups you have listed have equal status?
4. Whose interests do identity categories serve?

According to socialist feminist theorists, there are many political (feminist) reasons why we should identify as a sex group but no intrinsic 'natural' reasons for giving our biological sex more status than any other aspect of our experience. The fact that most people do attach enormous importance to their femaleness (or maleness) and regard it as 'the most vital determining factor in the development of identity (see box 2.1 on 'Theories of identity formation', pages 18–20) is explained as an effect of ideology.

Ideology can simply be understood as a set of ideas, values, and beliefs which are generally held to be true, natural, right, just the way things are or ought to be within a given social system. By seeming coincidence or in accordance with 'natural' or 'divine' law, these sets of commonly held ideas, values and beliefs, always serve the interests of the dominant group. The term 'dominant ideology', then, suggests both the widespread acceptance of one set of ideas, values and beliefs over others and their relationship to systems of power. (There are other adjectives to describe ideologies that aren't commonly held or supported by dominant institutions, but these are not the focus of attention here.) Dominant ideologies are transmitted through religion, law, education, sport, the family, the media, and so on. Through exposure to these institutions we come not to *understand* ourselves (since this would suggest that we were ready formed and awaiting explanation) but to *be* who we are, to hold the beliefs that we cherish as our own, to recognize and maintain our affiliations, differences and relative positions in society. Looking back at your notes about your own relationship to identity categories, you may well find that sometimes (perhaps as a white and/or economically privileged person) you are identified with the powerful group, and at other times (as a woman, as a lesbian) with a subordinate group. How can we understand the different and sometimes contradictory positions we occupy?

For socialist feminists it cannot be just patriarchy, as a social system, that needs to be interrogated and challenged, but the interlocking systems of race and class oppression as well. This doesn't mean that all Black and/or working-class women will align themselves with socialist feminist thought. It is, however, within this body of knowledge that women who feel it is insufficient to see the world as simply divided into two unequal sexes may find some useful tools for conceptualizing and theorizing the interlocking oppressions that shape our experience.

To finish off the notes under 'social construction and the sexual division of labour', how do *you* feel about there being no such thing as 'natural femaleness'? Paying close attention to history certainly demonstrates the ways in which dominant ideology can incorporate or exclude, value or diminish, the 'natural', depending on the requirements of the powerful group at any given time. Now women are fragile and dependent, now we're the backbone of the nation at war, now we're the queens of the kitchen, and so on. You have already come across numerous examples of the ways in which shifting notions of what constitutes 'natural femininity' have been used to justify and maintain women's subordination and the section headed 'The Historical Context' in chapter 12, 'Women and Spirituality', is certainly worth rereading in this respect.

To entertain the idea, though, that gender is entirely a product of the social isn't easy and there are a lot of feminists who are, at very least, wary about giving up on the idea of a 'natural femininity' altogether. There are parts of our gender identities that many of us like and feel very attached to. It's what the 'outside world' does with gender, or the way 'men' take advantage of our gender, that concerns us. Unfortunately we can't have it both ways, rejecting those bits that we don't like as false constructions and preserving those bits we do like as natural and true. If, for example, we don't feel any desire to mother then a theory that says that the mother instinct is an ideological construction that serves the interests of men will be very appealing. But what about those women who do feel a strong desire to mother and are happy doing it? False consciousness versus enlightenment again? The same, too, with sex. If we don't like sex, then we'll be happy to find a theory that seems to be saying that there's nothing unnatural about our lack of interest. We need to bear in mind, though, that this same theory can also be used to support women (ideologically constructed as passive) who actively want to have sex. Certainly we need to ask where our preferences for certain versions of ourselves come from but the matter cannot be decided on the basis of truth or falsity.

Precarious Subjectivity

We come, now, to the last of the broad headings I asked you to consider. Without necessarily picking up a definition of what is meant by this, you will probably have included some reference to post-structuralism, post-modernism, and psychoanalysis in your notes. You might also have noted an important contrast. Let's take the first word, 'precarious'. If, by this, we mean insecure, risky, dependent on circumstances outside of our control, then the fixed, unified individual at the centre of things that humanism proposes (see box 2.1 'Theories of identity forma-tion') is clearly an opposition. The second word, 'subjectivity' also requires some thought. How is a 'subject' different from an 'individual'? What theory does the use of this terminology suggest? It is very often the case that, unless someone is talking specifically about theory, we have to work out where their ideas are com-ing from. Words such as 'natural', 'true', 'real' help us to recognize essentialism. Words like 'subjectivity' and 'discourse' help us to recognize post-structuralist thought. Chris Weedon explains post-structuralism like this:

> The terms 'subject' and 'subjectivity' are central to post-structuralist theory and they mark a crucial break with humanist conceptions of the individual which are still central to Western philosophy and political and social organizations. 'Subjectivity' is used to refer to the conscious and unconscious thoughts and emotions of the individ-ual, her sense of herself and her ways of understanding her relation to the world. Humanist discourses presuppose an essence at the heart of the individual which is unique, fixed, coherent and which makes her what she *is*. [. . .] Against this irreduci-ble humanist essence of subjectivity, post-structuralism proposes a subjectivity which is precarious, contradictory and in process, constantly being reconstituted in dis-course each time we think or speak. (Weedon, 1987: 32–3)

Essentialist maxims such as 'boys will be boys' or 'that's human nature' that we looked at earlier are regarded as guaranteed change-stoppers by feminist post-structuralists. At the same time, the liberal humanist concept of individual auton-omy, free will, choice and responsibility is criticized for creating an illusion of power and control that cannot be supported. Does this emphasis on process, instability, contradiction, change, becoming rather than being, excite or disturb you? Much will depend on how problematic your identity, your sense of yourself, has been to date.

It is perhaps easier to think about post-structuralism as not just a challenge to notions of personal identity but as a challenge to notions of unified power struc-tures which emphasizes their contradictions, too. What if power isn't as unitary or as stable as we had thought? What if the slogan 'Smash the State' has remained precisely that (a slogan) because there is, in fact, no readily identifiable, single entity called 'the State' to rally forces around and destroy? Think for a moment about the way that you conceptualize power and make a note of any images that come to mind. Large men in grey suits, perhaps? The machinery of war? Walls?

Continuing with our images of power, we can further understand one aspect of feminist post-structuralism like this. If feminism is to 'change existing power relations', it has to avoid the erection of a White House, Kremlin, Houses of Parliament or any other fixed, solid structure. Attractive though the idea may be, building even a metaphorical 'feminist power house' would involve choosing one stone, one style, one site over another. Access would necessarily be limited; exclusions inevitable. Such a 'building' would be inflexible and unable to respond to changes, even the positive changes brought about by its own influence. What's more, if feminism were ever to become 'set in stone', it would be a relatively easy task to dismantle or 'smash' it.

Post-structuralist theory is, of course, far more complex than this and feminists are certainly not in agreement about the extent to which it is useful in the fight for change. What problems and possibilities do *you* think there might be with a theory that emphasizes multiplicity, process, fragmentation, instability, the provisional rather than the permanent, the local and immediate rather than the timeless universal?

Whether feminists describe themselves as post-structuralists or not, the fact remains that feminism, to date, has resisted building a 'power house' of fixed ideas with hierarchical organizational structures and it is arguably for this reason that it has not only survived, but flourished as a force to be reckoned with. The predominantly white middle-class heterosexual feminists of the 1970s who, in good faith, believed they could speak for and build a power house for all women were challenged. Black women, lesbians, working-class women, women with disabilities, questioned everything from the proposed location of this metaphorical power house to the interior colour scheme before even the foundation stones could be laid. Challenges like these, which involve a recognition that not all women, or even all those who share a particular group identity, share the same experiences, aspirations, or priorities, necessitate a repeated return to the 'drawing board' of theory. The theoretical framework, the set of ideas, the way of understanding and resolving the perceived problem, needs to be thought through again.

Feminism doesn't have a Bible or a Koran, a Marx or a Freud, or a single source of any description. Much as we may long, at times, for a Grand Theory, or even just a clear set of membership rules and procedures, there is reasonable agreement among feminists that (a) such a book can never be written, and (b) that, in general, feminism is more concerned with breaking rules and challenging procedures than with creating a new set. This might put you off altogether. On the other hand, it might excite you to realize that far from having 'been done', feminism demands constant renewal and re-engagement at every level. In this sense, feminism shares common ground with post-modernist social theory since post-modernists, too, place emphasis on plurality, conversation and continuation rather than on universalistic theories and closure. Whether any closer association with post-modernism is useful to feminism in the fight 'to change existing power relations between women and men in society' is the subject of intense, ongoing debate. I have offered a point of connection, rather than an objection or opposition, here, because it at least provides a reason to look further, find out more, and develop *your own* opinions.

Conclusion

This whole book, in fact, has been designed to encourage you to go on. Each contributor has introduced issues, theories, and debates in such a way as to demonstrate that you don't need to know everything that has gone before in order to join in and make your own contribution. As well as fleshing out some of the ideas in these chapters and inviting you to engage with a number of the theoretical terms and concepts they introduce, this final chapter, too, has placed the emphasis on asking questions and challenging assumptions rather than simply amassing and cramming in 'authoritative' information. This approach is favoured on most Women's Studies courses and the Women's Studies classroom is notably a place of keen, critical engagement and interaction. Exhilarating, challenging, and exhausting at times, each of us – the writers of this book – feel that it is an important and rewarding place to be and we wish you well in taking *your* next step.

REFERENCES

Concise Oxford Dictionary 1990: Oxford: Oxford University Press.
Fuss, Diana 1989: *Essentially Speaking: Feminism, Nature and Difference*. London: Routledge.
Stacey, Jackie 1993: Untangling feminist theory. In Diane Richardson and Victoria Robinson (eds), *Introducing Women's Studies*. Basingstoke: The Macmillan Press.
Weedon, Chris 1987: *Feminist Practice and Poststructuralist Theory*. Oxford: Basil Blackwell.

INDEX